A Love Journey
with
GOD

A Love Journey
with
God

From Pain to Love,
Captivity to Freedom,
Iran to the US

Marziyeh Amirizadeh

Cover design: Diana Lawrence

ISBN 979-8-9854631-8-7 (hardcover)
ISBN 979-8-9854631-7-0 (paperback)
ISBN 979-8-9854631-3-2 (Kindle)

My beloved, Jesus Christ, I wrote this story to honor you because you are my one true pride and joy in the world.

I dedicate my book to you, the love and true author of my life. Only you forgave all my sins by sacrificing your life without judging me. Only you have been ever faithful and never left me alone, even when I was unfaithful to you. You taught me how to walk with you, trust you, and forgive with your unconditional love. You raised me from ashes and gave me a new life. Now I see how masterfully you carved the beautiful image of yourself in me with love.

Contents

CONTENTS

Preface

I never expected to write a book. Now I've written two. The first one, *Captive in Iran*, co-authored with my friend Maryam Rostampour, is about our arrest, imprisonment, and death sentence for converting to Christianity and distributing Bibles after undercover government agents saw us handing out the Bibles. It traces a physical, emotional, and spiritual journey through a brutal Islamic regime determined to control the lives and thoughts of everyone within its reach. It is an account of God's mercy in my life and my boundless love for him, an account of a miraculous rescue from the most notorious prison in Iran and a new life in America. This story was translated into numerous languages and led to speaking opportunities across the United States and Europe, where I had the privilege of sharing my faith.

But that wasn't the whole story. To me that first book was an incomplete account of my life and my Christian journey. A reader couldn't possibly know me in full and understand those experiences without knowing what came before and afterward. Now I have written this book to fill in the gaps, share the details of my life—first in Iran and then in America—and put everything in perspective.

While my first book revolved around a very public series of events, *A Love Journey with God* is more of a personal journal from my childhood to the present day, more private and more subjective than before. I now have the advantage of more than ten years' distance to process and reflect on my evangelism work in Tehran and my time in prison. I also have ten years' more experience in speaking and writing in English, which was very hard for me when I started my first book. I have also reached a lifelong goal of earning a college degree and an MA in international affairs from the Georgia Institute of Technology.

This book gives me the opportunity to say exactly what I want to say, exactly the way I want to say it. I am the sole author and also my own publisher this time around, so I have complete control over what goes on the page. My only responsibility is to myself and my dear savior, Jesus.

This control allows me to write at length about my family dynamics, about life as a single woman in a Muslim world, about the highs and lows of human relationships, the power of dreams, and the miraculous resilience of the human spirit. It also allows me to speak frankly about the threat of radical Islam in the world today and the threat to the United States from Muslim enemies disguised as "advisors" and "consultants" to clueless liberal American politicians.

My hope and prayer is that through this book you will get to know me as someone who has emerged from the refiner's fire determined to share her knowledge and experience as a warrior for Christ and a survivor of Islamic terror. I love America with all my heart. It is the greatest country in the history of the world. But I fear for her safety in the hands of leaders who don't know what they're talking about when it comes to the dangers of liberal socialism, government control, and abandoning the Christian principles upon which our nation was built. The founders depended on Christian ideals to make our laws and institutions work and assumed that future leaders would be guided by them. To ignore those sacred ideals is to risk the future of our democracy.

PREFACE

I pray that as you read the pages that follow you will get to know me better; that you will understand how my faith in Jesus directs my life; and that you will see and experience the hope of Christ in your own life, in our great country, and in the world.

Marziyeh Amirizadeh
Atlanta, Georgia
January 2022

CHAPTER 1

The Iron Hand

We weren't supposed to be in the garden, and now somebody was coming. My brothers and cousins scrambled out of the neighbor's tree where they were eating Persian blackberries, jumped to the ground, and climbed the three-foot garden wall to escape. They ran toward the house my family had rented in the town of Shahr-e Babak while my father worked on a job assignment nearby. I remember a big house and a spacious yard with chickens in one corner.

Of course, the boys hadn't thrown me a single berry, even though I couldn't climb the tree and stood below them asking for one. They didn't want me with them at all and only begrudgingly helped me over the wall into the garden in the first place. As they vaulted to safety I was left alone, shaking with fear that the neighbor would punish me for being in the garden and picking his fruit.

My brothers and cousins thought the whole thing was hilarious. At the last minute, one of them ran back and boosted me over—not because they cared about me but because they might get in trouble for leaving me behind.

Though I was only five years old, the memory of that day is burned into my heart. It was more than a childhood prank played by brothers on their younger sister. It's one of countless family interactions designed to put me in my place. My brothers were cruel and dismissive to me because I insisted from early childhood that I could do everything they could do even though I was a girl. They mocked me for being the spoiled daughter of my father and not acting like girls were supposed to act.

By that they meant I didn't acknowledge that I was a second-class citizen and little more than the property of men according to the teachings of Islam and the laws of the post-revolutionary Iranian "republic."

I was born a few months before the revolution of 1979, in Rafsanjan, a small city in southeastern Iran. In those days it was one of the wealthiest cities in the country, with elegant villas surrounded by lush pistachio farms and some of the most beautiful desert in the world. Like most Iranians, members of my family were only nominal Muslims and never practiced the Islamic rules or sharia law at home. Those were safe, prosperous, happy times.

Everything changed after the Pahlavi dynasty of Mohammad Reza Pahlavi was deposed by the Ayatollah Khomeini. Iran, also known as Persia, is one of the world's oldest civilizations. Under Cyrus the Great in the sixth century BC, it became a vast and powerful empire stretching from Eastern Europe to the Indus Valley. The modern nation had a stable government, a growing economy, and great potential for the future. But since the revolution, my home country has been in the grip of ayatollahs and clerics, satanic beasts who have imposed their criminal regime on the nation. From its first day the Islamic Republic has arrested, imprisoned, tortured, executed, and murdered countless citizens in a bloodthirsty quest for control over every aspect of their lives.

They use their power above all to force Islam on the people of Iran. Islam is a brutal religion that calls on its believers to kill all who do not believe as they profess. It includes a long list of severe rules of moral and social behavior; violating them—even to be accused of violating them—can lead to imprisonment, beating, severe fines, and other punishment without due process or any sort of fair hearing.

Chief among the teachings of Islam is that women are inferior to and subservient to men in all things. Women were the main target of the Islamic regime in Iran and had their rights taken away immediately after the fall of the shah. We lost our respect, dignity, freedom, and personal identity not only in society but in our own homes as well.

For Muslim clerics and their followers, women exist only for cooking, reproduction, sex, and giving pleasure to men. Based on Quran verses, especially An-Nisa Surah, men should beat women if they disobey: "For women of whom you fear rebellion, convince them, and leave them alone in bed, and beat them. Then if they obey you, do not seek a way against them." In other words, if persuasion doesn't make women obey, abandon them. If that doesn't work, beat them into obedience.

The Quran is filled with such verses against women. Yet in Western countries, where most people have little or no practical knowledge of Islam, Muslims and politicians try to interpret these verses in a softer way to hide their true meaning. At the same time, Muslims in Iran and elsewhere brainwash young boys and men into believing women exist only for their pleasure and to do their bidding. Maybe Muslims in Western countries can deceive the public and manipulate the facts to try and convince the world that Islam is a religion of peace. But they will never be able to brainwash a woman who was raised in an Islamic country, lived under Islamic rules, and tasted the harshness of Islamic theology in her life.

If anyone wants to know the real truth about Islam, they should ask women who have experienced it firsthand. The first time I heard someone in the United States say Islam is a religion of peace I didn't know whether to laugh or cry. Only a woman who has lived under Islam can tell you the truth about its systemic oppression and abuse.

The iron hand of Islam begins controlling a girl's life at the age of seven when she is first required to observe hijab, the practice of completely covering her hair in public. I was seven when I started school. It was so exciting! Ever since I could remember, I had wanted to be a big kid and go to school. My school was only a short walk from my house, so I told my parents I'd walk by myself the first day. This was a dangerous trip for a child because there were no pedestrian crossings or school zones in our neighborhood and cars came flying from every direction. But I was confident I could make it safely.

During a break after our first class, a friend and I were running, laughing, and singing with excitement as we chased each other around the schoolyard. We climbed a dirt mound, and when we came charging back down, the school supervisor was waiting for us with a big wooden ruler. My friend ran faster than I did and could save herself, but the supervisor stopped me. With a frown she pulled my hands out in front of me and hit me hard several times on the palms with her ruler.

With the other students watching she said, "You are not allowed to climb that dirt mound. And your hair is not properly covered. If I see you climb that mound again or not have a proper hijab I will punish you again!"

I was speechless. I had no idea I was doing anything wrong. If someone had said not to climb in the dirt, I would never have done it. Why did the supervisor have to be so mean?

Embarrassed as I was at this public humiliation, I promised myself I wouldn't cry in front of anyone. When I found a quiet place to hide, I burst into tears. I'd waited years to go to school, and now this woman had ruined all my happiness on my first day. Looking back, it's like my desire for freedom and independence and my attitude toward Islamic rules marked me as a troublemaker from the beginning. I never shared that event with my father or anyone else, but I never forgot the bitter memory of it.

My two brothers and my sister were more traditional than I was, which meant that from a young age my brothers were domineering bullies who thought they had the right to control my life, and my sister was docile and subservient and did whatever they told her to do.

Arman was four years older than me and a disobedient, willful boy. Though my father gave him sound advice, he never paid any attention to it. He was a poor student and spent a lot of time hanging around with friends. His bad behavior revealed a cruel, even sadistic streak. When I was seven or eight years old, my mother asked him to go upstairs in our house and bring down some pillows. He and our brother raced up the stairs to see who could get to the pillows first. My mother waited at the bottom for Arman to throw them down. The stairwell overlooked a fish pond in our living room that had a metal fountain in the center of it. Instead of throwing the pillows down, Arman threw his brother over the stair rail and into the pond. Though my mother tried to catch him, he hit his head on the fountain. The injury almost killed him, but doctors saved his life. He still has the scar on his head.

Arman was cruel to animals, which always made me cry because I love animals. He shot at them, beat them, and killed them. Once he cut the whiskers off a cat to see if it would still be able to walk straight, because he heard that whiskers help a cat keep its balance. He injected alcohol into another cat to examine its reaction. Another time he hanged a cat in the yard with a sign around her neck that said, "This is my sister Marziyeh, who has been executed because of her crimes." I couldn't believe he would torture and kill an animal like that just for the fun of mocking me and laughing at my reaction. The sight broke my heart, and I cried for hours in my room. My mother always defended Arman and made excuses for him. She argued with my father to keep him from punishing her beloved son.

My brother Kaveh was two years older than me and not as vicious as Arman. However, while he was quieter and not as cruel, he also refused to obey my father and listen to his advice. Kaveh would rather spend time with his friends than do his schoolwork. Though he had lots of natural artistic talent and was chosen to attend a special school for his abilities, he had no motivation and wasted his time there. My father tried to correct and encourage him, but because my father traveled so much for his work, he was away a lot of the time and had little control over his sons' behavior and training. My mother took advantage of my father's absence to indulge and spoil her sons, which was part of the reason why Kaveh never succeeded in pursuing his dreams.

My sister, Marjan, was seven years younger than me, and her character was completely different from mine. It's like we were from two different planets. I had a better relationship with her than with my brothers, but she refused to stand up for herself and would not do anything against their bullying. She was afraid of them and would do whatever they told her to. Like them, she depended on our mother to spoil her and make excuses for her, and she did not have much of a relationship with our father.

Since Marjan did whatever they wanted, Arman and Kaveh were friendlier with her than with me. Marjan's humble, submissive behavior fed their egos and allowed them their role as dominant males in the household in keeping with the teachings of Islam. They took advantage of her and made her do errands for them, which she did to avoid fighting and criticism. She enjoyed going to parties with my mother and brothers and did whatever it took to be included in the fun. I preferred to stay home rather than give in to their demands. They could bully and mock me, but they couldn't make me their servant. And they were very jealous of the relationship between my father and me. I was the one he loved the most, and to me he is still the greatest, most honorable man who ever lived.

In a culture that degrades women, my father taught me to be confident and to defend my dignity as a human being from every challenge, whether from my brothers, my school, my community, society, the government, or any other threat. He always defended me, affirmed me, praised me, encouraged me, and showed me the importance of standing up for my rights. Everybody knew how much my father loved me and how faithfully he protected me. In the male-dominated society of post-revolutionary Iran, my father's unwavering support shaped my views on human rights and human faith. That process was the beginning of my preparation for a future I could never have imagined.

As a young girl I was always full of questions for my father, and he was always ready with answers and explanations. Some nights he and I spent hours outside our house in Rafsanjan looking up at the stars. We lived near the famous Dasht-e Lut, a large, salty desert that is the driest and hottest place on earth. The most beautiful nights belong to the desert, and I always loved them. The sky was crystal clear overhead, and my father and I could see thousands of stars shimmering above us. We tried to count them but never got them all.

He taught me the names of constellations like Dobe Akbar (Big Dipper) and Dobe Asghar (Little Dipper), and showed me how to pick them out among all the stars in the sky. I asked many questions about the stars, planets, Earth, the creation of the world, God, life, and death. My father patiently answered every question and never seemed to get tired of them, unlike my mother, who thought my questions were irritating and would tell me to stop asking them.

On these beautiful nights, my father and I spread a carpet outside and stretched out side by side holding hands. We talked about the universe and creation and everything I could think of. One night we talked about death. I told my father that if he died, I would die immediately afterward or else I would commit suicide.

"My dear daughter," he said kindly, "I know how hard it would be for you if we were separated by death. However, since I am older than you it is only natural that I may die sooner. If this happens, you should trust God, be strong, accept the truth, and live your best life going forward. Even if I am gone, you will never be alone. God will always be with you to protect you." Of course neither of us knew of the Christian God then, but we believed faithfully in God as the all-powerful creator and protector we understood him to be.

The reality that one day my father would leave this world was a bitter truth. He was the only person in the world I could lean on and trust to protect me. The thought of losing him made me cry. He was my inspiration, my rock, and I loved him so much. I always carried his picture with me in my school bag.

My father, Rouhollah Amirizadeh, was honored and respected by everyone who knew him. He was an accountant and auditor who traveled regularly to his company's branch offices in villages around the city to audit their books. He was often the guest of honor in people's homes. When he arrived, the host would serve a whole lamb and have an elaborate banquet in his honor. My father was hard-working, honest, and successful. We were relatively wealthy members of our neighborhood, always driving a nice car and having plenty of cash to spend.

In addition to his job as an accountant, my father owned a pistachio ranch in a village outside of Rafsanjan. He became one of the most successful and prosperous farmers in the village through years of solitary, back-breaking work. When he started putting pistachio trees in the middle of an empty desert, no one believed he would succeed. Working completely alone, my father planted thousands of trees with his bare hands and transformed acres of arid desert into fertile, productive land. It takes seven to ten years for a pistachio tree to begin bearing nuts, but after that it can produce for three hundred years. My father's dream was to create an eternal treasure for his children, a lasting legacy that would provide income for them and for generations beyond.

I will never forget his hands. When he got home after a long day of planting in the scorching desert heat, his hands were rough, peeling, and full of tiny thorns. I removed the thorns with a needle and tweezers. Sometimes that caused even more pain, but he patiently allowed me to do it, more for me to feel better than for himself. I was proud of him for working so hard. To me he was the best dad in the world.

Father was a strong, determined man who overcame many obstacles on his way to success. He grew up in the village of Ismail Abad near

Rafsanjan, the oldest of five children. Though his mother was Muslim, his father was Bahai and therefore considered an infidel. Prejudiced neighbors insulted my grandfather, spitting in his face on the street and throwing trash into his home. They also condemned my grandparents' marriage and pressured them to divorce.

My grandfather died when I was a child, and I remember hearing the story of his death from my father and grandmother. Grandfather was a farmer who left home one morning to work in his fields and never came back. Father, who was in his twenties, living and studying in Rafsanjan, returned to the village to search for him. Eventually, he found his father's body at the bottom of a high mountain called Kohe Shekam. The police never opened an investigation into his death, and we never found out what happened. Local residents said he probably committed suicide because he was so ashamed of being an infidel. After my grandfather's death they tried to destroy his grave and dishonored it by defecating on it. They said it was dirty and should be removed from the earth. Our family was afraid to go there to pay their respects. In time the headstone was stolen, and we could no longer even locate the grave.

My father knew the villagers would keep persecuting his mother and siblings. He bought a house in Rafsanjan and moved the family there. He helped his two sisters and two brothers continue their education and started working to support them and his mother. Among his other skills, my father became a professional wrestler and was wrestling champion of the state of Kerman.

As a teenager my father had been one of the smartest students in the village school. His teachers convinced my grandfather to let him continue his education in the city. He rented a room there from a single mother who struggled to earn a living.

He fell in love with the landlady's daughter. Seeing her mother's poverty, he offered to marry the daughter in order to help them both. My mother and father grew to love each other at first. Later, when my father traveled a lot, they wrote wonderful love letters to each other. Unfortunately, in time their marriage became strained because my mother's mother wanted to influence our family, control my parents' relationship, and allow my brothers to run wild without proper discipline. These conflicts would cause life-changing problems later on.

CHAPTER 2

One Essence and Soul

The bond between my father and me stayed strong as I grew older, even though my mother continued to criticize and mock our relationship. Some of her criticism was very petty. For example, from the time I was a young girl, my dad gave me a piggyback ride when he came home from work, no matter how tired he was. I always looked forward to seeing him at the end of the day and jumping on his back. This continued even into my teenage years. He would laugh as he carried me and praised me with many kind words, calling me "the beautiful daughter of Daddy."

My mother looked at us with scorn, saying, "You are a big girl now, and it's a shame for you to make your dad give you a ride like that!" My father answered that he loved his beautiful daughter and we were having fun. He seemed to ignore my mother's nagging the same way he ignored my brothers' jealousy at our wonderful father–daughter relationship.

My parents both had a lot of books in the house, and I enjoyed reading them. My mother had hundreds of magazines and books about the shah of Iran and the royal family. Those and many of her novels were banned after the revolution. Books by Persian author and journalist R. Etemadi were very romantic and made her liable to arrest and punishment by flogging and paying a fine. My father worried about her keeping these sorts of books, but she kept them anyway. She also had books by the Iranian social critic and folklorist Samad Behrangi, who was famous for his children's stories. Some of his stories were allegories, typically about children of the urban poor who were encouraged to change their circumstances through their own initiatives. When I was a teenager I read his book *The Little Black Fish*, the story of an old fish speaking to her twelve thousand children and grandchildren about a small black fish who leaves the safety of his local stream to venture into the world. The book was considered a political allegory and was banned in Iran after the 1979 revolution.

I liked *Kharmagas* (*The Gadfly*) by Ethel Lillian Voynich and its tale of faith, disillusionment, revolution, romance, and heroism. Other books I remember were *Papillon* by Henri Charrière, *Napoleon Bonaparte* by Emil Ludwig, *Désirée* by Annemarie Selinko, and a biography of Vincent van Gogh. I also enjoyed my father's books about the history of World War II, and I read lots of romantic novels.

My father thought I should spend my time reading better material than novels. When he saw me reading one of my mother's books he would say to her, "You are corrupting the minds of my children with your fantasy books. You should throw those sexy novels away."

Mother always answered, "These are my books, and I love them. It's their choice to read them or not."

To avoid arguments, I didn't read my mother's novels when my father was at home. I read his books instead. He wanted me to read things that would educate me, and encouraged me to study history, science, and famous Persian poets. His favorite was the thirteenth-century master Saadi, whose books are collections of poems and stories about his experiences and judgments upon life.

One famous Saadi quotation is:

Human beings are members of a whole,
in creation of one essence and soul.

If one member is afflicted with pain,
   other members uneasy will remain.
If you have no sympathy for human pain,
   the name of human you cannot retain.

In later years this reminded me of the apostle Paul in 1 Corinthians 12:26 (NIV): "If one part suffers, every part suffers with it. If one part is honored, every part rejoices with it."

My father spent hours reading and interpreting Saadi for me. We both enjoyed reading those beautiful poems and understanding the meaning behind them. I also read poetry with my uncle, who loved modern Persian poets including Ahmad Shamlou, Forough Farrokhzad, and Sohrab Sepehri. Whenever we met, we read those poems together and he interpreted them for me.

My father's encouragement and protection extended beyond our home and family to all aspects of life. He did everything in his power to make sure I was treated with respect and had the opportunity to improve and excel no matter what the circumstances. One example I will never forget happened in middle school. My math teacher started shouting at me in front of the class for not completing an assignment.

"You are one of the best students in this school," she said in a mocking tone, "but you can't even complete a simple math problem!"

It took all my willpower not to cry in front of my classmates, but I refused to show my true feelings even though it felt like one of the worst days of my life.

Unfortunately, teachers in Iran have the right to punish students any way they want, and parents are usually powerless to complain. My father picked me up after school as usual. As soon as I got in the car I burst out crying. I'd held it in all day, and now the tears came in a flood. My father was shocked.

"What happened to you, my dear daughter? Why are you crying?" he asked.

After I explained what happened, he tried to calm me down and encouraged me not to be disappointed or lose confidence in myself.

A few weeks later I was in the schoolyard during recess when I saw my math teacher leave the school in a hurry. She looked distressed, as though something bad had happened. The next day, her behavior toward me changed completely. She was suddenly friendly, respectful, kind, and encouraging. Even the other students noticed the difference. Despite her new attitude, she never said anything about the way she treated me in the past and never apologized for yelling at me in front of everybody. For that reason I ignored her efforts to show kindness and refused to talk to her. I figured she regretted her past behavior, was too proud to apologize, but wanted to apologize indirectly by changing our relationship for the better. I noticed similar changes in other teachers too. All of them were much more polite. Sometimes during recess I saw them pointing at me and whispering.

My father started asking me regularly how my math teacher and I were getting along. I told him enthusiastically that she had completely changed her behavior.

"She is trying to be friends with me now, but I ignore her," I said. "I will never forgive her unless she apologizes to me in front of all my classmates."

"You should forgive her and respect her effort to be friends," my father explained patiently. "Her new behavior means she's sorry for what she did. It's her way of apologizing. You should humbly accept her apology and not expect her to say something in front of the whole class."

I was a very headstrong child and insisted she had to apologize in front of the same people who heard her embarrass me. Eventually, I decided to take my father's advice and forgive her. It was years before I learned from another teacher why my math teacher had such a sudden and dramatic change of heart.

Not long after I came home crying, my father went to the educational department and demanded they fire the teacher for the way she treated me. Since I was a young child, I had won lots of awards and honors in sports, theater, and other areas and was one of the best students in the school. He told them they didn't deserve to have me there. How could they treat such an outstanding student with such disrespect? He used his connections and networking ability to insist the teacher be dismissed. It was the first time a parent had ever taken legal action against the local educational system. My father wanted not only to punish the teacher, but also to punish the school for allowing her to mistreat me.

In the end, the education department ordered the school to fire the teacher. The day I saw her leaving school in such a hurry was the day she went to the education department to meet with my father. She cried and apologized to him, promised to change her behavior, and begged him to withdraw his complaint. My father accepted her apology and dropped his complaint. From that day on, teachers and administrators treated me with respect because they saw what would happen if they did not. I was incredibly proud to have such a strong and supportive father who stood strong to defend me.

———— • ————

In middle and high school I made a point of helping poor girls in my class. I was fortunate to come from a relatively wealthy family and have pocket money to spend every day. I didn't want to embarrass my less fortunate friends or injure their pride, so I came up with ways to help without giving them money directly. Sometimes I invited a group of girls to lunch and bought sandwiches and snacks for everybody. We all had a great time, and no one had to go hungry or ask for a handout.

One day a friend said, "Marziyeh, I love you because you are different."

"I love you too," I answered. "But why do you think I'm different?"

"Even though you're wealthy, you are not proud," she said. "You are very humble. You treat poor people the same as everybody else."

"I don't see any difference between you and somebody who is wealthy," I explained. "Money never makes people more precious in my eyes. It's their true character that I respect. It's about all of us being equal as people, not who has more or less. The money we have is only a blessing from God, and he can take it from us in a second if he wants."

"But not everybody thinks like you," my friend replied. "As you can see, there are other students in the class that won't talk to us because they are rich and therefore think they are better than we are."

"I don't care what they think," I said. "I love all of you equally and respect you for who you are, not for what you have."

My classmates were very class-conscious and preoccupied with money and status, which I suppose makes them like teenage girls all over the world. One time I asked a friend who was poor why she was crying. She said it was because a wealthy girl made fun of her old, worn scarf. I went to the rude girl, grabbed her scarf in my fist in front of a group of students, and said, "The next time I hear you've mocked someone in this class, I promise to punch you in the face. Now apologize!" It took a while, but she apologized once she realized I would not leave her alone until she did.

One of my closest friends in school was from a poor family. Sometimes I went to her home so we could study together. She lived with her parents and sisters in a very small house, and at first she was afraid I wouldn't come back because the area was too low-class for me. Of course their house made no difference whatever. Once I saw their situation, I started bringing sweets and other food for them when I came over. While I was inside, neighborhood children came over to look at the car I was driving. People wondered why anyone with such a nice car would be in that neighborhood. To me the friendship was all that mattered.

Because I loved books so much and enjoyed reading and discussing them with my father, he gave me a very generous amount of money to buy a bookcase for my room. The next day at school I saw that the woman who worked as the school janitor was crying. When I asked what was wrong, she said her children wanted meat to eat but she hadn't been able to afford any for months because it was so expensive. The next day I brought all the money for my bookcase to school and gave it to her.

"This may not help you forever," I said, "but at least you can buy meat for your children for a couple of months."

She was astonished that any student would have so much money and was extremely happy and grateful for the gift. Later, when my dad asked me why I hadn't gotten my bookcase, I told him I decided to spend it on something else. I never told him exactly what I used it for, even though I knew he wouldn't be mad at me. By example, he taught me that the best way to give is to give quietly and without drawing attention to yourself. Too many people give in order to show off and feed their own egos. Those who have the right attitude give to help others, not for the sake of themselves.

Often during my years in school, teachers would appoint me student-in-charge and let me teach my fellow classmates. I was fortunate that learning came easily for me. I always had the highest grade in the class. After a while, my teacher would give me 100 on a test without even grading it. When the whole class objected to this, the teacher handed one of the girls my test. "If any one of you finds a mistake, show it to me," she ordered. "I know my students, and I trust them." There were no errors on the test.

While I enjoyed teaching, I was also sometimes ordered to discipline other students, which I refused to do. Once a teacher ordered me to kick a student out of class, by which she meant literally, physically kick her out of the room. When I wouldn't do it, the teacher shoved the student out of class. Another time, a teacher ordered me to get a ruler to hit a disobedient student's hands. I left the room but never looked for a ruler. Instead, I told the teacher that there was no ruler and no one around for me to ask.

I was grateful for my good grades and position of authority. Other girls were not so fortunate. Because of the revolution, every day, someone I knew at school was harshly reprimanded for some minor infraction of strict Islamic rules. Most Iranians lived two lives. Inside their homes they felt free to wear what they wanted and behave normally. But in public they had to follow Islamic sharia law or face harsh punishment. Students were routinely harassed for even a few stray hairs sticking out in violation of hijab.

Girls are not allowed to touch their faces in public until they are married. One day in high school a student was removing the hair from under her eyebrows to give the brow a more attractive shape. When the school principal found out, she confronted her in front of other students, hit her repeatedly in the head, then grabbed her by the hair and pulled her around the schoolyard, cursing all the while. She said she would expel the girl from school, but after the girl's family pleaded with her she changed her mind and allowed the girl to stay. The girl had to keep her eyebrows covered with a scarf until the hair she removed grew back. I never forgot the sight of that poor girl being beaten, insulted, and cursed for the horrible crime of shaping her eyebrows.

Of all the demeaning and humiliating Islamic rules imposed by the school, the most offensive one to me relates to Namaz, the prayers Muslims are required to pray five times a day. Girls have to wear the long black chador during the ceremony. Since my friends and I weren't really faithful Muslims, we laughed and whispered under our chadors instead of praying or repeating those nonsense Islamic verses. Because girls were allowed to skip Namaz if they were having their period (and thus ritualistically impure), students would sometimes use this excuse even when it wasn't true.

That led to the principal requiring any girl who wanted to be excused to come to the office, take down her pants, and show her bloody sanitary pad. This rule was disgusting. School administrators decided that religious law gave them the right to check girls' underwear to make sure no one was escaping the harsh dictates of Islam. I hated their rules and figured my classmates did too. I decided I would rather attend all Islamic prayers at school than allow those beasts to check my underwear.

Even something as carefree and innocent as riding a bicycle was a dangerous risk for me just because I was a girl. From the age of seven, girls are supposed to stay indoors according to Islamic law. I loved riding my bike through our neighborhood. This irritated some of our neighbors, a mullah (Muslim cleric) and his nosy and prejudiced wife who appointed herself as the morality police. She would knock on our door and ask if we were praying Namaz and following other Islamic rules.

I asked my mother why she allowed the neighbor to interfere like that. "You should shut the door in her face," I said. "Who is she to come to our house and ask these questions?" To me, what we did at home was none of her business. Mother lied about our religious observances (we didn't do them) and said she was trying to be respectful and avoid any animosity between neighbors. It was also true that as the wife of a cleric, she could make trouble for us. Every time this woman saw me riding my bicycle she stopped me and said it was shameful for women to ride bicycles and I shouldn't do it.

She criticized me for wearing a T-shirt and jeans outdoors and not having a proper hijab covering my hair. I ignored her and kept riding. Seeing that I refused to stop my indecent behavior, she kept complaining to my mother and me. Finally I had enough.

The next time she stopped me in the street I looked her in the eyes and said, "It's none of your business what I do or don't do. I do not have time to listen to your bullshit. And the next time you stop me, I won't be so nice. Stop sticking your nose in other people's business. Otherwise, I will find a way to shut your mouth myself."

She was shocked, furious, and flushed with anger. The next day she told my mother what I said. When my mother asked me why I talked to her like that, I said, "Someone needed to shut her mouth, and since you could not, I decided to do it for you."

Mother later apologized to the neighbor, explaining that unfortunately I behaved badly and wouldn't listen to her. I realize now that my mother's kindness kept this woman from reporting us to the authorities. But she never said another word about my bicycle. Every time she saw me after that, she put a scowl on her face and continued on her way.

As I got bigger and traveled farther from my house, I started dressing like a boy whenever I went for a ride. It was the only way I could ride legally.

"If people find out you are not a boy, we're in big trouble," my mother warned. But I didn't care. Even though I did feel afraid sometimes, I was ready to take the risk. I was willing to pay the price—and be a bit sneaky—to enjoy my freedom.

The mullah and his wife were not the only neighbors who condemned my family for failing to observe Islamic rules. Ali Akbar Hashemi Rafsanjani, fourth president of Iran since the revolution and a founder of the Islamic Republic, was born in one of the villages of my home city of Rafsanjan. A number of his relatives were our close neighbors. I remember from the time I was a small child that every time my friends and I wanted to go outside, these relatives' children would curse us and throw stones at us. Even the children in the family believed the whole city belonged to them and they could do whatever they wanted.

One family near us were the parents of Rafsanjani's daughter-in-law. Every time Rafsanjani came to visit, sweepers arrived beforehand to clean and scrub the streets. He and his family enjoyed everything that was forbidden to the rest of us. When they had a wedding, men and women wore Western clothes, with no hijab for the women, and men and women mixed freely together. If anyone else dared to have a wedding like that, revolutionary guards would raid the party and arrest people for being mixed and dancing together.

The family was above the law in many ways. The daughter-in-law's brother slept with a poor girl and got her pregnant. Under normal circumstances, he would have been arrested, flogged, and forced to marry the girl. But because of his family connections, the boy was sent away to Tehran without being punished, the girl's family was threatened to keep quiet about the situation, and the brother was appointed to be a government minister.

One day when a friend and I were walking home from school, one of our classmates from the Rafsanjani family and her mother drove by. The mother stopped the car, rolled down the window, and started shouting and cursing at us for not having a proper hijab. She said we should be ashamed for such behavior and she would report us to the school. I told her what we wore was none of her business. Her daughter smiled with pride as her mother kept yelling.

I have no good memories of the Rafsanjani family. They always acted like they owned the city. And they did, plundering its wealth and taking over its institutions for their exclusive benefit.

CHAPTER 3

The Day Will Come

As a girl in an Islamic world, everywhere I turned there was always some law or neighbor or family member telling me what I could not do. Girls were considered weak, timid, and helpless, always in need of a male to monitor their behavior. Even with my own brothers growing up there was always tension because I wanted to do things they thought I shouldn't do, and Islamic law gave them the right to control me. Sometimes the situations seemed like innocent sibling rivalry, but underneath them ran the undercurrent of strict Islamic rules and the assumption that girls simply couldn't measure up to what boys could accomplish.

When I was ten or twelve years old, my brother Kaveh challenged me to climb down a well some men were digging in our back yard. It was about thirty feet deep, and my father was having it dug so the city could pump out our underground septic system as part of its regular maintenance. There was nobody home but Kaveh and me. Kaveh climbed down the well and back out again without using a rope, then challenged me to do the same.

Looking over the edge into the dark hole, the thought of climbing down scared me. But I decided to prove to him I wasn't a coward and could do anything he could. There were shallow footholds cut into the sides of the well so that I could put one foot on one side and the other foot on the other, going down one step at a time with my body like an X. I dared not think of the consequences of falling. I concentrated completely on using the footholds and keeping my balance.

To Kaveh's wide-eyed astonishment, I went down the well and came back up just as he had. My whole body was shaking as I climbed out, but I felt a sense of triumph. I told him I was no coward and he should quit challenging me. I chose to risk disaster rather than allow him to underestimate me for being a girl. There was no doubt in my mind that God's angels saved and protected me that day.

Though my family were only nominal Muslims, the influence of Islamic teaching on my brothers was clear. Even my mother believed they should have more rights than my sister and me. Arman and Kaveh assumed they could bully and mock me and make decisions for me without my permission. I always resisted them and stood up for myself. When they ordered me to do their errands like they were my boss, I refused. They only did this when my father was out of the house and they considered themselves in charge. They knew that when he was home he would not stand for them bullying me and would punish them if they tried. When he was away, they thought of endless schemes to try to put me in my place.

One day at breakfast Arman ordered me to bring him sugar from the kitchen. Because he demanded it in such a rude, bossy way I refused. "Are you paralyzed?" I asked. "You've got two feet. Go get it yourself."

"If you don't do what I say," he shouted, "I won't let you eat breakfast."

"I'd rather not eat than tolerate your behavior," I said. Though I got no breakfast that morning, I refused to allow him to treat me like a slave.

Sometimes the conflict turned dangerous. I was watching cartoons one afternoon when Kaveh walked in and changed the channel to a soccer game.

"Hey!" I said. "I'm watching cartoons."

"I don't care what you're watching," he answered.

I changed the channel back to cartoons. He changed it to soccer. I changed it back to my show. He changed it back to the game. I turned off the TV.

Kaveh disappeared into the kitchen and returned with a knife, which he pointed at me, screaming, "I'm going to kill you!"

My mother came running and made him put down the knife. Then she allowed him to watch his soccer match. This was typical behavior for her. She always defended her sons no matter what they did. She knew my father would never allow my brothers to be so mean. She would be in trouble if he knew what she let my brothers get away with when he was out of the house.

Dad was away when one time for no reason Arman came outside where I was playing and started hitting me. Mother made no effort to stop him. Finally I got away, ran crying to my room, and hid behind the bed.

My mother came in and said, "If you tell your father what happened, I'll let Arman beat you again."

There were times when I wondered whether she was really my mother. I scarcely ever got any love or affection from her, never a hug or a comforting word. She was jealous of my relationship with my father and always sided with my brothers against me.

When my dad returned from his trip the next day, he asked me why my eyes were red and swollen from crying. At first, fearing what my mother might do later, I didn't want to tell him. When after a while I told him, he punished my brother immediately despite my mother's efforts to stop him. He told Arman, "If I ever find out you or your brother has touched my dear daughter again, the consequences next time will be even worse." It was the first time I remember my father physically disciplining one of my brothers. However, it didn't change their behavior.

Arman and Kaveh never missed an opportunity to belittle or criticize me. A favorite topic of theirs was my "big, ugly mouth." From earliest childhood, they had me convinced that my mouth was ugly and I should hide it. As I got older, I measured it sometimes with a piece of string and promised myself I would have plastic surgery as soon as possible to make my mouth smaller. I got into the habit of covering my mouth whenever I smiled or laughed because I thought it was so huge and unattractive. Years later someone asked me why I didn't open my mouth naturally when I laughed. I realized then that all my life I had been self-conscious and thought I should hide my expression. From then on I tried to laugh like a normal person.

My brothers made fun of my success in school and my study habits. To cover their own shortcomings as students, they branded me a nerd and disturbed my studying by turning the TV up loud so I couldn't concentrate. To do my homework I would go into the closet with a flashlight or sit outside on the roof. Of course, they only bothered me like this when our father was away. His kindness to me made them furious. "You should learn from Marziyeh," my dad said. "While you skip your studies and misbehave, she is working to get ahead. The day will come when you will bow before her. She will be successful, and you will waste your life. You won't be fit even to clean her shoes."

When I was fourteen I asked my mother to teach me how to drive. "She's a girl!" Arman insisted. "You should not allow her to drive a car." To my surprise, my mother agreed to teach me. In retribution, whenever I was on the road Arman would buzz me with his motorbike and try to make me have a wreck. He knew if I damaged the car it would be a good excuse to forbid me to drive any more. I didn't care. I also didn't care that as a woman I was required to wear a manto, a long, lightweight coat, over my regular clothes whenever I took the wheel. Most of the time when I was driving I did not wear one because nobody could see from outside that I was improperly dressed. It was risky because if the morality police pulled me over and saw I was not wearing a manto, I would be in violation of the law. On the other hand, Rafsanjan was a small city where almost everyone knew each other, so the police never stopped me.

My brothers weren't the only people who tried to intimidate me and keep me off the road. Boys in the neighborhood didn't like to see me driving. To teach me a lesson they started playing chicken whenever they saw me in the car. They drove toward me head on, forced me out of my lane or off the road, and enjoyed scaring me in order to remind me I shouldn't be there in the first place. One night driving home from a friend's house, I saw a car full of boys pull into my lane and start accelerating straight toward me. I decided I'd had enough. If I had a wreck it would be their fault because they were in my lane. The worst that could happen is that I wouldn't be allowed to drive anymore. I not only held my place in the lane; I sped up. We were headed for a big smash-up. At the last instant, with only inches to spare, the boys pulled over, almost lost control, and barely missed sideswiping another car. That was the last time anybody played chicken with me.

I longed for the day I turned eighteen and could get an official driver's license. The driving test in Iran is much harder than in America. There, the roads are narrower and parking places closer together, so drivers have to be skilled at navigating with only inches to spare. I passed my written exam, then scheduled the driving test. I asked my mother to have it as early in the morning as possible so my brother Arman wouldn't come with us. He was a student by this time in the state of Kerman, and I didn't want him showing up and causing trouble on test day.

But Arman was one step ahead. He asked my mother what day my test would be, then came home the day before. Since it was early when we left, I was able to sneak out of the house without waking him. We got to the test site and waited for my turn. My name was called, and the testing officer and I got in the car. Then the back door opened and Arman got in! I asked the officer to make him leave, but he said he could not. In my father's absence, my brother had the right to be there to "protect" me in public. The real reason he was there was to distract me so I would fail the test. He had failed on his first try and couldn't stand the thought that I might succeed.

Arman laughed at me, criticized my driving, and ruined my concentration the whole time we were on the road. I failed the test.

I made sure he was out of town the day I scheduled my re-test and told my mother not to tell Arman when it was. The officer gave me a very tough driving test. I would say it was harder than usual because I was obviously a good driver, which meant I might pass even though I was a woman. Most of the applicants who took the test that day failed. Only a handful passed, including me, the only woman in the group. To my surprise, everyone gave me a round of applause as I drove away.

———— • ————

As a teenager I was popular with the boys in Rafsanjan because I was so different from other girls. I was proud, confident, and unwilling to be pressed into the mold of a submissive Muslim woman. I heard I was one of the most popular girls in the city and that the boys had a competition to see who could date me. In those pre–mobile phone days, boys called me at home every night to see which one I would go out with.

The answer was: none of them. I didn't date anybody. This irritated my mother, who told me over and over that I should accept their offers and go out with them. Maybe she simply wanted to get me out of the house. The truth was, there just wasn't any boy in town who interested me.

I could scarcely imagine my mother thinking that I had to date someone. When I was a student, having a boyfriend was like being a prostitute. People would talk behind your back if you were dating someone. Decent girls didn't date, and many parents wouldn't allow it. Only immoral girls went out in mixed company. Sometimes girls who had secret boyfriends would be beaten by their families when they found out. Some girls were even murdered. It was for the sake of the family honor and perfectly legal under sharia law to kill girls who were considered morally corrupt. The law actually encouraged it.

While girls couldn't have boyfriends, boys could have all the girl-friends they wanted. There must have been plenty of immoral girls around. Arman had as many girlfriends as hairs on his head. No one criticized him in the least. Yet he made it his business to see that I never dated or even had contact with boys, and he tried to keep me from talking to them when they called the house. As always, my father took my side whenever he was home. He trusted me more than his own eyes and never questioned my purity and decency. I wasn't interested in boys anyway because I knew sooner or later they would treat me like my brothers did. They all thought they were so superior in their selfish, male-dominated world that it gave me pleasure to turn them down.

One day I was home alone, studying for a difficult math exam, when I discovered another way Arman had decided to take charge of my life. I needed to call a classmate to work on some problems with her and realized the phone didn't work. Arman had disconnected it so I couldn't talk to boys while I was there by myself. He was doing that every time the rest of the family left the house, but I didn't notice it until then.

It was an insult to me that he doubted my decency, especially considering by that time he had had a long list of girlfriends, immoral relationships, and adulterous liaisons. Now this morally corrupt bully dared to tell me what I could and could not do!

Knowing how Arman used the telephone constantly to set up dates and meetings with his various romantic interests, I proceeded to tear the wires out of every phone plug in the house. When he got home and saw what I did, he flew into a rage, screaming and swearing nonstop.

Unfazed by his outburst, I declared, "If you disconnect the phone on me again, I will not let you touch a telephone in this house anymore." I wanted him to see what it was like!

He couldn't beat me for fear of getting in trouble with our dad. But if not for that safeguard my brother might have killed me that night. He was completely within his rights according to Islamic law and was brainwashed from boyhood to believe it would have been the honorable thing to do.

It was part of a well-established pattern. Since the Islamic Revolution of 1979, when people inherit their parents' estate, women are entitled to only half the property men in the family receive. Divorce courts always grant custody of children to the fathers regardless of the circumstances. Women are not issued passports without permission from their guardians or male relatives. The legal age of marriage for girls is thirteen, although fathers can get permission from the courts for them to marry even younger.

The morality police have the authority to intrude into every part of a family's private life. Even people having parties behind closed doors could be arrested, flogged, and charged with crimes for dancing together, listening to Western music, drinking wine, or watching satellite TV or foreign movies, and their satellite dishes and movies could be confiscated.

I could never accept the way Islam described God. I saw God as my heavenly father who protected me when my earthly father was away. I wrote letters to God in a notebook and called him Daddy. I was very curious about God's character and wanted to know him better. But our teachers at school told us we could never have a personal relationship with God because we are sinners and God is holy.

They taught us that God punishes us as soon as we sin or disobey the rules of Islam. He sends sinners to hell, where he tortures them, especially women. If a woman does not cover her hair, God will hang them by their hair until their scalp rips off. If a woman fails to cover her neck or breast, God will peel the skin off those areas, hang her by the breasts, and drive hot swords into them. He pours hot lead down the throats of sinners, women in particular.

Islamic teachers describe women as candy and chocolate that has to be kept covered so it will not spoil or be fouled by flyspecks. Some mullahs characterize women as only responsible for feeding the family, bearing and nursing children like a cow, and existing solely for the pleasure of men. They are responsible for covering themselves so as not to tempt or arouse men. It is always the women who sin in a relationship, never the men.

Islam creates the horrible image of an ugly, cruel God who sits waiting in heaven like a bloodthirsty dragon to torture sinners for the slightest wrongdoing. The God of Islam is a misogynist as well, giving double punishment to women as compared to men. There are no equal rights for Islamic women on earth or in heaven. From a young age, boys are taught that heaven is a beautiful garden with cool streams and rivers of honey, full of naked angels for the pleasure of men. Martyrs for the Muslim cause have even more naked angels available, a point mullahs emphasized during the Iran–Iraq war to recruit young impressionable soldiers. There is no word anywhere of naked male angels for the women.

In America and other places in the West, I hear constantly that we should respect all religions and faiths. People who say this have no idea what they are talking about. They speak from a position of fear and political correctness. Politicians are especially careless and dangerous because even though they know how horribly criminal and barbaric these religious ideologies are, they close their eyes to the terror for the sake of money and political power. As a woman who has lived under Islamic law, I will never condone any such ideology, religion, or faith that disrespects me as a woman or considers me less than equal to a man. Though I respect human beings from every religion including Islam, I do not respect and will not stand for Islam's barbaric, shameful, murderous practices.

CHAPTER 4

"Your Proof Means Nothing"

In Iran today there is no distinction among military, political, and religious rule. In 1979 Ayatollah Khomeini and his satanic followers came to power by covering their hands with the blood of many innocent people, killing any and all who opposed them. Their political coup was the direct result of the infamous Cinema Rex fire a year before. Islamic militants chained the doors of a crowded movie theater in the city of Abadan, doused the building with gasoline, and set it on fire, killing more than four hundred people; the exact number was never known. The militants cast blame on the shah of Iran's security force. The shah was deposed, the terrorists took over, and the nation descended into darkness. It was decades before the terrorists' guilt was revealed.

The more brutal someone was during the revolution, the richer his reward in the new regime would be. After a massive purge of the government and media, most jobs were taken over by Khomeini loyalists—including murderous, illiterate thugs called *basijis*, uniformed street hoodlums accountable to no one, who took American hostages and murdered Americans and Iranians alike.

One of these criminal loyalists is Masoumeh Ebtekar, whose son now lives openly in the United States. In interviews Ebtekar has proudly stated that she was one of the hostage takers who imprisoned American citizens in Iran during the early days of the revolution. Later, after heaping condemnation on America, Ebtekar and numerous associates have sent their children there, where they got some of the best and most expensive education in the world and enjoy a life of freedom and luxury. In some cases, they give advice to liberal American politicians.

American political leaders also heed the counsel of the National Iranian American Council (NIAC). What the Americans either don't know or fail to admit is that NIAC is despised by the Iranian people because it badly misleads America and other Western countries into thinking Iranians support the Islamic regime. NIAC has deeply infiltrated American politics and yet spreads nothing but falsehoods and misinformation.

The revolution left Khomeini's most brutal and savage supporters in power, growing richer by the day from bribes from every branch of government. Well-connected people could get anything they wanted by passing enough money into the right hands. New judges came to the courts who had no training or experience in the law but were faithful to the new regime. Sadegh Khalkhali, a Shia who became chief justice of the revolutionary courts, was known as the hanging judge. He was also a founding member of the Military Clergy of Iran, committed to Islamification of the country at all costs. His trials of many of the shah's leading lieutenants were broadcast in classrooms. Some proceedings lasted only a minute, after which the accused was executed on a school rooftop. Khalkhali ordered hundreds of executions a week, more than eight thousand in the first months of the regime. Other judges, including Abolqasem Salvati (who later ordered the execution of my best friend) and Mohammad Moghiseh, followed in his bloody footsteps.

Before the revolution many Iranians took their freedom for granted and failed to stand up against corrupt opposition while they still had a chance. Those who were truly serving the country and building Iran into the greatest nation in the Middle East did not get the support of their countrymen. Instead of speaking out and defeating the cruel mullahs, they were passive and silent. Soon, an evil but laser-focused and well-organized minority was making decisions for the whole country. Even many who supported Khomeini at first were ignorant of his background and motivation, blind to the truth about him and his co-conspirators. One of the early slogans of the revolution was, "From exile the Beloved Leader has returned. At the approach of the Angel the Devil has fled." Now the world knows who the real devil was. Citizens of Iran allowed him to take over the country and did nothing until it was too late.

Today, a lot of former Khomeini supporters realize their tragic mistake, making the excuse that they didn't educate themselves enough about him and his policies and couldn't see what was happening. That excuse is ridiculous. It doesn't take a lot of research to realize that ignorant, evil mullahs with their demonic beliefs should not be in charge of a national government or anything else. They even look evil, with brutal scowls on their faces, scraggly beards and mustaches, and stilted mannerisms.

As the regime's power has faded, some former supporters who worked years for the radicals are realizing they were deceived and have now seen the light. Others remain faithful to the revolution. People both inside and outside Iran owe it to themselves to learn the hard truth about the country's past and the Islamic terror that has transformed it.

———— • ————

My father earned his position as a highly respected and successful businessman through many years of hard, honest work. Before his career as an accountant and auditor he served in the army under the shah, where he built a reputation as a trusted and responsible high-ranking functionary. By the time of the Islamic revolution, he had been in his civilian career for a number of years. Through his audits, he discovered that some of his work colleagues were corrupt and cheating the company. He warned them to stop, saying he would have to turn them in if they continued to steal from their employer. They refused to listen, and eventually he had to report them. Some were fired, while others were demoted.

After the revolution everything changed. Under the new regime, one of the demoted executives saw a way to get his revenge.

This executive was the father of two soldiers who died as martyrs during the Iran–Iraq war. The revolutionary government rewarded families of martyrs with promotions and financial benefits in order to keep enlistments up and the public's spirits high. As a result, this thief my father had caught and reported became my father's boss. This man joined forces with another worker at the company to plot my father's destruction.

The other worker was not a rich man. He told my father his daughter had been engaged for years but couldn't get married because he could not afford a proper dowry. This was destroying his reputation, relatives were humiliating him, and his daughter was shamed and embarrassed. In tears, he asked to rent my father's pistachio ranch for a couple of years to raise money for the marriage dowry. When my father agreed, the two of them drew up a contract with very low payments. The man gave my father checks to hold for future payments. Every year after the harvest, the man would honor checks for that year from the money he earned for his crop. Thanks to my father, the man not only saved the dowry money and saw his daughter married, he also bought a new house and raised his entire standard of living.

But after the third year's harvest, the man refused to honor the checks for that rental payment. My father met with him to find out why.

The man took the checks, tore them into pieces, and said, "I'm not giving you anything. This property belongs to me, and I'm not paying for it or returning it."

"You know this land and these trees are mine!" my father exclaimed. "I planted them with my own hands and waited seven years for them to start producing. I have proof."

"Your proof means nothing," said the man. And tragically, he was right.

When my father started planting trees in the middle of the desert there was no system of documenting land ownership. Who would ever want to own it? People like my father who wanted to develop property there paid the government some money in exchange for a piece of paper with signatures of witnesses who affirmed the land belonged to him. This was the common practice, but it didn't have the legal authority of a title or deed. My father's vengeful boss knew this and hatched the scheme with his coworker to take the pistachio ranch from my father. After the revolution there was no law. The government could confiscate my father's property and hand it over to the poor man, the boss whose sons died as martyrs, or anybody else who supported the regime.

My father was shocked and furious. After his coworker tore up the checks the two of them got into a fight, during which my father tore up a photo of Supreme Leader Khamenei that was hanging on the wall. The police came to the office and broke up the scuffle. Then they arrested my father and took him to jail.

During the weeks my dad was in jail, his brother got married. His family decided not to postpone the festivities since they had spent so much time planning them and had invited many guests. It was very hard for me to be there watching everyone dancing and celebrating while my father was in jail for trying to reclaim his own property. It broke my heart to see how no one thought about him or seemed to appreciate his hard work and sacrifice to build and defend this valuable legacy for us. At home that night I lay in bed and cried at the thought of my father so lonesome and unfairly condemned.

After my father was released, he immediately started legal proceedings to get his ranch back. The process would take years. His boss and the other man knew how valuable the property was and how much it meant to my father. They would stop at nothing to steal it from him permanently.

I was devastated at my father's condition when he got out of jail. One man went in, and a completely different man came out. He never would give me details of what they did to him. I know he was insulted, threatened, and beaten. Since then, he has never been the same.

Authorities learned that my grandfather was Bahai and tried to insist my father was also Bahai. After the revolution, mullahs persecuted all religious minorities and Bahai in particular. The government confiscated their property, fired them from government jobs, and expelled their children from universities. Many of them left Iran after 1979 for a new start somewhere else. If my father's enemies could convince the court that he was Bahai, they could easily confiscate everything he owned.

My family had always been nominal Muslims and did not observe strict religious rules or attend mosque. My father preferred to sing, dance, and have fun. Now he believed the only way he could save his property for the future of his family was to adopt all the outward signs of a faithful and devoted Muslim. Immediately, he started attending services and some Friday prayers. Through our neighbors who were related to President Rafsanjani, he connected with local religious leaders and attended some of their meetings. He believed it was the only way he could defeat those who were trying to steal the family legacy he spent a lifetime building.

Attending all these meetings and religious services caused his behavior to change. I could see he was being brainwashed. To save his wealth and property, he lost himself.

After a while he wasn't pretending to participate. He was becoming a true Muslim who observed all the rules. He started pressuring me and other family members to practice the rules, attend mosque, and so forth. He wanted to show the community we were all dedicated Muslims.

My father was a new character, a stranger I didn't recognize anymore. Though he finally won his court case and took back his pistachio ranch, the years of struggle left him severely depressed. He couldn't trust anyone, not even members of his own family. During this time, another former colleague tried to steal his car and some of his other property. Enemies seemed to be everywhere, and they never let him rest.

One day as I was walking home from school through an alley, a car entered from the other direction. When the driver saw me, he sped up and headed directly for me. I saw a small space in front of a house ahead of me and jumped into it as the car roared past, missing me by a fraction. My heart was pounding and I could scarcely catch my breath. I ran all the way home and told my father what happened. This, he told me, was a warning from his boss, who had threatened him many times in the course of their long legal battle.

Though he had only a few years left until retirement, my dad had to leave his job because of the threats, traumas, and pressures. He couldn't sleep at night and kept a knife under his pillow in case someone came after us at home. I think the car attack on me was the last straw. Because he retired early he received no pension for all his years at the company. All he had left was the pistachio ranch. At least now his ownership of that valuable property was legally secured.

All the difficulties he had been through made my father more and more depressed. Doctors diagnosed him as manic depressive, which today is called bipolar disorder. Yet despite Dad's sickness, with his legal troubles behind him and retirement years ahead, this should have marked the beginning of a quiet, satisfying season for him, tending his trees and enjoying himself in care of the family he had faithfully and selflessly supported for so long.

Instead, my mother and brothers saw a chance to take control of his assets. Mother cooperated with some of my father's old enemies and bribed court officials to find him incompetent. She petitioned the court to declare him insane and give her guardianship of all his assets. At the same time, she pressured my father to divide the pistachio ranch, by far his most valuable property, among his children to protect it from future threat. He was not in his right mind. Otherwise he could easily see that the biggest threat was not the future but my mother and her schemes.

Privately, my father had his own ideas about dividing his property. "I want you to have it all, dear daughter," he told me, "because my boys are not wise. They will destroy what I have spent years to achieve. They take everything for granted and don't appreciate the treasure I have prepared for them."

"It would be better for you to divide everything equally," I suggested. "Your sons are your children too, and if you leave it all to me they will hate me even more than they do now. They will be mad at you and be my enemies forever."

My parents argued for months. Father still controlled his assets at the time and insisted that all the children should get an equal share. Mother insisted my brothers should have more than I. The Quran and Islamic law require that an "equal" share for a woman be half as much as a man's. At last Dad decided he would give two-thirds of a share to my sister and me and that my share would include the best and most profitable section of trees, one that other villagers had tried to buy from him for years. He gave my mother a share and kept a small portion of land for himself.

My mother and brothers were enraged at his decision. In their eyes, I stole their inheritance. From that time forward they never missed a chance to vent their hate, animosity, and desire for revenge. "Islam gives us the right to have more, and we will take it as soon as our father dies," they said. "Don't think for a minute you are his 'dearest daughter.' We won't allow you to have a cent. As soon as he dies we will suck that property out of your throat!" This last threat was an old Persian saying with an obviously sinister message for me. I have no doubt that if my father had left me everything as he originally intended, my brothers would have killed me without a second thought as my mother looked on with approval. Though my sister got the same share I did, the rest of the family was convinced my father did what he did for both daughters out of special love for me. They were like angry lions waiting for my father to die so they could tear me to pieces.

Although at the time I tried to convince my father to split his estate among us, today I understand why he wanted to leave it all to me. The simple truth is that my brothers would not appreciate it and did not deserve it. What my father predicted became true: Arman and Kaveh not only failed to appreciate their inheritance, they wasted every penny and never spent a cent of it to take care of our father or thank him for his gift.

As my father's depression worsened, my mother and brothers began transferring his properties to my mother. My dad took medications that made him so sleepy that he spent most of the day in bed. I lost my champion, my only supporter in the household, the only one I could trust and lean on. The rest of the family knew my father couldn't protect me anymore. My brothers, especially Arman, were delighted with this development because it meant they were in charge.

This all happened during my last year of high school. My friends and teachers knew something was wrong. I wasn't the same student as before. I became depressed myself and lost my motivation to study and excel. I had been the best student in the school. Now I didn't care. My encourager and protector was gone and along with it my passion for success.

My brothers' cruelty to my father knew no bounds. When he was in the hospital and we went to visit him, my brothers and mother would argue in front of him about how they would control and handle his property after he died. "We will take back the extra land he gave Marziyeh," they said, knowing he could hear but was powerless against them. They would get their revenge against him. At times I saw tears in his eyes as he watched me silently during these awful visits.

The pain in my heart was indescribable. Sometimes it made me sick to my stomach. I didn't care anything about the inheritance for myself.

All I wanted was for my father to be comfortable and respected. I thought about how cruel people could be toward each other because of money and wealth. Often I stood watching my dear father and listening in silence to my family's raving treachery and scheming. I felt helpless and alone.

Arman never missed an opportunity to demean our father and brag about being in charge of the family. One afternoon he invited his volleyball coach, a man we all knew and respected, over to our house. Arman started talking with pride about "his" pistachio garden and how he was going to manage it and spend the money it earned. When the coach asked if my father agreed with these plans, Arman laughed derisively and said, "Don't worry about him. He's a crazy old man. He has no power to interfere in my decisions."

Insulting our dad in front of everyone like that was inexcusable. "What are you saying?" I demanded. "How dare you talk about him like this? If it weren't for him, you would be nothing. You should be ashamed talking about him this way. Whatever you have, all the source of your pride is because of his lifetime of hard work. I refuse to let you talk about him with disrespect!"

Arman blushed, not with embarrassment but with anger, and shouted, "It's none of your business how I talk about him. Shut your mouth or otherwise I'll do it for you. And get out of here!"

"You're the one who ought to shut your mouth," I said, standing my ground. "You have no right to talk about him like this. I'm not afraid of you, and I refuse to let you insult our father in his own house."

Arman jumped up and hit me in the face with his fist. Blood gushed from my nose and spattered all over my clothes. With all the power I could gather, I slapped him as hard as I could.

As everyone tried to separate us, my father, who had been sleeping in another room, came in to see what all the commotion was about. When he saw my bloody face he didn't need any explanation of what had happened. He walked up to Arman and slapped him hard. "Get out of my house!" he ordered. Arman left without a word.

My father looked sick, and his hands were shaking. He had used all his strength to protect me. He couldn't believe what Arman had done. My heart was pounding, and for a minute I thought I would faint. Once I felt better I went into Arman's room and started throwing his things outside through the window.

"I will never let Arman in this house again," I told my mother. "If I see him here again I will make it hell for him. The next time he attacks me like that I'll kill him." I felt unsteady on my feet and ended up going to the hospital for a couple of hours for an IV and oxygen.

Mom called Arman and told him to go back to the state of Kerman, where he was in college, and not return home for a while. It was two months before he visited us again. I never washed my blood-soaked T-shirt. I hung it on the wall of my room to remind me of my brother's cruel ways. All my life he had mocked, teased, insulted, and offended me, but this was different. When he did finally return, I stayed in my room whenever he was in the house, and the two of us never spoke or even saw each other.

One positive result of Arman's attack was that later on, it clearly showed me how God protects me and that I have God's favor. It wasn't long after he punched me in the nose that somebody punched him in the nose. Then he could see how it felt! There have been other times in my life as well when God has shown his sense of justice by bringing his judgment upon people who hurt me.

Meanwhile, Arman kept making my life miserable. Right before my high school final exams, he brought one of his college girlfriends over. In Kerman she was a notorious prostitute, so inviting her over brought shame on our whole family. Arman didn't care. He said she had a drug addiction, and he was going to help her quit. My mother welcomed her and joined them whenever they were in the house. Because of his medication, my father slept most of the time and had no idea what was going on. There seemed to be loud music, dancing, and drinking all the time. I wanted to tell them I was trying to study for finals but knew it would only start another fight. I spent the whole day in my room preparing for my exam, trying not to think about how they were ignoring my father and defiling his home. I felt powerless to do anything.

Family wounds from that time in my life are deep, but I hold no hatred toward any of my family now. Even then, God was shaping my life for a purpose. The pain of those years gave me strength and resolve for the future. The experience of fighting for my rights, fighting for my freedom, enduring times of trial, and rising to the next challenge and the next worked together to prepare me for a season I could never have imagined.

CHAPTER 5

The White Horse

It was during these dark days, through my tears of anger and frustration, that God spoke to me in a dream for the first time. He let me taste his love when there was no love for me at home. His love was so sweet and totally different from anything else I ever experienced in my life. The feeling was so intense that I felt I was on fire for him after tasting his love because I had never tasted such love before. I did not want to be home anymore. I cried to God and asked him to save me. I wanted to be with him and taste his love forever. After that, he became my father, and every night I talked to him about all my difficulties, pain, and loneliness.

All my life I had been curious about God and asked my theology teachers at school lots of questions about him. Because I challenged their teachings about God, they never liked my questions. I thought of God as a kind father who was closer to me than members of my family. I believed the God who created my body was closer to my heart than my own flesh and blood. I was taught Islamic beliefs and debated them with friends and teachers at school, but I could not accept the Quran because its teachings did not seem true. I could not accept the Muslim image of God as a harsh ruler over the human race who punishes us for the slightest sin. This is a terrifying image of God. I believed the daily

Namaz prayers, bowing five times a day in front of a God who was already in my heart, were unnecessary and a waste of time.

I also questioned why I had to speak to God in Arabic instead of Farsi, my native language. *Doesn't this God who taught me my mother tongue know it himself? Why can't I speak to him in my language? Why do women have to wear a long black or white veil while they pray Namaz? Why should I have to cover myself in front of the God who created me? Why should I pray to him as if he's a great political leader or ruler over me and repeat the same words every time throughout the day?* These questions had long occupied my mind, and the answers I got at school were unconvincing. They tried to tell me I had to follow the rules of Islam if I wanted God to be satisfied with me.

Despite my reservations, I did my best to fulfill my religious duties. I told myself that I might be wrong in questioning Islamic teaching and the truth would show itself one day. As I searched for the truth, I changed my approach to Namaz. For two years I prayed Namaz without fail, read the Quran, and sometimes even woke up in the middle of the night and prayed some more. But none of it made me feel any closer to God. The God I knew was a kind father, kinder even than my own dear father. And so I started calling him Daddy. After my own dad got sick, I started writing letters to my heavenly father in a notebook. In those letters I always called myself a daughter of God.

I knew nothing about Jesus at this time of my life. Even so, for some reason I always loved crosses. Whenever I saw a cross or a necklace with a cross on it in a store I would always buy it. I had a collection of crosses and wore one all the time.

It was my last year of high school, when I was seventeen, that I had my first dream about God. I was trying to study for finals while my brother entertained a notorious prostitute in the house. My father was sick and depressed, heavily medicated, and helpless to keep my mother and brothers from taking over his estate. I felt alone, helpless, and defeated. Then I met the White Horse.

One night I had a dream. In my dream I was praying to the sky when it opened up and a White Horse came down and spoke to me.

"Sit on my back," it said.

I obeyed. The horse took me to a city where worshipers were coming out of a mosque performing Tasua and Ashura ceremonies. Tasua means "ninth" and Ashura means "tenth." These are the ninth and tenth days of Muharram, the first month of the Islamic calendar. It is a time of mourning when all people have to wear black clothes. Some of them chant and flagellate themselves. Some sacrifice animals to imams. I never liked this ceremony because the morality police were on closer watch than usual and were more brutal to anyone who failed to follow the rules.

When the horse and I first arrived the people couldn't see us. But suddenly they changed into wild animals with savage features, no longer like people at all. As soon as I saw them they could see me and tried to kill me. The horse ran like the wind to save me. As I held fast to the neck of the White Horse, I felt its love pouring into me with a power and purity I had never known.

After we eluded our pursuers the horse came to a fork in the road where one path turned up to the sky. As the tired horse started on the upward path, I woke up. For a week after that, all I could think about was the deep love I had experienced in the dream. I have never since experienced love like that in this world.

Every night for weeks I cried, *God, why did you let me wake up? I wanted to be in that dream forever!* After some thought and consideration I concluded that the most important part of being a believer is my heart. So I decided to put aside my religion. That dream was the beginning of my journey with God. After the dream I became more curious about God and finding the truth. And though I could not have known it at the time, the White Horse would return.

In America and other Western countries, people, including many Christians, are suspicious or skeptical when it comes to inspired dreams. The idea that God would communicate with anyone through dreams sounds unbelievable or even crazy to them. Some are quick to label this experience as "charismatic" in a derogative sense, a product of an overactive imagination, an overly emotional expression of religious belief, or the response of someone easily influenced by other people's words and behavior.

It's important to realize that these Western preconceptions come from practical and cultural differences that most Westerners don't understand and have never even thought of. In America, God speaks to his people through the Bible, church services and sermons, and prominent organizations ranging from Catholic Charities to the Southern Baptist Convention. There are Christian lobbying groups in Washington and Christian broadcasting networks across the airwaves and internet twenty-four hours a day. The word of God is everywhere, and he has endless channels for communicating with anyone he chooses.

In Iran, as well as much of the Middle East and Asia, none of that exists. In some countries churches are illegal. People can only worship Christ in secret in their homes. To possess or to read a Bible is to risk your life. Anyone that God wants to reach has to be able to communicate in a way that is safe, private, and secure. Dreams are the perfect solution.

God has spoken to Persians in dreams for a very long time. It is a gift from God to the people he chooses. I would never have thought to reach out to God in some sort of subconscious way. God chose me in a dream because in revolutionary Iran that was how he could reach me. He had a specific plan for his purpose, which was the life-changing dream of the White Horse. I longed to see him and feel his inexpressible, otherworldly love again.

CHAPTER 6

Evidence of a Crime

During my last year of high school, Arman returned to his studies and his crazy lifestyle in Kerman, Kaveh left for his compulsory military service, and the household became somewhat quieter as a result. That was when I got to know a very kind boy named Ali who was a year older than I was. He had a broad, open face, thick eyebrows, and a wonderful smile. He was handsome and ambitious, and he fell in love with me. A lot of boys were interested in me at the time, but I ignored them all. Unlike the others, Ali was very polite and also very persistent. While at some point the others got tired of chasing me and begging for attention, he had a quiet determination to keep trying. After my father got sick, I felt so lonely at home that I eventually started talking with Ali when he called rather than hanging up on him. I had seen him a few times in front of my school and felt he had genuine respect for me. He didn't tease me or show off in front of other boys like everybody else. He wouldn't compete for my attention.

Even though I liked him, I never thought for a minute about marriage at that age because I wanted to continue my education. I didn't want anything, even love, to stop me from pursuing my dreams. Ali had finished high school and was ready to take his college entrance exam. In

Iran these tests, called Konkur, are very difficult, but you have to pass them to be accepted. For certain fields like medicine or engineering, applicants have to have one of the highest grades. Ultimately, the state, not the student, decides where and what they will study. Unfortunately, since the revolution, student quotas for the most prestigious fields are reserved for lazy, stupid children of government officials or for families whose children were war martyrs. Few students without connections, no matter how smart they are, win places at the top schools.

With Ali, I was looking for a companion in my loneliness and a trusted friend in a time when I felt I couldn't trust anyone. Ali clearly wanted more. I wasn't serious; he was. I didn't want to encourage him but also didn't want to lose his friendship. My solution was to give him impossible challenges so he would lose interest in a romantic relationship.

I said I would continue our friendship only if he majored in engineering. I knew how hard it was to be accepted into an engineering program and did not expect him to make it. If he failed, I then had a solid excuse for rejecting him as a romantic interest. He took the Konkur exam and was accepted to study physics in Tehran. This was a competitive and highly prized honor. Because he was smart and worked hard, he won the appointment. But, I reminded him, our agreement was that he would study engineering. I was shocked when he told me he would study for another year, then take a second round of Konkur tests to apply for engineering school.

A few weeks into Ali's tests his mother called me to explain how much her son was in love with me. She had never seen him like this, she said, and he was terribly stressed over his tests and the prospect of losing me. She asked me to be nicer to him. She also called my mother and told her how serious her son was and how much he loved me.

This was my mother's cue to start nagging. My brothers were living away from home, my father was in bed and medicated most of the time, so that left my sister, my mother, and me to coexist under one roof as best we could. And the sooner I was gone, the better.

"Why do you treat that poor boy like you do?" Mother whined. "I do not understand why these stupid boys fall in love with you in the first place. You break their hearts and still they praise and worship you. I only wish you deserved so much love and attention! You cruelly reject one after another after another. What's wrong with you?"

As my father's depression continued and my home life remained a disaster, Ali's selfless love and kindness attracted me more every day. After taking his second Konkur, he was accepted to study petrochemical engineering in Shahreza, a small city in the state of Isfahan. I began to feel love for Ali. This time I had no reason to argue against starting his college studies. However, I explained, I was not going to marry him until we both finished our educations. I still had to take the Konkur. When the time came, I passed the exam and was accepted as an English translation major at Ali's school in Shahreza. We were happy we could be in the same city and study at the same university. By the time I was ready to move to Shahreza, Ali would have already been there for a year and know all about the community.

In the meantime, as I finished my last year of high school, my mother built a beautiful new house for herself and our family in Rafsanjan. Of course, she used my father's money, though she made all the decisions with the architect and never asked my father about anything. It was a traditional style with a duplex floorplan. The first floor had the main rooms of the house and private quarters for my parents. On the second floor were bedrooms for me and each of my siblings plus another living room and kitchen. From our upstairs living room we could look down through the atrium to the first floor.

With Arman at college in Kerman and Kaveh, finished with his military obligation, now in Tehran taking classes to prepare for his Konkur, my mother and sister spent a lot of time out of the house, and I stayed there alone with my father. It made me sad to see how far he had fallen and how disrespectful the rest of the family remained. As a further insult to his good name, I began to suspect my mother was having an affair. My father also suspected her of being unfaithful, but whenever he brought it up, she said it was his depression. He was a pessimist and mentally ill. What did he know?

I believed my father was telling the truth, and eventually I learned the facts for myself. It started with overhearing bits and pieces of my mother's telephone conversations, which I could partially understand from the upstairs living room when she was talking downstairs. When I tried to listen in on her calls using an extension, I realized she used a secret wall switch to disconnect other phone plugs in the house when she was talking. Ali had given me a telephone of my own to keep in my room, which I hadn't used up to that point and that nobody knew about. One day when my mother was on the phone outside, I went around the house checking every switch with my phone until I found the one that secretly disconnected the lines. I also found a hiding place behind the wall in a closet where she had stashed money, documents, and other valuables that she could keep hidden from everyone else.

A while later I noticed she had activated the secret switch and was talking on a telephone out in the yard. I immediately plugged in my phone and started listening.

She was talking to her boyfriend.

I could only bear to listen for a minute or so, then hung up in disgust. I felt frozen in place. Nauseated. I couldn't move, couldn't think, couldn't talk. I couldn't even cry. I couldn't believe how easy it was for her to betray the generous husband who loved her and had done so much for her.

While I couldn't sit by and let my mother betray my father, I wasn't sure what to do. I couldn't possibly tell my dad. It would be a waste of time to tell my sister, Marjan. She constantly resisted me for trying to guide her and take an interest in her education and safety since my mother was willing to let her run wild. I couldn't tell anyone outside the family because in a small town like ours, it would bring shame on my father and the rest of us. If I told Arman, he would use the situation to try to take control of the family. Kaveh was no better. I'd rather have a showdown with my mother than face my power-hungry brothers.

Earlier, I had secretly cut the phone wires in the walls thinking that would show my mother that someone knew she was having conversations with her boyfriend. Now I decided to warn her and demand she end the affair. One day when we were alone, I confronted her.

"I know you're having an affair," I said. "I've heard your phone conversations. You've got to stop betraying my father and end this secret relationship immediately."

I thought she would be remorseful and at least a little ashamed. I was wrong.

"It's none of your business what I do!" she declared. "You have no proof, and Arman and Kaveh will never believe you."

She was right. So I bluffed. "I know about the secret telephone switch," I said. "I recorded your conversations. If you don't stop the affair, I'll play them for your beloved Arman and let him decide who's telling the truth."

"I don't care," she said, but I knew I'd connected. Her eyes were wide with fear, and her face turned pale. And yet after only a beat she countered, "If you do that, I'll make up a story for my friends that you're a dishonorable and immoral girl. It will destroy your character, and Ali's family will no longer accept you!"

I couldn't believe what I was hearing. Not only would she not apologize, but she was threatening me for revealing the truth. I could not imagine this evil woman was my mother. How could she ruin her daughter that way? She knew how selective I had been with a boyfriend and how both families were aware of Ali's and my friendship from the beginning. I felt ready to explode.

"You don't deserve to be called a mother," I told her. "You are a shame. Go ahead and say whatever you want about me. I don't care about my future. I know who I am, and God is my defender. I don't care if I never marry Ali or anybody else!"

She had not anticipated this turn of events. If I didn't marry Ali, she would never be rid of me and she knew it. After a long silence she started to cry. "Please destroy the recording," she begged.

"Never," I answered. "As soon as you continue with your affair I will give it to your beloved son." She couldn't believe I had recorded her phone calls with her secret lover, but she had no way of knowing for sure.

My mother and I had a bad relationship up to that day, but from then on, we were total strangers to each other. She became constantly cautious, canny, and devious around me while she figured out how to get out of the situation and get rid of me. I could never love her after that.

———— • ————

The city of Shahreza, where Ali had started college, is a very religious city known as "the small Qom" after the most religious city in Iran. The town is full of religious officials and their families who demand everyone follow the strict rules of Islam. I told Ali to be careful because the place was full of radical Muslims and *basiji* rabble-rousers who could easily make trouble for him. They especially resented students and were always looking for excuses to question or detain them.

Ali and I talked regularly by phone. He always shared his daily schedule and plans with me, and we looked forward to being closer together when I started college. One day during a call I could tell something was wrong. It sounded like he was whispering to somebody else in the room while he was talking to me. Suddenly he said, "I can't talk right now," and hung up the phone. Nothing like this had ever happened before. When I couldn't get him on the phone the next day, I got suspicious that something was wrong. For days I called without getting an answer. I called his family, but they didn't know what had happened to their son. He had completely disappeared.

Months later, Ali's brother learned through his connections with the ministry of intelligence that Ali was under arrest and in jail. Ali's father went to Shahreza to find out what had happened. Arman decided to go along to satisfy his curiosity. After a while I was able to put the whole horrible story together.

Ali had two roommates who liked to invite girls to their apartment. Ali explained to them that he had a fiancée and didn't want anything to do with their girls or their parties. But whenever Ali was away visiting his family in Rafsanjan, they would have girls over anyway. Ali knew how strictly Islamic rules of morality were enforced in their community and warned his roommates to be careful and not to have these women over when he was gone.

Once after Ali returned from a visit to Rafsanjan, his landlord asked him if he and his roommates were entertaining girls in their apartment. Ali explained that he wasn't involved in any of that sort of activity because he was in a committed relationship.

"But I've seen the girls coming and going myself," the landlord said. "I know what you're doing, and I'd like to join in the fun. I want you to invite me to your next party to share in the pleasure."

Ali confronted his roommates and argued that they had promised not to invite their girlfriends over while he was away. "Meet them somewhere else," he insisted. "If you get caught, I will suffer the consequences as well as you."

One of Ali's roommates was so angry that he left the apartment and moved in with some other friends. He started using drugs and alcohol and kept having girls over as before. He also joined a counterfeit money operation. When the police arrested him along with some other suspects, they tortured him and demanded he give them the names of all his friends. Since he wanted revenge on Ali, he gave the police Ali's name and address.

The security police raided Ali's apartment when Ali and I were on the phone. That was what I heard in the background the last time we spoke. They forced him to keep talking in order to trap me and arrest me too. He explained that I was almost five hundred miles away, and he couldn't arrange a meeting so they could arrest me.

"We know she's your girlfriend," they said. "You have to tell us where she is so we can arrest her for having an affair with you."

If the police had found any evidence of a crime in Ali's apartment they would have charged him at once. Since he had done nothing wrong and there was no evidence, they moved on to their next tactic.

"You have to confess to something," the police told Ali. "When we arrest somebody they have to be charged with a crime. We can't let people think we made a false arrest and jailed a suspect without any reason."

When Ali resisted, his interrogators turned up the heat. "Confess that you were drinking wine and making love to a girl. You have to say it whether it's true or not."

Ali still refused. "Even the strongest, most macho guys eventually confess to us," they warned, "so you may as well do it now and get it over with. We will not let outsiders judge us and accuse us of arresting innocent people. We will prove you're guilty!"

Ali still wouldn't confess. That was when the torture began. I'll never know everything that happened during the months Ali was in prison, but I learned some of it. Every day the police hung him by his wrists from the ceiling and beat him with cables for hours, stopping only for daily Muslim prayer. They tied him to a chair, then kicked him in the crotch and hung weights on his testicles. They stripped him naked and made him stand outside in the snow. Day after day, week after week.

Finally, Ali broke down and said he would confess to drinking wine but not to having an affair. He knew that if he admitted to an affair they would torture him again to give them a name. They demanded to know my name and planned to arrest me. They refused to believe he and I had a proper relationship. To put more pressure on him, the police brought in a local prostitute who wrote out a complaint that Ali had molested her. She worked for the intelligence police and regularly received payment in return for swearing in court that she had been assaulted or molested by whoever the police wanted to punish.

When Ali appeared before the judge, he claimed he had been tortured into making a false confession. He didn't know then that the judges and interrogators cooperated with each other to get their convictions. When Ali asked the judge for justice, the judge replied to the guards, "Take this prisoner back to jail and remind him how to confess to his crimes." The torture resumed as before.

It became clear to Ali that he had two choices: die of torture in jail or admit to crimes he didn't commit. When he saw once and for all that there was no hope for justice, he confessed to the charges against him of drinking wine and having an immoral sexual relationship. The court ruled he could not return to college for three semesters. And though I didn't know it at the time, before he could re-enroll he had to come back to the security police to receive a sentence of eighty lashes.

When Ali's father and my brother Arman saw Ali for the first time after his imprisonment, the sight made even my hard-hearted brother break down in tears. Ali was very thin, very depressed, and covered with marks. He had been beaten for months and also burned with cigarettes. He looked like the walking dead. He was a different person. His life was destroyed.

He had worked so hard to prove his love for me, and I had grown to love him too. After his release he was disappointed and felt he had failed me because, at least for now, he could not continue his education. He could no longer be the husband he and I thought he would be. He also revealed that he was addicted to opium. After torture sessions, the guards would sometimes give Ali and other prisoners painkillers so they could sleep. He became suspicious of the medicine and on the day of his release opened one of the capsules. He saw that they were laced with opium and knew he was already addicted.

Ali insisted he wasn't good enough for me anymore and that we should forget plans of marriage or any sort of future together. "I can never make you happy," he said. "You have to leave me because I have nothing for you. It's useless for you to wait for me to get better."

I believed he was waiting for me to leave him and then kill himself. He had done everything in his power to bring me joy during some of the worst days of my life. How could I leave him alone like this? He had lost everything, and I was his only hope. Leaving him would feel like a betrayal even though we weren't married yet. It was an impossible choice. If I married him, I could never be happy because he was only a broken shell of the man I once knew. If I left him, I would feel terrible guilt, and he would surely end his own life.

CHAPTER 7

Happiness versus Freedom

As I considered this incredibly stressful life-or-death situation, two people I wanted least in the world to hear from made it their business to advise me: my mother and older brother. Mother wanted me married and out of the house. With all of Ali's problems, she was afraid we wouldn't go through with our marriage. To pressure me into a decision she and Arman decided to use a little reverse psychology.

The two of them came into my room, and Arman started talking. "Ali isn't good enough for you anymore," he said. "You need to consider leaving him forever." Arman loved acting like the big boss. "He is no longer the right choice for you. His life is ruined, and he has no future. Unless you still want to marry him, you are not to see him anymore or contact him in any way."

This was an outrage. Two of the most disgraced and immoral people I ever knew were sitting in front of me talking about decency and honor and trying to control my decision. No doubt this was my mother's plot, and my brother relished his role in it as the all-powerful family authority.

"Are you crazy?" I said. "Don't you have a shred of humanity? Ali has lost everything, and now you expect me to abandon him in the midst of his depression and misery. I will never leave him!"

"Then you have to marry him," Arman ordered. He cared nothing for my future happiness, only for showing off his power over me. My father was too sick to rescue me, and my mother sat back with a smile and watched Arman's evil tactics.

The only way to get out from under my brother's control and have a life of my own, the only way to gain my freedom and stop Arman's relentless bullying, was to marry Ali. Under Islamic law I would be ruled either by my brother or my husband. I saw no future in a life with Ali, but at least I could be rid of my brother's constant, selfish interference and my mother's destructive scheming behind the scenes. I would gain my freedom by sacrificing my happiness. I would marry Ali.

"If you force me to choose, I choose to marry Ali," I told them. After Arman left the room I gave my mother an icy look. "I know what you did to me just now," I said. "I know you manipulated Arman, and the two of you set this whole thing up. Just be sure I will never forgive you for destroying my life!"

"Why do you think this is my fault?" she asked with a disgusting tone of fake innocence. "It is your decision to marry him. Your brother is in charge of the family, and I dare not disagree with him."

"You and I both know better who's in charge here," I said. "Don't try to deceive me!"

After Arman returned to college in Kerman, I told my mother exactly how I was going to marry Ali. "Since you pushed me into this marriage, I have some conditions," I said. "First of all, neither Arman nor Kaveh is allowed to witness signing the marriage contract because I do not want to see their ugly faces. Only Ali and I and our parents will be there.

"Second, there will be no wedding ceremony or party of any kind, because we are only signing a contract to be *mahram* [legally sanctioned partners] in order to satisfy you and Arman.

"Third, there will be no public announcement of our marriage. We are not telling anyone in Ali's family besides his parents. The marriage contract will be signed in secret and remain a secret until I am ready to reveal it.

"Fourth, after signing the contract I will continue living at home, and Ali will live with his own family."

Mother did not expect to hear those strict conditions, but she had to accept them for fear that if she refused, I would give my recording of her boyfriend's phone calls to Arman. I had no expectation she would keep her mouth shut about the wedding. On the contrary, she would blab it to as many people as possible. Her only hope was that I loved Ali so much I would leave home and move in with him after all.

I talked to Ali about my decision and the conditions I had given my mother for marrying him. He was upset and tried to dissuade me from going ahead with it. "This is the wrong thing to do," he said. "You will not be happy after marrying me. I can never give you the future we dreamed about. I've lost everything. I'm an opium addict."

"I know it isn't what we planned," I said. "I know it isn't good, but it's the best choice we have. By signing the marriage contract, I will be more able to help you recover. And with you as my husband, my brother can't bully me or control my life anymore."

I tried to convince him that he was helping me by signing the contract. Finally, he agreed.

Along with our parents, Ali and I went to a mullah in the middle of the night to sign the contract and pay the mullah's fee. Ali and I never imagined our wedding day would be like this. We were so sad and tired. There were no laughs, no smiles, no congratulations, nothing to celebrate. He and I signed the paper, said good night, and each returned home with our parents. The whole thing was ridiculous. The only change was that now I could talk to Ali without my brother's permission.

Ali loved and respected me. My father had protected and encouraged me as I grew up, and Ali would have done the same except for his experience in jail. He was like a dead man, unable to plan or focus or even take care of himself. He let me make decisions about my own future because he loved me but also because he was no longer able to think clearly or follow through on a plan.

My brothers were furious to be excluded from the contract signing. Arman came home from Kerman, had a violent argument with our mother, realized it was too late to change the situation, and went back to Kerman. Kaveh called from Tehran and cursed my mother over the phone for not including him. They were insulted that as family leaders they were not consulted. I was happy because they no longer had any control over my life.

A few months after Ali and I married, my brother Kaveh encouraged my mother to move the family to Tehran where he was living. I had always thought that eventually I would leave Rafsanjan. As a girl I sometimes talked about living in a foreign country. "The only foreign country you're fit for," my brothers would say, "is the bathroom in the far corner of the house!" Though those days of mocking and insult were gone, the sad situation with Ali changed my perspective about moving. The thought of leaving Ali now was very difficult. I still hoped that eventually we would be students together at the university in Shahreza, but the possibility of that was unclear. Ali couldn't return to college for three semesters because of his criminal history. We couldn't live together because our marriage was still a secret. As a young single woman I could not live alone in Rafsanjan. The only solution was for Ali to stay in Rafsanjan and me to move to Tehran with my parents and sister.

Soon after the move I got the good news that I had passed Konkur and could enroll at the university in Shahreza. As a student I would live in a dormitory, which at least temporarily solved the problem of finding an apartment as a single woman. Shahreza is famous for the Shrine of Shahreza, where Muslims pray for healing and leave money in hopes their prayers will be answered. This and other shrine-tombs, called *imamzadeh*, are pilgrimage centers all across Iran. I remember as a child hearing that these places offered miraculous cures and that so many people came to touch the graves, pilgrims were sometimes trampled to death. Even then I questioned the truth of all the miracle claims. My wits told me they were fake and belonged to Satan. After the revolution, mullahs realized they could trick poor ignorant people into giving money to imamzadeh. In time there were eight thousand of them all across the country, their rich offerings lining the pockets of the religious elite.

I registered at the university and rented a room in a private dorm owned by a very religious couple. There were four double bedrooms and a big living room and kitchen that all eight residents shared. My roommate was a nice girl from the city of Kashan, and she became a close friend.

The first day of classes, school authorities told us it was compulsory for all female students to wear a chador, the long black veil dictated by Islamic law. Not only did we have to wear them to class, we had to wear them any time we were out in the city. Otherwise, we would be expelled. I knew some universities required women to wear a chador to class but never imagined I would have to wear it on the street as well. I didn't even know how to manage it properly because I usually avoided wearing one in Rafsanjan. The first few months in Shahreza my friends made fun of my attempts. I put the cloth under my arms and half of my body was not covered properly. But I had to conform. I couldn't let my natural rebellious streak show, couldn't resist the rules, because I wanted to help Ali be readmitted to the university. For his sake I had to build a good reputation.

My roommate was a beautiful girl named Naghmeh, who arrived with her mother to help her move in. Since I was older than Naghmeh, her mother asked me to protect her like a little sister and give her good advice. I promised I would, and eventually we traveled together to visit both our families. Her family was very kind to me and treated me like one of their own.

Keeping my promise to protect her turned out to be harder than expected. Another girl in our dorm, Lyla, was the daughter of a mullah and one of the most immoral women in Shahreza. She wore heavy makeup, had sex with different boys at the university, and went with boys to parties in Isfahan, a big city of 1.5 million where she could enjoy her freedom.

Lyla also liked group sex and sex with girls, and began a sexual relationship with her roommate, Zohreh. Lyla set her sights on Naghmeh as well. Because I warned Naghmeh to stay away from Lyla and her friends, that made Lyla, Zohreh, and others angry. As much as they wanted their revenge against me for protecting my friend, they knew I would not stand any abuse from them. I had recently shown them that nobody got away with mistreating me, and I had taught a rude boy a lesson in the process.

Rude behavior from men and boys was commonplace in Shahreza. Despite the religious reputation of the city, men there were notorious for harassing women, exposing themselves to women and groping them in public. Sometimes my dormmates came home crying because, they said, some nasty stranger "grabbed my ass" on the sidewalk. A common technique was for a man or boy to cruise by on a motorbike, reach out for a quick feel, then drive away. As soon as I heard a motorbike or bicycle behind me, or the sound of anyone approaching, I would turn and stand behind a wall to let them pass.

One day a friend and I were walking home from a shopping trip. Because we were talking I didn't hear the bicycle behind me as a boy came by and reached toward my body. He misjudged the distance and only grabbed my chador, but I saw the smirk on his face as he pedaled by. Throwing down my shopping bags, I took off my chador and ran after him. I chased him through alleys to the main street, where I knew he had room to ride and I would never catch him.

"Stop him! Stop him!" I yelled. To my amazement, an elderly man who heard me stepped in front of the boy and grabbed his handlebars. I told the man what happened and asked him to bring the boy to my landlord. I was mad enough to beat my attacker right there in the street, but the landlord had warned all his residents that if we ever had any trouble in town to let him take care of it. He threatened that if we tried to settle an issue on our own, he would report us to the university and have us expelled.

The elderly man, the boy, and I walked to my dorm, with the boy insisting the whole way that he had done nothing wrong. "I'm innocent," he kept saying. "I never touched you!"

"Shut your mouth!" I ordered. "We both know what you were after." I was determined to punish him not only for what he tried to do to me, but for the harassment my roommates so often suffered. "I will teach you a lesson today that you can't go around harassing girls in this city!"

We arrived at the dorm, and the landlord came to see what was going on. I explained what happened and told the landlord to have this young nuisance arrested for harassment.

The landlord asked the boy his name and learned he was the son of a man he knew. He took the boy's identification and let him go. He didn't even scold him.

I felt disappointed and betrayed. The landlord knew my feelings and sent his wife to my room to talk with me. She tried to convince me that he would deal properly with the situation in time.

"Your husband is a weakling and a coward," I told her. "He didn't even say anything to him. I could have handled things better myself if your husband hadn't forbidden his renters to defend themselves."

The landlord knew he had made a mistake. He knew he had failed and that I was furious. He called all the dorm residents for a meeting and praised me in front of them as a courageous young woman who was bold enough to fight back at someone for harassing her.

"I admire her very much," he told the group. "I believe you should learn from her example and be able to deal with your own matters. I was wrong to ask you not to get involved and solve problems on your own."

The fact is, his masculine pride and insistence on supervising our lives had now gotten him into a tight spot. He knew the boy's family, and it was awkward for him to press charges even though he realized he should have. He knew that's what I would insist on. He never expected one of his residents to chase down an assailant and haul him in for justice.

Later he apologized to me in private and said he would report the boy to the security police if I wanted him to. It was my choice. He also said he was changing his rule and from now on we girls could handle our own business.

"I just want to teach the men in this town that they can't harass girls whenever they want to and get away with it," I said. "Whatever your rules are, the next time something like this happens I won't be so nice as to wait for anybody else to pretend they're my father. Anybody who bothers me, I will punch them in the face since you're too weak a man to protect me." I turned and left the room.

I decided not to press charges. If I had, the security police would have done nothing to the boy and it would only have created trouble for me. Under the Islamic regime, it is always the woman's fault. They would find something to charge me with—not covering my hair properly, immoral conduct, whatever they wanted. Even then I knew that women in Iran were routinely executed for defending themselves against rapists. Years later I would meet a brave woman named Ryhaneh Jabbari after she killed a rapist who was with the intelligence police. At her trial for murder, the judge told her she should have allowed the rape and filed a complaint about it afterward. She spent five years in prison before her execution by hanging.

In the case of Zahra Navidpour the rapist wasn't killed but still took his revenge. Salman Khodadadi, a member of the Iranian parliament, warned her that if she told anyone he had raped her he would kill her. Zahra made a recording revealing the whole story including Khodadadi's threats against her. Soon afterward she was found dead. The authorities ruled it a suicide.

———— • ————

I did my best to settle into a routine and pursue my studies, but it was hard to do. My father was sick, my mother was having an affair, my husband was struggling to recover from his horrible experience, my landlord was a wimp, and my dormmates were nothing but trouble. Lyla and Zohreh never missed an opportunity to get back at me for the crime of trying to protect Naghmeh from them.

One day I was in my room studying for a difficult exam the next day. Since Lyla and Zohreh knew I had an important test coming up, they went into the living room, turned their music up loud, and started talking with loud voices. When I came out and asked them to be quiet they laughed and ignored me, as I knew they would. It was the middle of the night before they went to bed and I could finally finish studying. This became a habit with them. Whenever they saw me studying, they made lots of racket on purpose to distract me.

After a while I decided to turn the tables on them. One day when I saw them studying hard, I turned on the TV in the living room and cranked the volume up high. After about five minutes, Zohreh came flying out of her room, screaming that I was an idiot, a jerk, a bitch, and more. Such rude and impolite words!

"Can't you see we're studying for an exam tomorrow?!" she shouted.

"A few weeks ago," I said, "I was studying for an important exam and asked you very politely to turn down your music, but you ignored me. Now you demand, using the ugliest words, that I turn down the TV. You need to know how it feels. I'm not turning down the volume, and neither are you. The TV sound will be wherever I want it to be."

She and the other girls had seen me drag a boy off the street for harassment and then stand up to the landlord when he refused to act. They were not about to cross me.

"I'll tell the landlord, and he'll throw you out of here," Zohreh warned.

"Tell him," I said. "He's not touching this TV either. When you learn to respect our rules and make requests politely, then I will change my mind. Not before."

While Zohreh went for the landlord, Naghmeh and some of the other girls warned me to turn off the TV before I got into trouble. I told them not to worry. After a minute Zohreh and the landlord appeared.

"Miss Amirizadeh," the landlord said, "may I ask what has happened here and why you disobey the dorm rules by refusing to turn down the volume?"

"I know better than anyone how to respect the rules," I answered. "She's the one who was disrespectful. You don't know the whole story." I told him what had happened. "Until she learns her lesson, no one is allowed to touch this TV, including you."

Then I added, "I respectfully ask you not to interfere in this matter and let me settle it. This is between us and is none of your business." He had already proven to all of us that when it came to solving someone else's problems, he was a complete failure.

After I finished, the landlord turned to Zohreh and said, "Miss Amirizadeh is right. You two need to sort this out on your own. I am not going to interfere in your disagreements anymore." With that, he turned and left.

Zohreh rushed to her room in tears. Though she never apologized, I turned the sound down then. All I wanted was to hold up a mirror to her rude behavior and demonstrate that everyone needed to follow the rules for our mutual benefit. I had made my point.

CHAPTER 8

Coming Apart

As I was starting college in Shahreza, my brother Arman fell in love with a girl he met in Kerman while he was studying there. Arman had lots of girlfriends. He was handsome, wealthy, and lavished money (our father's money, of course) on all his friends and girls in particular. Sima worked in a photography store. Her father was executed for drug smuggling when she was a child, so her family was poor. She lived with her mother, a brother who was a drug addict, and a younger sister.

She and Arman met when he was a customer in the store, and the two started flirting. She knew Arman was wealthy and set her sights on making him her husband. She and her mother visited a soothsayer to get specific spells that would lure him to her. It is very common in Iran for people to consult a sorcerer or fortune-teller for advice in making important decisions, especially about marriage. They shouldn't have bothered. Arman was easily tempted by a beautiful face and coquettish behavior and would have been pulled in even without a magic spell. He acted like a servant to the whole family and spent lots of money on them from the beginning.

It was no surprise that money was central to the relationship between Arman and Sima. Money was what Sima and her family wanted, and money was the way my brother kept his social position

71

and popularity since he was too selfish and rude to make friends any other way except by buying them. Usually, the father of the bride and the father of the groom agree on a dowry price. In this case, Arman negotiated everything himself. The day of the engagement, he told my family he and Sima's family had already agreed on the dowry and his family had nothing to do with it, even though the money would come from my father.

The families would meet later in the day to make a formal agreement. Arman warned that if my father or any of us said anything about the dowry price, he would humiliate us in front of Sima's family. It is hard for people in the Western world to understand how important it is in the Iranian culture to save face at all costs. Such a humiliation would resonate through the whole community and be an absolute disaster for our family for years to come. It was blackmail pure and simple, but my poor sick father thought he had no choice, and my mother couldn't have cared less.

Sima's family asked for more than $500,000. Arman agreed, both for the prestige that paying such a high price gave him and the degree of love for Sima that it demonstrated. (Huge as this amount was, it was about a year's income from the pistachio ranch and not an unimaginable figure for our family.)

My parents were shocked and outraged. They hadn't wanted this marriage even before the huge dowry agreement they had no say in. Sima's family had a bad reputation because of her father's criminal conviction and execution, while my father was a man of the highest reputation and success. Everyone who knew Sima and Arman knew she didn't really love him and pursued him solely for his money and for the prospect of my father's estate. To Sima's mother and siblings, this engagement was like winning the lottery.

The couple decided to have an engagement party that evolved into a celebration almost as elaborate as a wedding. Arman would spend a lot of money to satisfy Sima and her relatives. Like everyone else he attracted to his social circle, he would buy their respect with money since he could never earn it by his character. They didn't care about his character anyway.

In Sima, Arman found someone else who was as conceited, selfish, and shallow as he was. She wasted no time in treating me the way Arman always had. When I asked to see her pictures of the engagement party she admitted she had shredded them.

"Since you were so ugly in the photos, especially your big ugly mouth, I had to shred all of them," she said. Her words could have come verbatim from Arman.

From the beginning she was jealous of me. We were about the same age. Coming from a poor family, she had little while I had a lot, and she wanted to catch up quickly. She often asked to borrow my clothes until Arman bought her a closet full of expensive new things. When she learned I had a driver's license and a car, she insisted Arman arrange for her driving test and buy her a car. Whatever I had, she had to have too.

Arman not only allowed her to be rude to me, he encouraged it. I can only guess it made them feel superior to criticize me and try to embarrass me in front of others. Arguing with them or trying to defend myself was a waste of time. I decided to let it go, but I certainly would not be attending their wedding. When I told my mother I would not be at the ceremony, she insisted I go regardless of the way the wedding couple treated me. She wasn't worried about me. She was worried about the gossip that would come from friends and family if I were absent.

I changed my mind only for my father. I attended the ceremony after all because I didn't want him to experience any awkwardness or disappointment on account of my absence. However, I drew the line at posing for photos with the bride and groom. After they shredded the pictures of me at the engagement party I was not giving them another chance to insult me. When the photographer motioned to me to take my place as sister of the groom, I refused and the whispering began. I couldn't have cared less.

My mother pulled me aside. "Why are behaving like this in front of our guests?" she asked. "Arman is so mad at you!"

"I don't care how mad he is," I said. "Go tell him that whenever he learns to respect his own family I will give him the honor of posing for pictures. I'm not stupid enough to let them shred my pictures twice." I could see that Arman was mad at my rejecting him in front of his friends, but he couldn't let loose his savage temper at his own reception. As soon as the ceremony was over I went back to Shahreza to deal with my ongoing challenges there.

———— • ————

The first week of classes at the university, I went to the office of the dean to talk about Ali. I explained that Ali was innocent of the accusations against him and the school should allow him to come back and resume his education. The dean sympathized with the situation but explained the decision wasn't up to him or the academic faculty. University security forces, who were basiji goons, were the only ones who could allow him to re-enroll.

I kept pressing my case until the dean arranged a meeting for me with university security. These long-bearded, cold-hearted thugs refused to consider letting Ali return. Because he saw how insistent I was and because Ali was such a good student, the dean recommended I meet with someone at the national department of education in Tehran. If I could convince them, university security would have to let Ali return.

I made the eight-hour bus trip to Tehran and met with a panel of Muslim radicals who told me Ali had to be punished for disobeying the rules of Islam. I tried to explain that Ali was innocent and that even if he had drunk a glass of wine, that should not be grounds for expelling a student from the university. These heartless men were unconvinced. I made the eight-hour trip back to Shahreza and went straight to class.

I didn't want to take time to rest because otherwise my family would want to know why I was absent.

I returned to the education department in Tehran several times during the school year to make my case. Each trip was exhausting and put me further behind in my studies. My only hope was that I could help Ali get back to the university without having to wait the three semesters ordered by the police. At last the authorities decided they would allow Ali to come back after two semesters instead of three. That meant he could return to Shahreza right away.

Happily, I called Ali to give him the news. I moved out of my dorm and rented a small apartment for us. Now at last we would be in college together the way we planned so long ago. The day he arrived in Shahreza I was so excited I could scarcely wait to see him come in the door. But when he walked into our living room, I knew immediately that something was terribly wrong.

That was when I learned that before he could come back to college, he had to report to the police station to receive his sentence of eighty lashes. He had never mentioned this sentence to me or anyone in his family. He knew how hard I had worked for him to resume his studies and didn't want to reveal this terrible step he was forced to take as part of the process.

When Ali took off his shirt and showed me his back, I almost fainted. His flesh was blood-soaked and swollen from the lashing. It was disgusting how savagely they beat him. I had heard about lashings before but never seen the results firsthand. I couldn't believe my eyes. How could one human being do that to another?

"Why didn't you tell me about this?" I asked.

"I knew how much you wanted me to come back to school and how much you sacrificed to help me," he said. "I didn't want to disappoint you. I knew if I told you I had to have the lashes, you would not want me to return."

I was crying with shock and anger. I could not believe that a conviction for drinking a glass of wine could justify such violence and cruelty. How could they ignore all the talent and intelligence in this young man and beat him with a cable for ridiculous charges that were completely made up? How could they so easily ruin the life of someone with such potential and so many dreams? For nothing! How many lives, hopes, and dreams like Ali's had the Islamic regime destroyed with its barbaric rules? At that moment I hated Islam and its laws with every cell in my body.

It was clear before our "marriage" in Rafsanjan a year earlier, and even clearer now, that Ali was a different person from the energetic, ambitious, optimistic boy who pursued me my last year in high school and wanted nothing more than to make me happy. He felt hopeless and had no direction in his life. His captors ruined him physically, sexually, emotionally, and spiritually. They left him nothing but a broken body, a broken spirit, and an opium addiction.

We could never live together as man and wife. We were more like friends. As a friend who cared about him deeply, I wanted to help him as much as I could. He survived months of torture and a year of addiction because he knew I would not give up on him even if he gave up on himself. I put aside any thought of continuing my college studies. My only goal was to save Ali and help him recover what the police had taken away. I wanted to restore the old Ali from the ground up. Not only for Ali and myself, but for the people who did this to him, I wanted to prove he could triumph over all the evil they had caused.

A short time after Ali came to Shahreza, he wanted to go to the security police to pick up the belongings they confiscated when he was arrested. I went with him to see where they kept him and what the animals looked like who had tortured him.

A thin man with a black beard answered Ali's knock. When he saw me, he jumped behind the door so I couldn't see his face.

"You were supposed to come alone," he barked. "Tell your wife to stand away from the door."

I stood in that spot on purpose so I could see what this monster looked like. These evil men who torture and murder have much to fear if somebody recognizes them. That's why they hide themselves and have fake identification. Whenever the reign of Islamic terror ends, they will have to flee for their lives to escape retribution from all the people they have destroyed in the name of Allah.

The man handed Ali his belongings, and we left.

On the way home, Ali took me by an old, abandoned house.

"That's where they tortured me," he said. Even though he was always blindfolded when he came and went from the building, he figured out which one it was.

"You must be kidding!" I exclaimed. "This place looks abandoned, like nobody lives there."

"That way nobody gets suspicious," he said. "There are underground rooms where the police torture prisoners every day. Down there no one can hear them scream."

Another way I tried to help Ali was to buy an exemption for him from military service. An exemption is very expensive, and there has to be a reason acceptable to the military authorities to grant one. Ali was already a year behind in his studies. Considering his condition, it was going to be hard enough to make up that time without adding another eighteen months to two years for his mandatory enlistment. His psychological problems and depression would be even worse after living the life of a soldier. I was determined to have him excused.

To do this I faced the same sort of roadblocks with the military as I had with the security police. At first they said an exemption was impossible. Time and again I walked boldly into the defense department offices, where women practically never go, to meet with various authorities. Dealing with military officers was a man's job in a man's world, and they were shocked to see a woman there arguing her case. I didn't care what they said about me or how they judged me. All I cared about was achieving my goal. Finally, a year after I first envisioned it, the military approved my request, and I bought Ali's exemption.

Though this victory gave Ali new hope, he stayed in a deep depression living in Shahreza and attending the university. The trauma of being in the community where he had been so horribly abused, and the frustration of seeing his classmates moving ahead of him into upper levels, were more than he could bear. In addition, because of his beatings he still had convulsions and headaches. Sometimes he pounded his head with his own fists in desperation for the pain to stop. Other times he resorted to opium for relief, which helped the pain but always brought back his addiction.

In tears he would tell me I had to leave him, had to save myself and look out for my own future. "I'm a dead man," he sobbed. "You're wasting your life trying to help me."

I couldn't give up that easily after all we both had been through. But I was near the end of my rope. Constantly looking after Ali, I didn't realize my own depression was growing deeper and more dangerous. Whenever Ali went back to Rafsanjan to visit his family he would start using opium again. He felt worse than ever knowing he was unable to make me happy anymore. That was what really crushed him. His trips became longer and longer until I was spending most of my time alone in our apartment. I know now that he stayed away hoping I would get tired of waiting and leave him. He wanted me to break free and enjoy my own life. But I wasn't ready to accept defeat. I believed that together we could get through it all somehow. Yet my own life was coming apart.

I stopped going to class. I hated school and hated Shahreza. The only reason I was there was so Ali and I could finish college and live our lives together. What chance did we have of doing that now? I hated the loneliness and stress of my life. I started smoking cigarettes and also started taking sleeping pills. The more pills I took, the more I slept and could escape the living hell of my life.

I started having weird symptoms and frightening health problems. Once when Ali returned from a visit to Rafsanjan I was asleep and he couldn't wake me for a whole day. When I finally got up, I thought he had just come home and was amazed when he said I had slept so long. There were times when I lay down that I felt dizzy and like I was shaking in an earthquake. I had what seemed like electric shocks running from my head to my toes and couldn't catch my breath. I would start crying loudly and couldn't stop. Sometimes I had these symptoms in public, which was an embarrassment. There were times when I felt so bad that Ali took me to an urgent care clinic, where I got sedatives and oxygen. I always felt better afterward but never knew when my medical problems would come back. I wasn't sure how much longer I could hold on.

CHAPTER 9

A Follower of Christ

S ince Ali was out of town most of the time and I was no longer in college, I sometimes went to visit my family in Tehran. As rocky as the
relationship was with my mother and siblings, I still needed to escape
from Shahreza once in a while. Life there was lonely and depressing.

The one bright spot in my world was the closeness I felt to God. In
the White Horse dream, I had tasted God's love and knew from that
moment how he loved me more than anyone on earth did. I felt his
presence every time I reached out for it. I continued writing letters to
him in a special notebook.

During one of my trips to Tehran, I had a conversation with a friend
who had talked with me before about God. She knew how much I loved
him and how I was searching for the truth about him. We both felt God
was our father, not the cruel Muslim master sitting in judgment over
sinners and condemning them to torture. I believed God is love.

This friend confessed that she had converted to Christianity. Since
this was a serious crime, she was afraid to tell me at first but decided she
could trust me. She had prayed for me that day and asked God to show
her a sign if she should share her faith. When I started talking about
my love for God and how much I wanted to know him better, that was
the sign she needed.

She said, "Now it's my turn to share my faith with you." She explained that she and her husband converted to Christianity years ago. "Jesus is the son of God and has come to this world to save us from our sins."

I was surprised and curious and excited all at the same time. I asked one question after another because I had never heard such information about Jesus. I thought he was only a prophet, as our school textbooks said. Before I left, my friend gave me a Bible. I felt like a thirsty traveler who had just found a well.

As soon as I returned to Shahreza I started reading, and God began speaking to me through the scriptures. However, what I read raised many questions. How could Jesus be God? How can I know if what the Bible says is true? Why is Christianity right and all the other religions in the world wrong? I knew little or nothing about other religions and began reading and learning about some of them.

The more I read, the more complicated the questions became. Then I realized the person I should ask to guide me was God himself, my dear, loving, heavenly Daddy. I knew he was out there. "Daddy," I said, "I know you are alive and can hear me. I really do not know what the truth in this world is. If Jesus is the truth, you must guide me to the right path and save me from being misguided. How am I supposed to find the truth without your help?"

God answered with a miracle. On my next trip to Tehran my friend invited me to worship with her. My first church service was an incredible experience. Worshipers were so joyful, full of hope, and free to pray and worship in their own language instead of the Arabic that was forced on all Muslims. The message of God's love and grace through the power of Jesus Christ filled me to overflowing.

Later the same day, I had an appointment with a doctor to see about my dizzy spells, insomnia, and the sensation I had sometimes that the ground was shaking under me. Suddenly, in my heart I heard a voice. *Marziyeh, you are healed.* The message repeated a little louder, and again louder still. The repeating continued, with the message louder every time. I tried to ignore this strange voice, but I could not. I told my friend what was happening.

"It is Jesus," she said. "He has healed you."

I appreciated her faith and encouragement, but I did not believe her. I had to leave right after the service to make my medical appointment. The doctor asked me questions, examined me, and then picked up his pen to write a prescription. Then he hesitated. After a minute he said, "I don't know why, but I cannot write a prescription for you now. Would you please come back another time?"

I was somewhat irritated by the request because I did not want to go back to my apartment in Shahreza with these uncomfortable symptoms. At that moment, I felt the presence of God reminding me of the message I heard in church and telling me to trust him and not insist on a prescription. I left the doctor's office empty-handed. But by the time I got back to my apartment, my symptoms were completely gone.

Had Jesus healed me? Maybe, but to me it wasn't enough to convert to Christianity. I asked God to show me more proof that I should believe in Jesus.

Though at the bottom of my heart I had begun to believe in Jesus, I still had my doubts. I read in the Bible about the Holy Spirit but could not fully understand it. I was fascinated with the story of the apostles' supernatural experience of speaking in tongues. I heard the same story from my Christian friend in Tehran and was very curious about it. What must it be like?

One day when I was praying, I found out. At that moment the Holy Spirit came on me, and I started to pray in tongues. Even though I didn't know what the words meant I could somehow understand what I was saying to God. It was the first time I had ever been so close to God that I felt I could touch him.

For a few seconds while I was praying, I actually saw Jesus in front of me standing beside a large throne covered with shining gold. At that moment I was not on earth. The middle of my forehead burned like some-one had branded it. In an instant all my doubts disappeared and God removed a curtain from my eyes. I could now see the truth. I could not control my tongue but kept worshiping him in an unknown language.

I prayed and sang in tongues nonstop through the night until the early hours of the morning. My jaw ached, but I did not want the expe-rience to end. The sense of God's love was so powerful and the experi-ence of singing and praying so incredible that I cannot describe it. No one hypnotized me. No one cast a spell on me. The only explanation I can logically derive from the experience is that I had met God through his son Jesus Christ.

From that day to this, I have dedicated my life to Jesus.

Since that experience, I have always felt God's presence with me. Jesus is the only person who has been with me every single day of my life. Even as I've gone through very difficult times, Jesus has walked next to me and been my guide in life.

After giving my heart to Jesus, I found hope. I wanted to share this hope with Ali. I believed Jesus could save him and change his life. We saw little of each other. He spent most of his time with his par-ents in Rafsanjan and still struggled with opium addiction. My parents thought I was still in college, but I couldn't pretend forever. Ali and I both hated our school and hated Shahreza. When I told him about my experience with Jesus, he seemed interested and said he wanted to know more. We could move to Tehran and get away from the bad memories of Shahreza. We could attend some house churches together and maybe Ali could get better help with his addiction. My only concern about moving was telling my father I had quit school. His dream was for me to finish my education, but I knew I had to tell him the truth.

Meanwhile, I considered whether to share my newfound Christi-anity with anyone in my family. My brother Kaveh had moved back to Rafsanjan and gotten a job there. God put it in my heart to visit him and share the message of Christ's salvation. Since no one in my family was a practicing Muslim at heart, I hoped Kaveh would be open to the good news of Christianity.

I met him in his office and explained what it meant to be a Christian and that I had become a follower of Christ. At first he seemed very interested. I told him how I met Jesus and how he had changed my life. Before I left, I gave Kaveh a Bible. Unfortunately, my visit had the opposite effect of what I had hoped. After our discussion, he started reading the Quran and other Islamic books. He met with an ayatollah to ask questions and tell him I had shared my faith in Jesus. The ayatollah advised him to kill me as soon as he had the chance. It was his duty. I was an infidel and lower than dirt, so Islam would protect my brother from any murder conviction.

Kaveh's initial curiosity about my new faith had turned to anger and hatred. I asked God why he led me to talk to my brother if it only fed his deadly Islamic prejudice. The Quran teaches that the command to kill infidels comes through Mohammad the prophet directly from God. Jihad, the killing of non-Muslims, is the right and responsibility of Muslims. This teaching is repeated every day by mullahs all over the world. Mosques and schools in Syria, Yemen, Afghanistan, Lebanon, and other Muslim countries are portrayed as cultural humanitarian agencies while their real purpose is to recruit and radicalize converts.

During a later visit to my family in Tehran, Kaveh stopped by my parents' house to see me. I could feel his anger. The mullah had ordered him to talk me into renouncing my faith and turning back to Islam. If that failed, he was to kill me. Kaveh and I had a long discussion, poring over the Bible and the Quran until late in the night. He asked a lot of questions that I answered as well as I could, but he refused to believe that Jesus was the truth and stayed angry at me and my faith.

Exhausted, I started praying silently for Kaveh. I asked the Holy Spirit to open his heart because I had failed to show him the truth. We sat in silence for a few minutes, then he knelt on the floor and started to cry. He began answering out loud all the questions he had asked during our hours of conversation. God had revealed the truth and opened his eyes!

"God, please forgive me for not seeing the truth about Islam," he shouted. "Thank you, God, for showing me the truth about Mohammad and the imams!" He repented his past behavior and said that God had suddenly opened his eyes and allowed him to see the truth about Jesus. That night Kaveh gave his heart to Jesus, and I was so happy.

But things were not what they appeared to be. In spite of this powerful experience, Kaveh's character didn't change. Whatever I thought I saw that night, I don't believe he ever experienced the Holy Spirit and a new birth in Jesus. He told me later that based on his interpretation of the Bible, we should obey the government's rules and laws. That meant women were not the equal of men, I was not legally equal to him, and he still had control over our father's legacy. When it came to money, all his newfound beliefs were out the window. His behavior reminded me of Jesus's story of the rich man who would find it very hard to get into heaven because of his greed. If we do not practice and obey God's commands, our faith is meaningless.

I had a similar experience with Arman. We were in Tehran together, and he asked me about my faith in Jesus. As we talked he was eating fruit, cutting it with a knife. I noticed that as I spoke, his face turned red and he started sweating, clutching the knife handle in his fist. Then he threw the knife across the room.

"What happened?" I asked. "What's wrong?"

"I was holding the knife tightly to keep from killing you," he said. "While you were talking I felt a strong power driving me to put this knife in your neck. I had to throw it away to stop myself."

I knew Satan was mad at me and that God had protected me against the dark powers working through my brother. Some time after I went back to Shahzera I heard that Arman had given his life to Jesus, but I never saw any difference in his behavior or attitude. If the Holy

Spirit had come to him, it would have been obvious. As with Kaveh, he said the right words, but the actions of a Christian never followed.

Years later I was incredulous to learn that in America and other Western countries, schools and professors try to teach that jihad means something besides "killing infidels." They try to soften and "contextualize" this, the main command of Islam. That was when I myself attended a college class where the teacher tried to insist that people misunderstood the true meaning of jihad. When I started to explain that my own brother was commanded by a mullah to kill me for converting to Christianity, he changed the subject and refused to let me finish. Of course, he had no firsthand knowledge of what he was talking about. It is tragic to see how ignorant people in positions of authority continue to mislead the world about Islam.

CHAPTER 10

A Big Lesson

Ali and I moved to Tehran. Since nobody outside our immediate family knew we were married, we couldn't live in our own apartment. We moved in with my family until we could figure out a better solution. As I had expected, my father was heartbroken to learn I had not finished my education. I couldn't explain my decision to him because he didn't know anything about my and Ali's problems in Shahreza. I promised my father I would earn a PhD but failed him because I was trying to help Ali.

I needed to get a job. Few careers are open to women in Iran, but one available option is cosmetology. I could learn to be a hairdresser and give beauty treatments. Ali managed to get a job in business and went to work every day. We started attending a house church in Tehran, and in time, Ali gave his heart to Jesus. He expected a miracle and cried and prayed for Jesus to deliver him from his addiction. Despite both of our prayers, he failed again and again to stay away from opium.

I believe his hopelessness did not allow him to experience healing. He called himself "the walking dead" and believed he had lost everything. Ali knew how much I wanted to continue my education and was sure he was ruining my happiness. I tried to put up a brave front and pretend I was satisfied with our life together, but he felt my disappointment. We once had such dreams of happiness. Now Ali was desperate. In addition to his addiction he was taking psychiatric drugs to help with the problems caused by his beating and torture.

Ali had been an addict for two years. His doctor told me there was only a 5 percent chance he could overcome his addiction and return to a normal life. The lingering effects of torture made his prospects for recovery even worse. With tears in his eyes, the doctor said, "I cannot believe these bastards could destroy the life of such an intelligent person as Ali."

"Five percent is chance enough for me," I told him. "I'm not giving up."

"I can see that," the doctor replied. "I have never seen such a strong and loyal woman. You are willing to sacrifice everything to help him. But I believe you're wasting your time. Ali will never be the person he was."

True, I was sacrificing everything—time, money, education, health, my own happiness—to help Ali. The effort was exhausting. Both of us were sinking. At times I felt like giving up but resolved to keep fighting. My last resort was Jesus. I asked one of our Christian friends to pray that Ali would be healed from his addiction. We both prayed for a miracle.

This friend introduced me to a very faithful Armenian Christian family: Onnik, who was a pastor of several house churches; his wife, Karmella; and their two children. Karmella was the kindest woman I had ever met. The family was not rich but had the kindest hearts to serve others. We immediately became fast friends. They moved out of the house where they lived so Ali and I could stay there while Ali concentrated on quitting his addiction.

In spite of all the sincere prayer, Ali did not get better. I was desperate and didn't know what to do. When I asked God for guidance, I felt he was telling me that Ali and I should go our separate ways. But I couldn't imagine God would ask me to do that instead of helping him. I believed Ali had given his heart to Jesus, so I tried to ignore any message that I should leave him.

Finally, after many stressful months of trying different methods, praying, and continuing to ignore God's message to leave Ali and save myself, I asked God for final assurance that I should separate from my husband. I promised this time I would obey his will. The next morning I woke up early and, before leaving for cosmetology school, I prayed, "Jesus, if you want Ali and me to separate, please send him away yourself because I cannot leave him." Then I went to class.

That night Ali and I were supposed to go to the theater. In the afternoon my sister, Marjan, called to ask if I was still going to the theater and what time I was leaving. "Yes," I answered, "we're still going. You can ask Ali what time works best for him."

"Don't you know?" she asked with a note of surprise. "Ali left this morning after you went to school. He said goodbye to me and went to Rafsanjan."

I was shocked. I knew nothing of these plans and could not believe he was gone. Since I didn't want Marjan to know I was unaware Ali had left, I said, "Yes, I know he left this morning, but I thought he might change his plans and travel tomorrow instead. That way we could still go to the theater."

It was the first time Ali had ever gone to Rafsanjan without telling me. I knew immediately this was an answer to my prayer. God made it happen. When I left for school that morning, Ali was still asleep. Later that day God sent Ali away just as I had prayed for him to. Now I was sure God wanted us to be apart and would not try to bring him back again. This was God's will. Even so, my heart was broken because I had tried every way possible to help Ali. His captors had ruined him beyond recovery. After two years of trying, I surrendered to God's will and stopped trying to save my husband.

———— • ————

Once I became a Christian, God spoke to me many more times in dreams. As I had realized earlier, this was not because I was especially holy or loved more than anyone else. God chose this method because of my personality, my faith, and the condition of my country. It was one way of communicating that no Iranian authority could prevent.

I had many different kinds of dreams. In some of them I heard the voice of God speak directly to me. Some were about future events. Some were about the people around me, when God would reveal the truth about them and also their destiny. Some dreams were clear while others needed interpretation so that God's message was revealed later.

In my White Horse dream, Jesus had shown me his love and the truth about Islam. During the years of struggle with my family, Ali, and my own depression and illness, I saw battles with Satan in some of my dreams. In one of them, Satan was trying to kill me. He was angry and determined to destroy me. Satan was like a vampire whose mouth and hands were covered with blood. His nails were huge and long like claws. Suddenly he plunged his nails deep into my heart, ripping it, and he dragged me across the floor.

Although I knew he had ripped my heart, I felt no pain because as he dragged me around, I was worshiping and singing to God. The sound made Satan furious. I could see how he hated me. He drove his nails deeper trying to stop me, yet still I felt no pain. I sang louder than before.

Then I woke up. The dream had revealed to me how angry Satan was about my faith. He would add more pain to my life in order to try to separate me from Jesus. He was desperate that I was worshiping God in the midst of all my difficulties. Even though I was under a lot of pressure, nothing could shake my faith in Jesus. With God and God alone we can endure any pain and go through to victory. Only God can protect us from Satan and his harm and deception. Through my dreams I could see how much power I had in the name of Jesus. Even saying his name terrified Satan. That was a big lesson to learn.

———•———

Azadeh had been one of my best and closest friends since middle school. We shared everything with each other, never imagining our destinies would be tied together in the future. She was the only person I confided in completely—all the ups and downs, all the hopes and heartaches and family drama. She did what she could to comfort me and distract me from my struggles. We were like sisters. She was a beautiful girl with light eyebrows and long hair that Iranians called "blonde" because it was much lighter than average, though to Americans it would be auburn or dark brown.

Though her family lived in Rafsanjan, her father was a veterinarian whose office was in Tehran. After Azadeh finished high school, her family moved to Tehran so they could live together. I missed her so much then, and we talked a lot on the phone. When my family decided to move to Tehran I was very happy because I could see Azadeh again. We ended up living near each other on opposite sides of a small park. God had brought us back together, and we swore we would never be separated again.

After I gave my heart to Jesus, I shared my faith with Azadeh, and she became a Christian too. We attended house churches together and prayed for each other. She was the only one who knew the whole story about my mother's affair. She couldn't understand why I allowed my mother to go on like she did. Why did I stay silent?

Azadeh would scold me, saying, "If you don't tell everybody what she's doing, I will! Your mom is destroying you and your family, and you allow her to keep it up with your silence." I couldn't make her understand that revealing my mother's behavior and confirming it as true would bring unimaginable shame on our family.

I didn't hear from Azadeh for a while. When I tried to find out why, I became suspicious of her behavior. I knew her well enough to know she was hiding something. Then I learned she was dating Hamed, a private English tutor who taught Azadeh and her sister at their house. Hamed knew the family was very wealthy and that Azadeh was vulnerable. He started deceiving her with his fake love. Hamed was divorced, had a child, and was from a lower-class, highly prejudiced Muslim family. He was a terrible match for my friend Azadeh, but she was too blinded by his promises and charms to see the truth.

Azadeh decided to marry Hamed. When she introduced me to him, I was extremely disappointed that she could have fallen for such an arrogant, overbearing man who obviously cared only about her family's money. Azadeh had never had a romantic relationship before and was very naive. Soon Hamed convinced her she was lucky to have such a great boyfriend. He became more and more controlling and selfish. I prayed and argued and tried to warn her she was making a terrible mistake. But she had no interest in my advice. "I don't want your opinion," she said. "You sound like my own family." She was determined to ruin her life. Because she got tired of my warnings, she started to avoid me and we drifted apart.

I could not stand by and let her destroy her chances for future happiness. I decided to try talking with members of her family who felt the same way I did. When I spoke to Azadeh's mother, I realized all of them were desperately trying to keep Azadeh from marrying this dangerous opportunist. Her mother found out that Hamed had psychological problems during divorce proceedings against his first wife. He was brainwashing and controlling Azadeh more and more. When Azadeh learned that I had talked to her family, she cut me off completely. I knew I ran the risk this would happen but considered it worth trying in order to save her. I loved her and wanted to help her. She didn't see it that way. She and Hamed were married, and they disappeared from my life, though I never stopped praying for her.

Years later, when I was living in the United States, she called me. I was delighted to hear her voice, though I was sad—but not surprised—at the story she had to tell. After their marriage, Hamed took complete control of every aspect of their life. He sold her property without permission and kept the money. He refused to let her leave the house. He beat her for even the most inconsequential matters. She got pregnant right away, and the beatings and abuse continued in front of their young daughter.

In desperation, Azadeh filed for divorce. She hired a lawyer and started the process, but the courts refused to hear the case without her husband's permission. Every time he beat her, she went to the police station to show authorities the latest set of bruises. They said being beaten once or twice was not enough to justify her complaint. She had to have more bruises before they would take action on her case.

"Do I have to be murdered by my husband to convince you my daughter and I are in danger?" she asked. "How can I get a divorce after I'm dead? And how can I protect my daughter from being beaten too?"

"Do you have any evidence the child was beaten?" the police asked. She didn't, but even if she did, under Islamic law mothers have no right to sue fathers for beating their daughters. Fathers own their children and have the right to punish them as they see fit. If they went so far as to murder a child in cold blood they would be sentenced to only two or three years in prison.

Even after the divorce case began, Azadeh had to keep living with Hamed. According to the law, her leaving the house would be a sign of disobedience to her husband, which would weaken her legal position. Every time Hamed got a letter from the court, he beat Azadeh again in front of their child. She was a regular witness to her mother's beatings, but the authorities would never bother to interview her.

After long years of suffering and effort, Azadeh got her divorce. However, the court granted custody of the daughter to Hamed from the age of seven, as allowed by Islamic law. Though he promised to let Azadeh visit their daughter, he failed to keep his promise. By law she was allowed twenty-four hours a week of visitation, but Hamed didn't even permit that. When she complained to the court, the court said they could not get involved because her husband now had custody of the child. She would have to convince him herself to allow visitation. Hamed told Azadeh that if she would give him some property, she could visit twenty-four hours a week. Then he wanted a car. Eventually, she gave up fighting and had not seen her daughter in years. She doesn't even know where she lives. In the world of Islam, a woman is a creature who must serve the man, and her cry is never heard.

It is infuriating to see international organizations today that not only ignore such institutionalized brutality against women but also elect the criminals and misogynists who promote these policies to positions where they monitor the status of women's rights. I cannot understand how the United Nations, along with other similar groups that are supposed to defend humanity and fight against the violation of human rights, allow such a barbaric regime as the Islamic Republic of Iran to have a seat on their commissions on the status of women in the world. The UN and others are like a ridiculous circus with clowns and buffoons who care only about lining their own pockets and securing their own safety and wealth, not about the rights of women around the world. Human rights are meaningless to these institutions. They'd rather make a trade deal and look the other way when it comes to torture, murder, and institutional abuse of women.

Worst of all are European women politicians who sweep the whole terrifying subject under the rug. Either they are hopelessly ignorant of the facts or arrogant accessories to these murderous policies. They're far worse than the men politicians. How a woman can sit beside a male politician from a nation where gender-based murder is commonplace and shake his bloody hand, while the man sees the woman as half the human being he is and worthy only to satisfy his wishes, I cannot imagine. None of those smug, immaculately groomed women "leaders" would last a minute under the brutal and barbaric reality of Islam.

May the Lord open the eyes of those who close them to the injustices against humanity and sell their souls for money and power.

CHAPTER 11

Stolen Harvest

After Ali left, I made myself busy by taking some extra courses at cosmetology school. I would have to earn my own living in the future, so I wanted to prepare as well as possible. Meanwhile, the relationship with my mother remained strained. She kept finding ways to limit my father's recovery and cheat him out of his property. She discovered that I was bluffing about having a recording of her on the phone with her boyfriend and so flaunted her affair more openly than ever.

One day I found a bottle of pills in the glove compartment of our car that I recognized as strong sleep medication. In my mother's handwriting, the label read, "For treatment of allergy." I knew my father's medications and knew this was not one of them. I believe my mother got this from the pharmacy to mix with my father's other medicine and keep him groggy all day so he wouldn't interfere with her or ask questions. I believed she was gradually killing him with sedatives. This realization made me despise her even more than before. I felt I had no choice but to tell Arman and Kaveh what was happening, yet I was afraid they would only make matters worse.

This happened before Azadeh and I parted ways. Azadeh was the only person who knew the whole story, so I asked her what she thought I should do. This was also during a time when my mother claimed she wanted to be a Christian and was attending a home church with Azadeh and me. I hoped Jesus would change my mother's ways, but she never truly accepted Christ. She was too busy backbiting and criticizing me, telling others in the congregation that I was a pessimistic person who was suspicious of her for no reason. People in the church began to think I was a disrespectful daughter who unfairly mistreated her mother. As before, I did not tell anyone besides Azadeh the truth because it would bring such shame on our family for my mother's affair to become public.

Azadeh warned, "If I were you, I would tell everybody what's going on. You have to speak up for the truth. People at church believe your mother's side of the story because you're still protecting her reputation!"

I said I would pray for my mother to change by attending church but would remain silent even if it gave others the wrong impression. On the other hand, she played up her role as the mistreated, self-sacrificing mother, crying and looking for sympathy. One church member shared with me a dream about Mother, that during a service the heads of seven foxes appeared on her back. I'm not sure what this meant, but my mother was definitely sly like a fox when it came to pretending she cared anything about me or about the church.

The pastor of our home church, an Assyrian woman, invited her brother Asu to worship with us. She said he was a heroin addict who was saved by Jesus. The rest of their family had abandoned him when he became addicted, so he lived alone and sometimes stayed with his sister. Asu seemed like a kind, humble, spiritual person, and everyone at church liked him. He knew a lot about the Bible. He had memorized long passages of scripture and told biblical stories with impressive passion.

My mother and I became friends with Asu and invited him to our home. Even my father, who had no real interest in Christianity, listened carefully to him and was impressed by what he had to say. While I was happy that Asu's Christian testimony appealed to my father, my intuition told me something about him wasn't quite right. Yet as soon as he started talking about the word of God, I repented in my heart and asked God to forgive me for my judgment. How could someone who talked so passionately about God and the Bible be evil?

But I couldn't shake my suspicions. I had already caught my mother having an affair. Now I believed she was romantically involved with Asu. One day after church, Azadeh and I followed the two of them and saw them go off together. This heightened my feelings even more. I was sure they were seeing each other behind my father's back. (Later I learned that my father shared my suspicions, and when he confronted my mother, she said he was mentally incompetent and convinced the doctor to send him for shock treatments.)

I told my pastor about my concern and asked her not to have Asu attend our church. She told me I was mistaken and that her brother was of the highest moral character. She believed this at least in part because my mother kept spreading her gossip that I was a pessimist and that my crazy assumptions about her and Asu were completely false. The fact is, God has given me the gift of discernment, and I can see through to people's true character. I knew I was right and was disappointed that the pastor insisted I was mistaken. She asked me to change my attitude toward her brother. I agreed that we should not be judgmental, but at the same time I couldn't pretend to be stupid and close my eyes to what was happening around me. My accusations irritated the pastor, and I knew it was pointless to say any more about it.

I tried to solve the problem myself by keeping Asu out of our house. He was luring my mother away and betraying my father's trust and admiration for him. I called Asu and said I knew about his affair with my mother. I warned him that if he ever came to our house again, I would tell my brothers and members of the church what he was doing. But my mother kept inviting him, and he ignored my threats.

Eventually, I couldn't take this lying, pretend-Christian another minute. I came home one day when he was in the living room with my mother and sister. My father was asleep in his room.

I opened the front door and yelled, "Asu, get out of this house right now, or I will kick you out myself!"

My mother jumped up. "You have no right to insult my guest in my home," she said.

"Tell him to get out," I ordered. "Otherwise I will tell everybody you know about your dirty relationship!"

Without a word, Mother looked at Asu and pointed toward the door. She knew she could not resist me in this.

As he passed me on the way out I said, "This is the last time I will ever see you here," and slammed the door behind him. My whole body was shaking. He never came back. While he never again betrayed my father in his own home, he and my mother continued meeting elsewhere in secret.

Though my pastor was angry at me for throwing Asu out, her husband was on my side. "Marziyeh is right," he told her. "Your brother and her mother are having an affair behind her father's back." The pastor still refused to believe her beloved brother could act that way. That being the case, I decided it was best for me to stop going to that house church.

The affair continued. Not only was I angry at my mother, I was worried that she would eventually dose my father with enough sleeping pills to kill him and get him out of the way. I saw no alternative but to tell my brothers what was going on. They wouldn't care about my father. What would interest them about the situation is that if my mother left, they could sue to end her guardianship of my father and get control of his estate. As always, all they cared about was money and being in charge.

One fear I had was that they would kill our mother. As much as I despised her, I didn't want to feel responsible in any way for that. I called Arman and Kaveh and told them I needed them to come to Tehran. We met away from the house, and I told them our mom was having an affair with the brother of my house church pastor. I didn't mention the previous affair I had discovered by phone or anything else that had been going on. They didn't have the capacity to understand or react properly to so much. The affair with Asu was plenty.

They went to the house immediately and angrily confronted our mother. They wanted her gone. They gave her an ultimatum: leave home on your own or get a divorce. Either way, she would no longer be in a position to keep mistreating my father. My mother moved out, got a divorce, and eventually married Asu.

My brothers wanted to move Father to Kerman. Since they would not be renewing the lease on the house in Tehran, I had no choice but to accept their invitation to move in with them. For the time being I would have to stop pursuing my cosmetology career, help my father get resettled, and deal with whatever self-serving plan my brothers came up with.

As soon as my father and I moved into Arman's house in Kerman, my brothers began the process of taking over my father's property. They filed a case in court to sue our mom for abusing her guardianship. A psychiatrist examined my father and certified that he was healthy enough to manage his own affairs. This made my father so happy! Little did he know it was only a trap.

The court ruled in favor of my father and ended my mother's guardianship. That put control of his estate back in his own hands. Of course, that wouldn't work for my brothers. They took my father to another psychologist and bribed him to say our dad was incompetent. Based on that report, the court gave control of the estate to Kaveh. My mother had never given me any of my share of income from the pistachio ranch. Now it was my brothers' turn to steal the rest of my father's wealth and property.

I wanted to go back to Tehran and get a job with my cosmetology degree, but I didn't have any money for an apartment or living expenses. My brothers told me that if I would stay in Kerman until the pistachio harvest, they would give me my share of the money and

I could return to Tehran. Since it was really the only choice I had, I remained with them until the harvest in early fall of the year.

It was uncomfortable living with Arman and his wife, Sima, who was as jealous of me and as hostile as ever. The weeks passed slowly, and at last the harvest was in and sold. It was then that my brothers told me they would give me my share of the income only if I agreed to live permanently in Kerman. There, I would remain under their control, helpless to manage my own life. The only reason to stay would have been to help my dad, but as long as Arman and Kaveh were around I had no power to do anything.

"You have no right to tell me where to live," I said. "This money is my property, just like your portion of the income is yours. Our father gave each of us our share. I never tell you how to spend your money or live your life, and you have no right to tell me."

I suspected that even if I agreed to stay they would still keep my money. They wanted revenge for all the times my father protected me from them.

"This isn't our decision," Arman said. "This is what our father wants."

What an outrageous, insulting, and ridiculous claim! First of all, he would never say that. Second of all, they had taken away my father's control of his business with a guardianship so his wishes didn't matter anyway. They had never given my father a cent to make him more comfortable or ease the burden of his illness and his wife's betrayal. And they would never give me a cent either.

"I'm leaving, with or without my fair share of the harvest income," I said. "I will stand on my own two feet and never ask you again for what is rightfully mine."

"You're not going anywhere," Arman said. "I will make the decisions about your life and your future. Father isn't around to defend you now, and you have to obey me whatever I tell you do to."

"You will never decide for me!" I yelled. "I would rather die than be bullied into acting like your servant."

Arman snapped. One minute we were scowling at each other and the next he lunged at me, beating me with his fists and gouging me with his fingernails as his wife looked on. I had to go to the hospital for treatment of stress and low blood pressure. When I returned home, Arman was gone. I started packing my suitcase.

As I gathered my clothes, Sima came into my room and sat in front of me.

"I have to confess something," she said. "I've always been jealous of you."

"This is nothing new," I said. "You've been jealous of me since the day we met, and you've never been shy about it. Now you don't have to worry. My mother has robbed me and abandoned the family, my father is sick and unable to stand up for what's right, and my brothers have stolen everything I had left. I have nothing. There's nothing to be jealous of anymore."

"I am jealous of your courage," she said. "You are fearless. I'm jealous of you because you're brave enough to live alone with no money and no support. You could stay with us here and be taken care of, but you refuse to give up your freedom no matter what the risk. I could never do it." She paused, then asked, "Where did you get that courage and resolve?"

"From God," I explained. "I know who my true Father is, and I trust in him. I am fearless because my faith is in him and not in this world."

"I'm so sorry I don't have any money to help you out," she said. "If I had any money of my own, I would gladly give it to you to help support you back in Tehran."

What a lie! She had access to plenty of money both in her own bank account and from her husband. Also, a few days earlier while I was in the house alone, I accidentally found a huge stash of cash hidden under the carpet in her room.

I didn't mention any of this. "Don't worry," I told her. "I don't need your money. I'm confident I will be able to support myself."

Later in the afternoon the door opened—and there stood Ali!

"What a surprise," I said to Ali. "Why are you here?"

"Your brother asked me to come and convince you not to go back to Tehran."

Obviously, Arman did not know Ali and I had been separated for months. When Ali saw scratch marks on my face, he asked what happened. "Arman attacked me because I told him I'm moving back to Tehran," I explained.

"Arman sent me here to stop you from leaving," Ali said. "He said I should beat you if you don't obey me." I could tell he had no interest in taking Arman's cruel advice. Ali continued, "I apologize for coming here without your permission."

"It's all right," I said, realizing once again what a dirty and vicious excuse for a brother I had. "Don't worry. There's no need for you to get involved."

Ali agreed. "I will support you in your decision," he said. "I know now what kind of bully your brother really is."

As we were talking, Ali's father arrived. Arman had called him too. Arman told Ali's father that Arman would give Ali and me lots of money if I would stay in Kerman. Ali's father liked that idea because if I stayed, maybe I would help Ali some more with his addiction and other struggles. "If you agree to stay in Kerman, Arman and I will give you all the money you need to live," he said.

"Thank you for your support," I said. "You should have supported me all those years I was trying to save your son and no one helped in the slightest. I'm leaving. Don't try to stop me."

Carrying my luggage, I walked down the street to find a taxi. Just as I left, Arman returned. I was still in sight of the front door, so he sent Ali after me. My husband caught up with me, took me by the hand, and said, "Marziyeh, don't you think it would be better to stay at least a few more days?"

Two minutes ago we had agreed that Arman was a cruel bully and the best thing I could do was leave his house as soon as possible. Now Arman had forced Ali to come after me.

"Leave me alone," I shouted. "You have no right to stop me!"

He grabbed the handle of my suitcase. I slapped him with every ounce of power I could muster. "How dare you stop me when you know how horrible my brother is!" Arman and Ali's father stood watching in the doorway.

My slap brought Ali to his senses. "I'm sorry," he said. "Let's go." He waved down a taxi, and we both got in. "I'll go back to Tehran with you to make sure Arman doesn't try to stop you again. Then I'll return here and leave you in peace." Since Ali was legally my husband, Arman was powerless to stop us. My brother could only stand in the doorway and seethe with fury. Ali and I rode to the bus station and took a bus back to Tehran together.

While living in Arman's house I had prayed a lot about my future. The Holy Spirit assured me I should leave that place. That was one reason I was so anxious to move back to Tehran. Also I had a dream during that time that reinforced this sense that I should go.

In my dream, I was looking at the sky. God opened the sky and dropped three big boxes down to me—gifts from my heavenly Father.

"These are yours," God said.

While the boxes were coming down, one of them opened. Inside was a small carpet with unbelievably beautiful flowers on it. As it got closer, I could see that the flowers were fresh and natural. It unrolled, moved under my feet, and took me up into the sky.

"This is not the time to see the other two gifts," God said to me. "They will be open in the future for you."

I was leaving Kerman with nothing. I had no money, no family, and no support. I knew I had chosen a difficult path and anything could happen. However, I trusted in a mighty God who would never leave me alone. I knew he would be with me and protect me everywhere. This dream added to my confidence that God was with me, that I definitely needed to leave Kerman, and that I could always trust God to be close by no matter where I was.

CHAPTER 12

Step by Step

Ali and I found a cheap hotel for me to live in for the time being. Even among the low-budget options, no reputable hotel would let me register as a woman traveling alone. The clerk checked our identification cards to make sure we were legally married, and then Ali registered on my behalf. He needed to get back to Rafsanjan for more addiction treatment and could only stay a few days. We made sure the hotel employees saw us together as man and wife. When Ali returned to his home, he left his ID card so the clerk would not think I was living there by myself. However, after a few days the staff realized Ali was no longer around and began to suspect I was on my own. I had to find a permanent home immediately. I had no idea then that it would be five years before I returned to Kerman and saw my father again.

I spent the days looking for an apartment, returning to the hotel only at night so the staff would see me alone as seldom as possible. I had no job and very little money. When I left my family in Kerman I brought a few silver dishes of mine with me. I sold them for money to pay my hotel bill, but that left almost nothing for food. I couldn't afford a taxi, so I spent the day walking from one rental office to another. The first thing the agents would say is, "Where is your husband? Where is your family?" The assumption was I was a prostitute.

Almost every day, an agent would proposition me as soon as it was clear I was living alone, asking for sex or an Islamic temporary marriage. It was insulting and degrading. I started wearing old clothes and no makeup in order not to encourage them. I also still had Arman's scratches on my face, which I hoped made me less desirable.

The process was discouraging because even the smallest room or basement apartment was more than I could pay. I ate only a pastry or a piece of bread all day to conserve what little money I had. I was hungry all the time and started losing weight. I wore out my shoes so that my bare feet touched the ground through holes in the leather.

I had to find a new place soon. The hotel workers were starting to harass me. Besides, my room was awful—dark, damp, filthy, and infested with cockroaches. Suspecting I was alone at night, someone started knocking on the door in the middle of the night. When I asked who it was, they never answered. Every night I stacked my luggage against the door and prayed to God to protect me.

One night after yet another terrifying midnight knock, I couldn't go back to sleep. With all my heart, I prayed to God for help. "Please protect me, Daddy," I begged. "I don't have anybody but you. I left behind my family, my wealth, pride, and social standing. All that's left is my trust in you, that you will bless and protect me.

"I promise that no matter what happens, I will never let need and desperation allow me to choose the wrong path. I will be loyal to you even if it costs me my life. Help me, protect me, and guide me to the right path."

After crying for hours, I fell asleep and had a dream. I was sitting alone in the middle of a dry desert, surrounded by angels dressed in white. I was praying with my hands lifted to the sky. I heard the voice of God. There was no sound in the normal sense, but I could hear his beautiful voice crystal clear.

God said to me, "My daughter, don't be afraid because I am watching you. You are not alone. My angels are watching you and protecting you from all harm."

When I awoke, I couldn't believe that my heavenly Father had talked directly to me. He had heard my cries! I was overwhelmed with gratitude. I was more confident than ever from that moment on that God would be with me wherever I went. Through tears of joy I thanked God and praised him for his promise. I knew I could trust him to help me through any hardship.

A few days after my dream, someone agreed to rent a room in his house to me even though he doubted my character. In the house was a two-bedroom apartment where the landlord's eighty-year-old mother lived. She was infirm and not in the best of health, so he was looking for someone to keep her company and help her during the day. Everyone called her Maman Moulook. I fell in love with her from the first day I met her.

Maman Moulook was a short woman who was always cheerful, always smiling. She had had many hardships and disappointments in life, including the death of two children. But she was a survivor who saw the good in every situation. For a woman of her age in Iran she was very open-minded and ready for adventure. Her motto was, "Let it go!"

Though I was relieved and grateful to have a home at last, my room was small, windowless, and cold. I had no furniture, not even a bed. All I owned were my clothes and luggage. I made a sleeping pallet on the floor out of some clothes and used other clothes as covers. It was mid-autumn by now and the nights were cold. I was embarrassed by my situation and hid from Maman Moulook and her family the fact that I was in need.

Since hairdressing was one of the few jobs available to women in Iran, I thought with my training I could easily find work. But day after day I spent hours walking from one salon to the next without success. My single status was still a problem because some salons and some

111

hairdressers were fronts for fortune-telling and setting up relationships with men. I did get several job offers. Desperate as I was to support myself, I turned them all down because I was suspicious of their true nature. I had promised God I would choose only the right path.

On weekends when most salons were closed, I stayed in my room. Maman Moulook's daughter, who lived upstairs and brought her medicine down several times a day, also brought her meals. At lunch and dinner time, the smell of her delicious hot food drove me crazy. One Saturday Maman Moulook invited me to bring my lunch into the garden and join her. I said I wasn't hungry and only brought a glass of milk to the table. After watching her savor her lunch, I went back to my room and cried out of hunger and frustration. I had been a rich girl with a nice car, a pocket full of money, and anything I wanted. Now I couldn't even buy enough to eat.

I soon fell asleep and had a dream. I saw the hand of God open my door and put a plate inside. On the plate was heavenly manna such as God provided for the Israelites as they wandered in the desert. As I looked at it, I heard God say, "Do not worry, my daughter. I will feed you every day." The dream was so real that when I woke up I could still feel the presence of God in my room.

In tears, I fell to my knees to thank God for watching over me and caring about me. I thought of Jesus's words in Matthew 6. Beginning at verse 25 Christ tells us not to worry about "what you will eat or drink; or about your body, what you will wear. Is not life more than food, and the body more than clothes? Look at the birds of the air; they do not sow or reap or store away in barns, and yet your heavenly Father feeds them. Are you not much more valuable than they?" (NIV). God promises to provide for us when we trust him. He asks us to seek his kingdom and righteousness first.

This dream reassured me that I could depend on God for anything and everything. It made my faith stronger because I could see God was with me, talking to me, protecting me, and guiding me step by step. Even though I was separated from my earthly father and all my material wealth, I had a heavenly father who was always with me. God heard my cries and felt my wounds. I was not alone. In obedience to God I had left my family behind. From the first step of the journey, God was with me. Jesus himself was walking with me every day. From that moment, I had a renewed sense of feeling God's presence wherever I went and whatever I did.

After that dream God started blessing me in new ways. The next night, when I came home exhausted after another long day of job hunting, there were blankets in my room. Maman Moulook noticed I was sleeping on the floor and brought them for me. Later, her son brought me a bed. When Maman's daughter learned I was trained as a hair stylist, she hired me to do her hair at home instead of going to a salon. She told others in her family, so that before long I had a customer almost every day. With the money I earned I could buy real food for the first time in months.

I started thinking of Maman Moulook as my grandmother. We grew closer as the days passed, and I began sharing stories of my life with her. No matter what happened she was always cheerful. Whenever I was upset she smiled her radiant smile and said, "Let it go, my dear. Life isn't worth being sad about." Often she would add, "Come, dance for me!" and with her encouragement I would do a little dance around the room. After the pain of her own life, she found joy in everything.

The one trait about Maman I had to get used to was that she was very hard of hearing. I had to shout for her to understand me, and for her to hear the television she had to turn it up extremely loud. Sometimes she would start watching at 4:00 a.m. The TV would shock me out of a sound sleep and scare me half to death. The few times I asked her to turn it down, she always apologized and lowered the sound immediately. But in a few minutes it was back up again. Well, she couldn't help it if her hearing was bad.

Because Christianity meant so much to me, I shared it with Maman Moulook and her family. They seemed grateful and interested, and asked questions about it later. Whether Christ ever came into their hearts, I do not know. But I was grateful for the opportunity to speak with them about it and for their willingness to listen.

As my job search continued, I had another dream. In the dream, God showed me the cosmetology school where I had trained. I was unable to stand and was falling to the ground. Then the owner of the school, Madame Taheri, reached out her hand and lifted me up. God's voice told me, "This is where you should start your work."

I had thought of going there before, but my pride kept me away. As a student, before my mother's divorce and before my brothers took my father to Kerman and stole my inheritance, I was a wealthy, self-assured young woman from a respected family. Now I was penniless and had zero social standing. Yet that was where God told me in my dream that I should go. I hesitated at first but finally decided to follow God's leading.

As soon as I walked through the door of the school, everyone there who knew me flocked to greet me, Madame Taheri most enthusiastically of them all. Mrs. Taheri had wild, bright-red hair and stylish glasses, and always wore expensive Western clothes. She was slim, modern, and the envy of many women in the community. Her salon and school were big, thriving businesses, proving that with enough work and carefully avoiding the limelight, it was occasionally possible for a woman entrepreneur to succeed even in Tehran.

"When you left for Rafsanjan you said you'd be back soon!" Madame Taheri teased. "Where have you been all this time?"

She couldn't help noticing how thin I was, my worn clothes and scratched face. She invited me into her office for a talk. I didn't tell her everything, only that I had a falling out with my family and was now financially on my own. I didn't ask for a job. It was obvious she had plenty of employees, and I didn't want her to think she had to hire me out of charity. I told her I missed her and had come by to purchase some hair products for my own customers. I bought a few items, said goodbye to everyone, and went back to my tiny room.

A few days later Mrs. Taheri called. "Are you ready to come to work for me?" she asked.

"Are you asking me because you think I need a job, or because you really need more help?" I asked. "I know you don't need any more staff."

"One of my best employees is leaving at the end of the week," she said. "I have to replace her right away with someone I trust who can work as well as she did. It's Mrs. Rose."

"Mrs. Rose!" I exclaimed. "She has been with you almost since you started the school. I'm amazed she would want to leave."

"It was a complete surprise," Madame said. "I never expected her to quit, especially on such short notice. She said she found another job and asked to leave as soon as possible."

"In that case, I will be delighted to accept your offer."

"Great. I'll see you next Monday morning at eight."

God had worked a miracle. There was no other explanation for it. Through my dream, God sent me to Madame Taheri at exactly the right time. He knew Mrs. Rose was leaving, and I was the perfect replacement.

The school was on the top floor of a building in an upscale neighborhood. There was a big open space for the styling stations, a separate classroom, a private office for Mrs. Taheri, and a kitchen. My job was to handle the administrative duties and also to clean the salon whenever the cleaning lady was absent. I woke up at 5:00 a.m., took a bus to the salon by 7:00 to prepare the rooms and make breakfast, then opened the doors at 8:00. This was far from my dream career—I was still determined to get a college degree—but I could earn a living, have some fun, and save money for college in the future. I never forgot the promise I made to my father that I would earn a college diploma. My old friend Azadeh had once told me nothing could stop me from pursuing my goals. She said, "Even if you get to be fifty, you will never give up. You'll still be taking your Konkur to enroll in college."

I hoped it wouldn't take until I was fifty. I was only twenty, and fifty sounded like an awfully long way off. I decided to order some books and start studying at night for another Konkur entrance exam. Between my work at the salon, the long bus commute every day, and Maman Mou-look cranking up the TV volume in the middle of the night, it was very hard to make time for study. Somehow I managed to do it, passed my Konkur again, and was accepted at a university in Tehran.

My excitement didn't last long. I could only attend class at night, but because of my work I often missed the sessions. Also, it was very difficult to pay my living expenses and tuition on my modest salary. After two semesters I gave up.

For the second time, I had passed the very difficult Konkur exams and been accepted by a university. Now for the second time, personal challenges forced me to drop out. The first time it had been me trying to help Ali after his imprisonment and addiction. Now it was the lack of time and money to go on.

I began to question why God would let me experience all these difficulties and disappointments. Why did I want an education so desperately if it was always going to be out of reach? Why did I have to go through all this humiliation and deprivation? What would happen to me in the future?

God answered me in a dream. In my dream I saw a city of brick buildings. Rising up out of them was a tall tower made of gold that shone bright and beautiful above everything. The main part of the tower was built, but some of it was still unfinished.

The voice of God asked, "Can you see that tower? Can you see how beautiful it is?"

"Yes," I said. "It's stunning."

"That tower is you," God said.

"How is that possible?" I asked in surprise.

116

"That tower is you," God continued, "and it is not yet completed. As beautiful as it is now, can you imagine how beautiful it will be when it's finished?"

Then God showed me a spider spinning its web. "Can you see how this spider is building his house?" God asked. He showed me a liquid coming out of the spider's mouth. "A spider builds his house with a liquid from his own body. If you allow me, this beautiful tower, this house, will be built out of your own essence. If you allow me, I can design it and finish it with you."

I awoke realizing why God was taking me through so many difficulties. He wanted to change me, train me, and build me over again. It was so hard that the thought of continuing with these trials made me cry. Yet, difficult and painful as it was, this was God's plan for my life.

"Do whatever you want," I prayed. "I will not complain anymore." God was leading me through these hard times for a reason. Though I still didn't understand his purpose I decided to trust him. I knew he loved me because he sent this dream to explain his plan. Step by step he was walking with me and teaching me. Even though I couldn't see him with my eyes or touch him with my hands, I realized he was my true Father. He had planned a destiny for me alone. I had to trust that God chose me for a specific reason and would reveal it in his own perfect time. He would build me himself. It was up to me to trust him and yield to his will. I trusted him because I was in love with him.

CHAPTER 13

Dreams and Nightmares

As I got into the routine of working at the cosmetology school, God continued to communicate with me through dreams.

Though I hadn't seen any of my family since moving to Tehran alone, I thought about them often. One night I dreamed that all of them would be punished if they refused to repent for the wrong they had done to my father and me. I continued to hold a grudge against them for the way they treated me. After the dream, I prayed that God would forgive them and that I could forgive them too. I didn't want any of them to suffer the holy retribution they truly deserved.

Another dream was about the Assembly of God church. This was the only church in Tehran where nonmembers were allowed to attend openly. The pastors were Armenian and preached in Farsi, so it was very popular with people interested in learning about Christianity. However, the government discouraged visitors from attending. The intelligence service opened an office in front of the church entrance so they could monitor everyone who went inside. After Mohammad Khatami won election as president of Iran in 1997, the rules were more relaxed in keeping with his relatively moderate politics. Even so, in the past I only worshiped there once in a while so as not to be recognized as a regular visitor.

Now I decided not to attend this church anymore, but it wasn't because of the intelligence police. The bishop of this church taught that Armenians should marry only Armenians and Persians should marry only Persians. Several mixed couples begged him to allow them to marry, but he always told them it was forbidden. Yet after his wife died of cancer, he fell in love with a Persian woman despite his own insistence that this was against the teachings of the church.

I dreamed that the Assembly of God church was completely destroyed. This bishop was running around among the debris of the building, very anxious and stressed, trying to repair everything, but he could do nothing. As I watched the bishop, an angel in white approached me and handed me a huge, heavy key about three feet long.

"This is the key to the Church of Iran," the angel said, "and we will give this key to you. Take it." As I looked at the key and at the bishop stumbling around, I woke up. I started reading the Bible, and God spoke to me through the verses in Jeremiah 10:21–23, warning that stupid shepherds who fail to seek the Lord will not prosper and their flocks will be scattered. God put it in my heart to send this message to the bishop.

I talked about it with my friend Pastor Onnik, the kind Armenian Christian who pastored several house churches in Tehran. I told Onnik I believed God wanted the bishop to repent and pay attention to the example he was setting by his own action. He did pass my message on to the bishop, who ignored it. The time came, though, when the bishop had to leave his church and leave Iran. Eventually, he married his Persian girlfriend without any thought of the many disappointed lovers whose relationships had been destroyed by his senseless and misguided rules.

Onnik respected the messages that came from my dreams. He and his wife, Karmella, had been like family to me since they had worked so hard and so faithfully to help Ali with his opium addiction. Though Ali returned to drugs after a few months, Onnik and Karmella remained two of my best friends, and I was grateful to reconnect with them in this new season of my life. Onnik was the humblest pastor I ever saw and would do anything in his power to help someone in need. People would come to his house in the middle of the night asking for prayer on a particular matter, and he would always go to help them. They welcomed visitors to their home any time of the day or night.

The couple reminded me of early Christian believers who lived together and shared what little they had freely with each other. Onnik and Karmella lived very frugally and worked hard to support their two children, yet always reached out to help anyone in need. I could see the true love and passion they had for serving others. They stood by me through some of the hardest times of my life. Even though my family had abandoned and hurt me, God brought me this wonderful new family to love and help me and for me to love in return.

During this time I often prayed for the people of Iran who suffered under the criminal Islamic regime. It broke my heart to hear and read reports of people being arrested, tortured, oppressed, and murdered day after day. One night I had an astonishing dream that I was dressed in white, standing on top of a high mountain and holding a staff in one hand. Around me at the base of the mountain millions of people were standing. I began to pray and lifted my free hand to the sky, which was dark and overcast. As I prayed, the clouds parted and a bright light shone through to the huge crowd below. The people rejoiced because through my prayers they could see the light and miracles of God.

The people of Iran were surely desperate for light and miracles, as the summer of 1999 revealed to the world.

On July 8 of that year, a peaceful protest was staged in Tehran over the government shutdown of the reformist newspaper *Salam*. Authorities closed the paper because the day before it had published a secret intelligence ministry report about plans to censor Iran's pro-reform press.

Following the demonstrations, riot police raided a student dormitory at the University of Tehran, killing one student. This death sparked six days of demonstrations and riots resulting in three more deaths, more than 200 injured, and an estimated 1,200 to 1,400 arrested. Five of those officially detained, along with more than seventy other students, disappeared without a trace. One of them was twenty-three-year-old Said Zeinali, whose mother, Akram Neghabi, still carries a photo of her missing son and still seeks answers from government authorities about what happened to him that night. No one will accept responsibility for his disappearance. She has dedicated herself to exposing the atrocity and cruelty of the Islamic regime in Iran through awareness of his case.

I had just come home from work that horrible night when the protests began. The dormitory that was raided was very close to Maman Moulook's house. We heard shouting and screaming in the streets, then gunfire. Maman's daughter and I went up to the roof to see if we could find out what was happening. Through the smoke and darkness we saw basijis chasing students down the street and shooting at them. The students banged on random doors, begging to be let in to escape being captured or shot. Some neighbors bravely opened their doors to them, but others were afraid. If a basiji saw someone go through a door, they ran in after them and raided the house. Soldiers scanned the rooftops for witnesses, so we had to keep ourselves hidden as we watched. Though we couldn't see much because of the darkness and smoke, the sounds were heartbreaking. I prayed for protection of all those in danger.

After days of street fighting, our neighborhood looked like it was under military rule. Every night I sneaked home from the bus stop trying not to be seen. I heard that the dormitory raid was brutal and barbaric. Along with basiji, the Ansar-e Hezbollah plainclothes government agents attacked students, kicking down doors, smashing through walls, and setting fire to rooms. They pulled female students by their hair. They threw students off third-floor balconies onto the pavement, crushing their bones and paralyzing at least one victim. Students later said the uniformed police stood by and did nothing.

Tehran looked like a battlefield. Demonstrations spread to other cities including Tabriz, Mashhad, Shiraz, and Esfahan. Knowing what Ali endured for the crime of drinking wine in his own apartment, I could only imagine what cruel punishment these political protesters faced. Their fate was never reported, nor was the true number of deaths, casualties, and disappearances. The state media had to lie to cover the enormity of its crime against its own people. Other Iranians were helpless to expose the truth. Western media didn't care about the truth. It was a living nightmare.

Ali had told me that when he was in prison he met many students whose arrests weren't reported and no one knew about. Did anybody know how many people's lives were ruined during and after that horrific week in July 1999? Of course not. Did any of the media report the full story in all its murderous reality? No, not one. Families were left on their own to find out what happened to their loved ones. By this time, there was scarcely a family left in Iran who had not been affected by the arrest of at least one member at the hands of government agents for some frivolous infraction.

———— • ————

Through all the violence and military occupation of my neighborhood, I kept working at Madame Taheri's cosmetology school. Each semester we had thirty to forty students working toward their cosmetology diplomas. We also had a steady stream of fifty to seventy customers a day who allowed students to work on their hair and face. Our services were inexpensive because the students provided them in order to learn. It was good for students to have these opportunities, and it was also good for customers because they got the services very cheaply. A teacher always checked the students' work to make sure it was acceptable and correct any mistakes as necessary.

I worked both the morning and afternoon shifts every day, managing all the school's administrative matters. I answered the phone, scheduled appointments, collected money, made bank deposits, and handled communication and paperwork with the cosmetology board. Morning was the busiest time of the day because we had a lot of customers and a lot of students working. In the afternoon, Mrs. Taheri saw her own clients and taught advanced lessons to experienced students who already had their basic diplomas.

I learned new skills by watching Mrs. Taheri teach her advanced students in the afternoon. After a while she sometimes allowed me to check a student's work before a customer left the salon. I tried at every opportunity to show Mrs. Taheri how hard-working I was. I always arrived early and left late. It was my job to turn the cash over to her every night, and I was never even a penny short.

After a while, Mrs. Taheri invited me to study for certification as a trainer and manager. I was excited at the opportunity even though it meant late nights of study at home. Sometimes I didn't get back to Maman Moulook's house until 10:00 or 11:00 at night, and then studied until long past midnight. After six months, I took the trainer and manager written tests and passed them both.

The last step to certification was a practical exam. This concerned me because I had very little practical experience as a stylist. I spent most of my time at a desk. The practical exam was geared toward stylists who had been already working for years.

When I told Mrs. Taheri how nervous I was, she quickly reassured me. "While you were doing administrative work, your eyes and brain were watching closely and recording my lessons with students," she said. "Besides, I know how talented you are. I have no doubt you'll pass with ease."

The first thing I noticed at the test site was that I was by far the youngest woman there. Many of the applicants had their own salons.

Some of them I knew by reputation. I would be tested with these experienced professionals! Nervously, I prayed simply, "Jesus, help me."

The test took all day. Each applicant had to do several stylings as the examiners watched. As I worked I could see the examiners looking at me and whispering to each other. What did that mean? All I could do was concentrate and focus on the task at hand.

When I finished, I went into the manager's office to retrieve my ID card.

As she handed back my card, the manager asked, "May I ask how old you are, my dear?"

"I'm twenty-one."

"You're the youngest applicant of all, and your work was absolutely the best," she said. "Everyone else who took the test today already owns her own salon, and some of their work was awful! You were the best of the bunch, and I congratulate you, my dear."

I couldn't believe what I was hearing. Those words made my day and did wonders for my professional confidence and self-esteem. Back at the salon I shared the good news and kind comments with Mrs. Taheri.

"I had no doubt that you were the best and would easily pass," she said.

Now that I was certified, I began taking on more and more responsibility at the salon. With me working, Mrs. Taheri did not need as many other employees as she had. She let them go one at a time until only she and I were left to do everything. I found myself doing the work five or six women had once done, with only a small increase in my salary. However, I didn't complain. I had no doubt I was where God wanted me to be.

———— • ————

Students often shared their personal stories, traumas, and difficulties with me. This gave me the chance to tell them about Jesus. While some situations were the sort that anyone might face, others were serious and needed immediate attention. One student told a frightening story about her sister, claiming the sister sometimes sounded like a wolf and the shape of her mouth changed to look like a wolf.

The student asked me to come home with her and pray for her sister. I felt that something was wrong with the family and I should not go alone. I was afraid the sister was possessed. I asked my friend Pastor Onnik to go with me. I knew he had the gift of casting out demons because I saw him use his gift on the wife of a church member.

The wife had come to a church service and sat quietly at first. But when Onnik and others started praying for her, as soon as she heard the name of Jesus she started screaming and cursing, beating and attacking the people who prayed. Her voice changed completely and became very rough, like in a horror movie. The shape of her body started to change. Even though she was thin, Satan gave her a lot of power. Several strong men tried to hold her down. The noise got so loud that we stopped praying for fear someone nearby would complain about a house church holding services there. Some men took her to a quiet place outside the city in order to continue their prayers. A few weeks later the woman came back to church to share her testimony. She had suffered terribly because of the demons that possessed her. After her deliverance she became one of the strongest believers in the congregation.

Knowing this story gave me hope that Pastor Onnik could help my student's sister. He agreed to meet me at the student's house. I arrived first. The house was a run-down place in a poor neighborhood. My knock was answered by a woman whose face terrified me. It looked almost inhuman and was covered with scars. I wasn't sure whether to go inside or run. "My daughter said you were coming," the woman said, inviting me in with a gesture.

The house was very eerie, with witchcraft tools and symbols everywhere. I prayed silently until my student arrived. A minute later Onnik joined us, and we two exchanged glances. There were sinister forces at work in this house. After Onnik and I started praying, the mother left the room and never came back. The sister never appeared at all. Onnik told the student we should meet with her sister somewhere else to pray. We also told her she should move out on her own as soon as possible. If her mother was a witch of some sort and her sister was possessed, she was in grave danger.

The student told us the rest of the story. Her father was in prison for dealing drugs. Her mother had been terribly burned in a house fire and almost never left home. The only way she saw to earn a living for herself and her daughters was through fortune-telling, casting spells, and dealing drugs.

To me the fact that neither the sister nor the mother would pray with us was clear evidence they did not want our help.

"You need to move out as soon as you can," I advised.

"I know," she said. "That's why I'm learning hair styling. I want to be able to earn my own living and move away from here."

After that she and I prayed together privately at school. She gave her heart to Jesus, and we prayed for her protection as long as she lived in that house. I gave her a Bible and encouraged her to read it every day and to trust God in her difficulties. She also started attending the house church from time to time. I was grateful for the chance to show this student that whatever challenges and dangers she faced, Jesus would always be with her.

CHAPTER 14

Looking for the Light

Most of the stories I heard from students were not so dramatic, but to each of the women their struggles were very real. I encouraged them to be strong and not despair. I told them everyone in this world will pass through difficulties and hard times. Some people respond by losing hope. They get addicted to drugs or alcohol and choose the wrong path in order to comfort themselves and relieve the pain. Other people respond by getting stronger and learning how to improve their faith. They learn from their difficulties and never lose faith, never give up. They turn their difficulties into a bridge to raise themselves to a higher level. They learn from failure and transform it into a ladder to help them climb up. When they fall, they get up again and try even harder.

Then I would ask, "Which group do you want to belong to? Hopeful or hopeless? It's your choice."

I also shared some of my own life journey to encourage them not to lose hope. Even women who were much older than I was came to me with their stories and asked for advice. I was happy that I could inspire them through sharing my difficulties and, most important, my faith in Jesus.

One night when I was in the shower, the Holy Spirit whispered that one of my students was going to have a dream about me that night.

I had no idea why the Holy Spirit would tell me that. I had already talked to this student about Jesus, but she still had doubts. The next day I was sitting at my desk and had completely forgotten about my experience the night before. That particular student came into my office and said with excitement, "Miss Amirizadeh, guess what."

"You had a dream about me last night."

She was shocked. I explained that the Holy Spirit had told me what would happen. That made her more interested in Jesus than before. It was a lesson to me that God has many different ways to convince his children of the truth. She needed to see the power of God and his miracles before giving her heart to Christ. Later, that incident helped her to make her decision.

Mrs. Taheri knew I was a Christian and that I shared Christ with many students. She appreciated the passion I had for my faith but worried that it could get both of us in trouble.

"I can't stop you from talking about Jesus," she said, "because I see the positive effect of your faith on these poor women. Your faith encourages them to lean on God and trust him. It inspires them and gives them hope. However, you should be careful. I'm concerned about you and about my business.

"Please don't give anyone a Bible at school. You could be arrested, which would cause problems for you and also for me. Moreover, I don't want to lose you! I need you here. You're welcome to give people Bibles outside of school. Then if something happens, I can say I knew nothing about your faith and you never gave anyone a Bible in the salon."

I understood and respected her position. After our conversation I still shared my faith with those who needed to know God and to experience his love in their lives and were thirsty to know the truth. For women who wanted to give their hearts to Jesus, I arranged to see them outside the school and gave them a Bible and prayed for them then.

One student I shared my faith with was a beautiful, bubbly, fun-loving girl named Sara who said she was interested in knowing more about Christ and wanted to attend church with me. During the service, I noticed her attention wandering as she looked around the room. When a good-looking boy started to sing, she stared at him, watching closely, and said, "He's very handsome. I should try to get to know him."

That was a typical comment for Sara. Though she was basically a good girl, she loved to flirt. "I brought you here to worship God," I whispered, "but all you're doing is looking for another boyfriend." She apologized and promised to focus on God and her relationship with him. But it didn't happen.

The pattern continued for nearly a year. I talked to her about the love of God and the truth about Jesus and prayed for her faithfully, but she was too preoccupied with her romantic pursuits. I believe she loved God and wanted to get to know him, but she couldn't stop chasing boys.

Eventually, I got tired of praying for her and gave up. I lost contact with her and didn't know where she had gone. About a year later I answered the phone at the salon, and it was Sara! When she heard my voice she shouted with joy because she didn't know if I was still working there. She called to tell me she was now a strong Christian. She told me she had given her heart to Jesus and that it transformed her life. In tears, she admitted she was "blind and deaf" when I tried to tell her about my faith. "Now I understand why you were so eager to share Jesus with me," she said.

Sara went on and on about how she had experienced the love of God, sharing stories about her relationship with Jesus and the miracles that had happened to her. I was so happy that she had finally found the truth and that God had changed her life.

Sara's story taught me another important lesson. After a year of sharing and praying, I had given up trying to help her find Christ. Through Sara, God taught me that there is a time for those we pray for and that time is chosen by God, not by us. Even if we get tired of praying when nothing seems to happen, God never gets tired of waiting for his children or for those we tell about Christ and the message of salvation.

Sara not only found the truth about Jesus but also became a very strong Christian. Her life totally changed. She experienced the love of God and shared that love with heartfelt passion. From Sara I learned that I should never get discouraged, never give up on people once God puts it in my heart to pray for them. Never let people disappoint you with their mistakes, because Jesus came for the sinners. He loves them and will bring them to himself in his own perfect timing.

For every uplifting story like Sara's there are others without such a happy ending. Another student was a beautiful young woman with a wealthy, cruel husband who beat her almost every day. She had plenty of evidence of her abuse, but because her husband was a powerful and influential man with connections in the government, the court repeatedly refused her plea for divorce. Her husband said the only way she could get a divorce was to die. The student went to court time after time without success. The beatings and torture continued. Sometimes he bit her.

One day the student came to class with a box of cookies and happily told me she had finally been granted her divorce. I was amazed and asked her how she had done it. Her face started to change. Her smile turned to sadness and the tears began to flow.

"I slept with the judge," she said. "It was the only way. From the first, the judge said he would help me with my divorce if I would go to bed with him. I couldn't stand the thought of being with that lewd, immoral, filthy old mullah, but it was my only choice if I wanted the beatings to stop."

On one hand I was happy she had finally gotten her divorce and the abuse would stop. On the other hand, I was aghast at the idea of such a beautiful girl sleeping with a dirty old mullah to save her life and restore her freedom. I could see in her face that she was deeply broken by the experience, yet she was happy to be released from the cage of her cruel husband.

Later I would learn that in the courts of Iran it is commonplace, even expected, for women to sleep with the judges—these "holy" mullahs—in exchange for getting help with a divorce or other legal proceeding. Most courts pressure women for Islamic temporary marriages or simply sex services in exchange for favorable treatment. Otherwise their case will never make it through the system. I didn't fully believe these stories until I experienced them myself. The family courts in Iran are headed and staffed by pimps, panderers, bastard mullahs, and radical Muslims who are always looking for ways to quench the fires of their lust. They target vulnerable women and put pressure on them for sexual favors in return for Islamic "justice."

———— • ————

Every morning when I arrived at the salon, I made breakfast while looking out the window at the beautiful sky and the mountains in the distance, and I prayed. I prayed for myself, for students and customers who would be there that day, for the opportunity to talk to them about Jesus, for Mrs. Taheri, and for protection of the salon from enemies. Among the students and customers were women with bad spirits and some who were fortune-tellers. In most salons in Tehran, fortune-tellers told the future by interpreting the patterns in coffee grounds. Every day I prayed that as long as I worked there, the salon would be filled with God's presence, not demons.

One semester we had a student about fifty years old whose bad spirit I could feel from the beginning. I felt her anger and hatred toward me and that we didn't get along because the Holy Spirit in me clashed with the bad spirit in her. Other students told me this woman's eyes had an abnormal power. One day when I was cleaning a table, the fluorescent light in front of me suddenly exploded. Luckily I wasn't hurt, but as I turned I saw this student behind me, scowling. Students who saw what happened insisted that this student was focusing her bad spirit on me and caused the light to blow up.

Over the weekend I had a dream that this student came into my house while I was in bed, sat on my stomach, and started choking me. "In the name of Jesus, get out of here!" I yelled. I woke up in a sweat. Later I dreamed again that she attacked me and knew that the demons in her life didn't like me because of my faith in Jesus. Satan was angry with me and trying to hurt me through her.

In another dream, I was in the kitchen at work, looking out the window and praying. Mrs. Taheri was there too. The student walked in, pointed angrily at me, and said to Mrs. Taheri, "Marziyeh has a power that I hate because it keeps me from doing whatever I want to here. The power inside her is stronger than I am and does not allow me to accomplish my goals in this salon." That dream convinced me that she had the power of demons and that was why she wanted to hurt me.

A while after that, this student left the school without finishing her course. Because she had the power of Satan, she could recognize the power of God in me and couldn't stay around me anymore. God's power protected me from the enemy. Through this experience, God built my faith and showed me how much power I have in Christ. No other power in the world can stand against the power Christians have in the name of Jesus.

My challenges with students came in many forms over the years I worked for Mrs. Taheri. We had a student named Akram who decided she wanted to take my place in the salon. She started spreading malicious gossip about me, hoping Mrs. Taheri would fire me and hire her. She began telling other students I must be immoral because I lived by myself. Akram tried to run a background check to see if she could find anything questionable about my past.

She tried to convince me to visit her friend Tahere, a fortune-teller who could reveal "interesting" facts about my past. I told Akram I had no interest in fortune-tellers. Furthermore, I told her there was nothing to reveal in my past because I had a strong faith in the true God.

"My life and my future are in God's hands, not people's hands," I explained. "Besides, God hates witches." To me, fortune-tellers were only witches by another name.

That made Akram angry. "Since you refuse to see her, I'm going to talk to her, and she will tell me everything about you without even seeing you!" she said.

"I don't know why you are so curious about my past," I said. "But as I already explained, neither your friend nor any other fortune-tellers can tell you about me because my life is in God's hands. I don't live with demons. Besides, this school is a place for learning and improving your skills, not fortune-telling or witchcraft. It's better for you to focus on your work instead of getting involved with satanic ideas."

A few days later the doorbell rang. I was busy, and the salon was very crowded. Mrs. Taheri ran to open the door. I couldn't see who was there because of the wooden partition all salons have just inside the entrance to keep men from looking inside. As Mrs. Taheri spoke to whoever it was, I felt the presence of an evil person who had a very bad spirit like a savage demon. I started praying in my heart in tongues, which I often do when I feel the need to pray but don't know specifically why or what for.

That afternoon when it was quieter, Mrs. Taheri told me it was Akram's friend Tahere who was at the door. Tahere had called her and asked if she could come by and talk, but when she arrived, she refused to come inside. She looked very distressed and anxious, apologized that she couldn't come in, and said she would return another time. When I heard this, I realized why I'd had such a bad feeling earlier and that the power of the Holy Spirit in me had kept Tahere out of the room. I was relieved and happy because I knew Akram had sent Tahere to the salon to see me. The next day I could see defeat in Akram's face, but I didn't mention Tahere. Akram stopped talking about Tahere's power, and I never saw Tahere again. I hope Akram understood that the power of God inside me was much stronger than whatever dark power Tahere had. However, even then, Akram continued her backbiting and animosity toward me.

At the end of each semester there was a practical exam. The board of cosmetology sent an inspector or examiner to review students' work. Whoever passed the exam was awarded her diploma. During the test of Akram's class, Akram was so nervous her hands were shaking and she had tears in her eyes. She had several children and really needed the diploma to support her family.

I walked over to her and said, "There's no need to be stressed out. You can do this. Focus on your work, and don't worry. You will pass your exam." I tried to calm her down, give her some confidence, and pointed out mistakes she was making with suggestions how to fix them. Thanks to my help, she passed.

After the exam was over, Akram stayed behind and came over to me. "Please forgive me for what I said about you," she said, in tears. "I said and did many things to hurt you. You could easily have let me fail my exam. You deserved to take your revenge, but instead, you helped me more than anyone. I can't understand your kindness. How could you help me instead of hating me?"

"Dear Akram," I said, hugging her, "you were just like every other student to me. I wanted everyone to pass, and I was concerned about you. I knew how hard you had worked, but you were so nervous today! With your children, it would be hard for you to attend more courses in order to retake the exam. I'm not here to focus on people's bad behavior. I'm here to help you get your diploma and also to help you learn bigger lessons of life. I have no grudge against you. However, my recommendation is that if you want to be successful in life, never try to ruin the lives of others. Try to improve yourself instead." She hugged me tightly and cried for a long time. Later, I talked to her about Jesus and gave her a Bible.

Mrs. Taheri saw me helping Akram. "I expected you to take your revenge and let Akram fail," she said. "I was surprised to see you paying more attention to her than to anybody else during the test." She smiled. "I'm very glad you work for me. You are such a good example to women here and teach them what true humanity means."

School wasn't the only place where God gave me unexpected opportunities to share the joy of knowing Jesus. I went to a photo shop one day to copy some images of Jesus for a friend. Behind the service counter was a beautiful, young, very slim girl who seemed to look at me in an odd way. I handed her the images and asked her to print copies for me.

She left to make the prints, and when she came back, said, "Could you please sit for a minute? I would like to talk to you, if you don't mind."

I was curious to know why she kept looking at me so strangely and said I would be glad to talk. The shop was empty, so it was just the two of us. Without another word, the girl started to cry. When I asked her what was the matter, she said she needed to share something with me.

"I'm usually not in the office at this time," she began. "Today I was supposed to leave an hour ago, but an unknown power made me stay longer.

"I had planned to kill myself today. I've been depressed and considering it for a long time. Just now when you came in, there was a bright light behind you. The reason I was looking at you strangely is because the light was so bright I could barely see your face. When you gave me these images of Jesus my whole body started shaking. It was a sign from God. When I saw the images I realized God was talking to me through you. Before you arrived I was telling God, 'You don't exist! You don't care about me and my suffering! I am going to end my life today!' I was supposed to commit suicide today if you hadn't come.

"Would you please tell me who you are? Where did you get these images? And why Jesus?"

I was speechless at first but so happy God had sent me to her. I asked her why she wanted to end her life.

Her name, she said, was Rahele. She was born into a wealthy family and grew up with a very comfortable life. "Then my father went bankrupt," she went on. "Because he couldn't pay his debts, he was arrested and sent to prison. The courts and creditors confiscated everything we had. Then a few months ago our house caught fire. Our mother became sick and had to go to the hospital. My younger brother and I are working to pay the hospital bill and support our family as best we can, but we barely have enough to keep going. I asked God why we have all these miseries and difficulties, and I have lost faith in him."

She went on to say a friend invited her to a meeting of Satan worshipers. There they sacrificed animals. She heard that some of them even committed suicide as offerings. She said Satan gave these people supernatural powers and that she wanted the same ability in order to change her life. Though she joined their group, some other force inside her prevented her from receiving satanic power. In despair that even Satan couldn't help her, she had decided to end her life.

"But today when you came," she said, "I felt the presence of God with you. I saw the light of God right behind you. That is a sign that God has heard my cries."

I was amazed to realize how God brought me into that shop and into her life at exactly the right time. She needed help, and God sent me there to help her. I shared my faith in Jesus with her and briefly explained how God had brought me safely through all my difficulties.

"Satan definitely wants to take your life," I told her, "but Jesus loves you and your family and wants to save you all. Promise me you won't harm yourself and that you'll wait a little longer. What you saw today was definitely a sign from God, who can change everything and bring miracles into your life."

I asked if I could visit her mother in the hospital to pray for her. Instantly, I saw her face light up with happiness and hope. The next day I went to see Rahele's mother. She was a very kind lady who was happy to hear I wanted to pray for her. After praying, I gave them a Bible and suggested that Rahele come to my pastor's home church rather than go back to the Satan worshipers.

Within days, Rahele's mother was completely healed and invited me to visit her at home. There she told me, "I believe God healed me because of your prayers. He is showing me and my family his mercy and miracles since we met you."

She and I became good friends. I introduced her and her family to a church to help them financially and assist them in getting Rahele's father out of prison. Church members made a special effort to surround them with love and kindness. In time, the whole family gave their hearts to Jesus.

Whenever I think of Rahele's story, it reminds me of the verses in Matthew 5:14–16: "You are the light of the world. A town built on a hill cannot be hidden. Neither do people light a lamp and put it under a bowl. Instead they put it on a stand, and it gives light to everyone in the house. In the same way, let your light shine before others, that they may see your good deeds and glorify your father in heaven" (NIV). God sent me as a light to Rahele, and she was able to see that light. It made me so happy that I had the light and power of God with me instead of darkness, bitterness, and hate.

CHAPTER 15

The Beauty Within

My friendship with Mrs. Taheri grew stronger every day. We became almost like a family. I was very grateful for her trust in me and did all I could to earn it. I worked hard, even in my free time, to organize the salon and make sure it was clean. She trusted me to order all the beauty products and keep the accounts. I managed the students and their work, made appointments for customers, communicated with the cosmetology board, and still took care of all the administrative duties. After a while, she trusted me enough to give me keys to her office, the supply closet, and her safe containing jewelry, cash, and other valuables. I believe she could see how God was blessing her and her business since she had hired me.

Late one evening when Mrs. Taheri was in her office and I was finishing up the day's accounting, a young woman came in with her mother. I tried to hide my shock when I saw that the mother's face was horribly disfigured by leprosy. At the same time, I saw the kindness in the woman's eyes. I could only imagine how hard her life was as she went through every day seeing people react to her appearance. I assumed the young woman had brought her mother here at night so no one would see them on the street.

The young woman told me she would like to have Mrs. Taheri give both of them some beauty treatments. When I went into the office to relay the request, Mrs. Taheri looked frightened. She had seen the women come in. The older lady's appearance scared her, and she wanted nothing to do with these two women. "I'm not doing anything for them," she whispered. "Please tell them to go."

I imagined these women were used to being rejected. I felt bad for them and hoped I could change Mrs. Taheri's mind. "Please don't send them away," I said. "I know the mother looks scary, but I have a good feeling about them. If you refuse them, they'll know it was because of the mother's appearance. Please don't break their hearts. And as you can see, only the mother has a problem. The daughter is fine."

"But the mother has leprosy!" Mrs. Taheri exclaimed under her breath. "How can we protect ourselves? I don't want to risk it." Like many people, she believed leprosy was highly contagious and incurable. The fact is it is neither (95 percent of people are immune to the bacteria that cause it), but she was still afraid for her health and the safety of the salon. Though I didn't argue that point with her, I still hoped she would take them as customers.

"I'm sure they are rejected all the time," I said. "I would appreciate it so much if you would treat them just like any other customer." To my surprise and delight, Mrs. Taheri said she would give them the beauty services they wanted.

I walked from the office back into the salon. I could tell by their expressions that the two expected me to ask them to leave. "Mrs. Taheri will be happy to give you the services you want," I said. They were elated. Their faces changed instantly from somber looks to smiles of delight.

The young customer went first. As she sat in the salon chair, she said that her mother did indeed have what she called "dry leprosy," by which she probably meant the less serious and less contagious form of the disease. She and her mother were used to being rejected, and she had intentionally brought her mother with her that night to see who would serve them and who would turn them away.

"I can't hide my mother because of her problem," the young woman explained. "She needs to get out and socialize. I don't want her to get depressed. I assumed that a salon with the reputation of Madame Taheri's would definitely reject us. To my surprise you not only did not reject us, you have treated us with respect. Thank you for treating us like normal customers."

While the daughter was having her treatment, I asked her mother if she would like a cup of tea or coffee. As I served her tea, I noticed how kind and respectful she was to me, how relaxed and comfortable she seemed sitting there. *The true beauty of a person is in the soul, not in their appearance*, I thought to myself. Some people with the most beautiful faces have the ugliest and darkest souls. Others in turn may not be physically beautiful but they have beautiful souls and personalities. Most people judge others based on what they can see, not on the soul inside. God sees our souls and our hearts. He therefore sees our true beauty and true ugliness. In my prayers I always ask God to give me discernment and his own eyes to be able to judge well. God has shown me many people who are not beautiful but have the kindest hearts. And he has shown me beautiful people with souls that are horribly ugly and dark.

As it turned out, only the young woman had any treatments that night. The mother was there strictly to test our salon to see if we would accept her even though she had leprosy. As I served the mother tea, I noticed her beautiful and very expensive diamond necklace. We later learned that these women were two of the wealthiest people in Tehran. Because we had welcomed her mother, the young woman became one of our regular customers and brought many blessings to the salon. She also paid top prices for even the simplest services. By showing we appreciated these women for who they were and not what they looked like, as God's example teaches us, we made new friends and a very profitable new customer.

Mrs. Taheri often invited me to visit her at home. She was divorced and lived with her two sons. Because of my mother's behavior I had nothing but bad thoughts about mothers for a long time. I even hated songs about mothers. Mrs. Taheri was about my mother's age and was a wonderful mother who would do anything for her sons. It made me wish I'd had a mother like she was. In fact, I started calling her Mother, which she very much enjoyed. We went on trips together, to the gym, to parties, and spent most of our time with each other. Mrs. Taheri was the mother I never had.

————— • —————

After two years of living with Maman Moulook and her family, I decided to find a new apartment closer to work. I could afford a better place now, and I wanted to shorten my daily commute. As much as I enjoyed my time with Maman, it was time to bid her goodbye and begin a new chapter in my life.

I faced the same problem as before in that few real estate agents or landlords would even consider renting to a single woman. Also, because I set my sights on a more exclusive part of town, many of them scoffed when I told them what I could pay per month and what I could afford for a deposit. One distinguished-looking older agent laughed derisively when I told him what I could spend. "My dear," he said, "it is useless to search for a home in this area on your budget." I didn't expect that kind of reaction from someone who was old enough, and should have been professional enough, to know better.

I said to him, "You should be ashamed of treating me so rudely. Second, my trust is in God who made heaven and earth and who makes all things possible, not in you or anyone else who mocks others and robs them of hope. I have faith that I will find a good apartment on a small budget because my eyes are set on Christ, not on you. My faith and hope are stronger than your arrogant criticism. I trust in God to guide me to the right place. I certainly don't need your help."

The man was surprised at my reaction. My words embarrassed him. "I'm sorry," he said. "As you said, I'm sure you will find a place in this area that fits your budget. Please forgive me, my dear. I never saw a person with such faith. I admire you for it."

As I left his office, I gave him a Bible and told him that yes, my faith was in the true God, Jesus Christ.

An agent told me about a place I should consider. It was a basement studio apartment in the neighborhood I wanted, in the home of a wealthy man with three daughters. At first the homeowner said he would not rent to any single woman or to a man because his daughters lived there with him. The agent was a kind man who knew how long I had been looking for a place. He also believed I was an independent, professional woman of good character and would make an excellent tenant. He told me the homeowner wanted a trustworthy person most of all and that the rental income wasn't important. "If only I can convince him to meet you in person, I'm sure he will rent his apartment to you," the agent said.

At the agent's request, the homeowner met with me at the real estate office. After only a few minutes, he agreed to rent his apartment to me at a price I could afford, which was much less than he was asking. It was a miracle. I was so happy that God had finally led me to just the right place.

My landlord and his family were wonderful people. We all became friends, and the daughters would sometimes visit me in my apartment. When the time seemed right, I shared with them my faith in Jesus. They were curious and asked a lot of good questions. I felt safe in my new home. It was my very own place, not a room in someone else's apartment as before, and it was much more convenient to the salon. The new space became a temple of God for me, a place where God gave me more dreams and where I could freely worship him, sing for him, dance for him, and live for him. There he built my faith and made it stronger than ever. It was my private haven where I experienced a love relationship with God.

Over the time I lived there I had amazing experiences with God in my solitude and loneliness. I continued writing poems and love letters to him. I longed for him every day and felt his presence everywhere in my home. Along with the apartment itself, my landlord and his family were also gifts from God. Once during a holiday I got so sick with an infection and high fever that I could hardly get out of bed. I didn't have much food in my kitchen. Though I was more financially stable than in the past, I still earned only enough money for rent, transportation, and basic groceries. I never had much extra food in the pantry. I often depended on snacks and treats that our students brought to share at the salon to supplement my meager meals.

I had eggs and a few things in the refrigerator but felt too weak to cook. All I could do was lie in bed feeling sick and lonely. I felt tears welling up in my eyes. "Daddy," I prayed to God, "you are my heavenly Father. I don't have anybody in this world to take care of me right now. Please take care of me and heal me. Please give me back my strength."

As I was praying there was a knock at the door. It was one of the landlord's daughters with a big bowl of soup in her hands. My appearance shocked her.

"Goodness, we had no idea you were sick," she exclaimed. "My mother cooked this soup today and asked me to bring you some. I'm so glad I did! I'll let her know you are unwell, and we'll bring you medicine right away."

She left the soup, dashed out the door, and returned quickly with several different medicines. I was speechless, weeping for joy. Her mother sent down different soups every day until I was completely healed. Later, when I thanked her, she said she rarely thought of sending soup to anyone outside the family but that day God put it in her heart to send some to me.

I had been in the middle of my prayer to God asking for help when he sent not only the food I wanted but the medicine I needed. I could not believe he was watching over me that closely with that much love. He truly cared about my needs. With the daughter delivering her soup, God demonstrated everything about my life is under his control. He assured me that he hears my prayers. That day God reminded me not to worry about anything in my life. If I will only trust him with all my heart and mind, he will always be there for me. He is closer to me than me.

That day God reminded me not to fear anything in this world when I have him by my side. It doesn't matter that I can't see him with my own eyes when I can feel his presence so strongly in my heart and in my life. I suspect that those who don't believe in God have closed their hearts to him. Otherwise they would know he is closer to them and cares more for them than anyone in the world. Denying God means denying our own existence.

———— • ————

Another way that I could share my beliefs about God was to volunteer for charity work. The Kahrizak Charity is an organization in Tehran that cares for old or disabled people who are abandoned by their families. Along with some other Christians, I decided to volunteer there on weekends when I didn't have to work. We brought the people snacks and fruit, sang worship songs for them, and tried to add a little joy and laughter to their lives.

Their stories varied, but all of them were heartbreaking. Some had not been visited by a family member in years. Some had been wealthy or well known earlier in their lives. One man had been very successful but lost everything as a result of an accident and ended up in this dreary and depressing place. Though the stories were difficult to hear, these people's lives taught me many good lessons. I learned how vain the world is. Some people live like they will never die or never face misfortune. There were people at Kahrizak who once had that attitude. None of them expected to be there. They were rich, proud, and selfish one minute, then destitute the next. Many of them had been betrayed by family members they once supported and cared for.

One middle-aged man was completely disabled and could not move from his bed. He had been a renowned carpenter, happy and making a good living. After he fell from a ladder and was paralyzed, his family left him at Kahrizak and rarely visited him. "You are like my daughter," he would say, in tears. "She hasn't come to see me in months. Yet you come every week without any obligation. You are so kind, while my own family has forgotten me. After you leave, I can't stop crying." I cannot imagine how a family could treat such a kind man so badly.

Another resident there had been one of the wealthiest men in town. His family betrayed him, took him to Kahrizak, and left the country. I could see the deep sorrow in his eyes. I felt his pain and loneliness. Several young women there were paralyzed during a 2003 earthquake that nearly destroyed the city of Bam in Kerman province of southeastern Iran and killed more than 26,000 people. Some survivors of the quake had lost their entire families.

People at the charity had to cope with a wide range of loss. While many residents were destitute and had lost their material wealth, many more had a variety of physical losses such as sight or hearing. Some seemed almost inert—unfeeling, unmoving, unresponsive, unable to communicate or receive any sensation from the world around them. Those who could respond were grateful to us beyond my ability to describe it. Whenever we visited them they begged us to stay longer and come back soon. They were desperate for company, for human interaction, to know someone knew they existed. They would hold my hand and never want to let go. Every time I went there I wished I could spend more time with them to show them the love of God. I talked with some of them about Jesus, and after each visit I always prayed for the people I met.

Everybody needs to visit a place like Kahrizak. No other experience will ever demonstrate so clearly to the selfish and greedy people of the world that nothing in their lives is permanent. Power, money, health, and beauty are blessings that come from God alone, and he can take them back at any time. Kahrizak taught me that a selfish, conceited, inward-focused life is meaningless. It taught me that listening to people's sorrows and pain with attention and respect can genuinely ease their burdens. It taught me that a simple smile can transform a life. It taught me that sometimes the best way in the world you can serve mankind is to let someone hold your hand.

I went to Kahrizak almost every week for two years to help the people there and learn the true meaning of life. I learned many lessons there I could never have learned anywhere else. Some of my friends at the cosmetology school criticized me for spending time at Kahrizak. "You're young," they said. "Instead of spending your weekends in a place like that, you should get a boyfriend and go enjoy yourself."

I couldn't imagine doing that when I could spend the time showing the world's outcasts that whatever else had happened in their lives, Christ would always love them and never leave them.

CHAPTER 16

The Power of Love

From the time I was a teenager I have always loved mountain climbing. When my family used to go camping outside the city, I would climb by myself for hours at a time, taking in the beautiful views and the calming silence. Even before I gave my heart to Jesus, I loved climbing up to a quiet, private place where I felt close to God and could talk to him out loud if I wanted, without anyone overhearing.

After I got so busy at the salon, I had no time for any mountain climbing. Besides, all the nearby public mountain areas were very crowded and noisy. I searched and found a mountain outside the city that wasn't easy for the public to reach, a place where I could experience God's world and God's love in a special way.

One cold winter night I got up at midnight to climb this mountain before anyone else was out. There were buildings under construction nearby, but my plan was to go there and back before the construction workers arrived. The air was crisp and clear, the ground covered with snow.

I hadn't gotten very far when I heard a rustle and found myself facing a pack of wild dogs. They stopped a few feet from me, barking and growling and baring their teeth. I knew that if I ran they would chase me down. Instead, I stood completely still and silent. The minutes seemed like hours as they passed, but before long the dogs stopped threatening me and walked away.

I started my climb as the sun began to rise. The scene was magnificent, with the sky turning bright and the fresh snow shimmering in the light of a new day. I was about halfway to the top when I saw three men in the distance. I couldn't believe anyone was out in such a remote area so early. I shifted my course to avoid them, but it was too late. They had already seen me and started walking my way. I said a quick prayer asking God to protect me.

As they came closer I saw the men were Afghans. I could tell they were as surprised to see me as I was to see them. I tried not to look afraid.

"Who are you?" one of them asked. "What are you doing here alone?"

"What are *you* doing here?" I asked in return.

"We're construction workers on those buildings you passed down below," one of them said. "We're up here hunting birds."

"I'm nobody," I replied. "I'm here just to enjoy climbing this mountain."

"Don't you know how dangerous it is for you to be here?" their spokesman continued.

I looked the speaker directly in the eye. "I see no danger because God is with me." After a moment I added, "If you'll excuse me, I need to be on my way."

Another of the group said, "Wait a minute. You can't go any higher with those shoes. There's too much snow." When I didn't say anything, he added, "Let me come with you."

I didn't hesitate. "All right, go ahead. I'll follow you."

He said goodbye to his friends and started walking ahead of me up the mountainside. The last thing I wanted was for this stranger to walk with me. But soon I realized he had been right. The snow was so deep I would never have made it with the shoes I wore. He stepped ahead of me, and I followed in his footprints. I began telling him about Jesus and the love of God, and he seemed to be listening, though he didn't say anything.

We both got tired, and I suggested we take a rest. While we rested I made a snowman. After we recovered our breath and I had finished my work of art, we started climbing again. I was determined to make it to the peak, and by this time we were close. Then the man stopped. "It's very dangerous to continue," he said. "I'm not going any farther, and you shouldn't either. We don't have the shoes or equipment to get to the top safely."

We stood there for a moment, and as I thought about his suggestion he said, "Let me confess something. The only reason I got as far up the mountain as I did just now is because I smoked opium a little while ago. How in the world could you climb this far without any drugs and in those ridiculous shoes? Are you truly a human being, or are you an angel?"

Now I understood why he hadn't said anything as we climbed. He thought I was an angel sent to tell him about God.

I tried to hide my laugh at his remark. "Thank you for coming with me," I said. "I see now that if you weren't here to pack down the snow so I could step in your footprints, I could never have come this far."

As we headed back down the mountain we met the other two men coming our way. They were amazed when they learned how far we had walked. The men had some bread and cheese and offered to share it with me. I was suddenly hungry and gratefully accepted their hospitality. As we sat on the mountainside, I shared the message of Jesus with them. I could still see the surprise in their eyes that I was there.

They told me they had never seen a woman as courageous as I was. One of them said, "We thought at first you were an angel from God. I still can't believe you're human!"

I laughed and said, "I'm a human being the same as every one of you. And because I'm human, I am very tired from our climb. I need to go home and rest."

They wished me the best and asked me to visit them on the mountain again. "You're the only Iranian woman who has ever treated us kindly and respectfully," said one of the men. "You even sat and ate with us. People in the city think Afghans are dirty and dangerous."

"We are all human beings in the eyes of God," I said, "and he loves us whether we're Afghans or Iranians or whatever. We should follow his example and love and respect each other. I'm sorry for the way other Iranians have treated you. I hope you know now that not everybody feels that way."

As I left them I saw tears in their eyes. I knew God had sent me to the mountainside that morning to comfort those poor men. I had gone there to speak with God, not knowing God had sent me there to speak in his name to three kind Afghan construction workers many miles from home.

———— • ————

God seemed to fill up my days more and more. I felt his presence with me in the salon, going about my daily routine, and especially when I was at home in my cozy apartment where I could sing to him, pray to him, and write him letters whenever I wanted. He spoke to me again and again in dreams. Most exciting of all was the reappearance of the White Horse.

In this dream, I instantly recognized the White Horse as the same one from my dream years earlier, very beautiful and very wild. His caretaker stood beside him. One by one, people approached the horse and tried to climb on his back, but every time the horse angrily shook them off. The horseman saw me watching and asked, "Why don't you come here and ride the horse?"

"Because the horse doesn't allow anyone to ride him," I answered.

"You're the only one he allows to ride," the horseman said. "There's no need to hesitate. Come sit on his back."

I trusted the horseman's word. As I walked up to the White Horse, the horse looked at me with his beautiful eyes, and I knew he wouldn't buck me off. Then I woke up. I could not believe it was the White Horse I was so much in love with from the first dream. I felt an indescribable closeness, a deep and powerful connection between us even more intense than the first dream had been.

Why had the White Horse returned? Later God gave me dreams that allowed me to understand the messages behind earlier dreams. Step by step he revealed his promise to me and the reason he had chosen me.

One of my many memorable dreams was about baptism. At that time I had not been baptized because I wasn't sure exactly what it would say about me as a Christian in Iran. Jesus came to me in a dream to explain what I should do.

About a year after I became a follower of Christ, the pastor of the home church I attended had asked me if I was ready to be baptized. This ceremony would be performed by an Armenian pastor of the Assembly of God church in Tehran.

Others in the congregation were thrilled for me. One of them said, "Marziyeh, you are very lucky they have decided to baptize you. I hope they will offer it to me soon so I can get the official document that proves I'm a Christian."

Excited as I was about being baptized, I hadn't even thought about my baptism certificate. I was thinking about how my heart had been transformed and how baptism was an outward sign of that transformation. Jesus demonstrated the importance of this sacrament by being baptized himself. But I didn't need a piece of paper to prove I was a Christian.

"Why is the baptism certificate so important to you?" I asked.

"Everyone is competing for the chance to be baptized," my friend explained. "It makes you an official Christian."

"I don't understand what you mean. What difference does it make whether you're an 'official' Christian or not? Jesus knows my heart."

"If you get baptized by the church, they give you a certificate with an official stamp that proves you are a Christian."

"I don't need a piece of paper to prove I'm a Christian."

"You still don't understand," my friend said, slightly exasperated. "If you have official proof that you are a Christian, you can use that to apply to emigrate to any country you want. Since you're a Christian, you can't continue living in Iran because Iran persecutes Christians. So other countries will let you move there. Without the certificate of baptism you have no proof you're a Christian. That's why it is so important."

I couldn't believe what I was hearing. These Christians were excited about their baptism because they got a piece of paper and could leave the country, not because they were symbolizing their covenant with God. The thought of this made me angry.

"If I want to emigrate I will do it on my own, without using God to achieve my worldly goals," I told my friend. "If the purpose of baptism in this church is to get a certificate you can use to apply for asylum in another country, I prefer not to be baptized and give my turn to you."

That day I promised myself I would never be baptized in Iran. I told the pastors I wasn't ready. I didn't give them any other reason because I didn't want to jeopardize someone else's opportunity. They were surprised, since others wanted to be baptized as soon as the church would permit it.

A year later, asleep in my quiet basement apartment, I dreamed that Jesus and I were standing beside a beautiful lake. He was dressed in brilliant white. He was beautiful, and his face shone. Jesus walked me to the lake and put my head under the water with his own hands. When I came out of the water, I saw individual drops cascading off my hair and splashing through the air. It was like watching the scene in HD slow motion. It was so clear I can draw it from memory. It is an unbelievably beautiful picture: me being baptized by Jesus Christ.

"I have chosen you," Jesus said to me. "You no longer belong to this world anymore. You belong to me."

I awoke with tears of joy running down my face. I thanked Jesus and praised him for what he had done. I didn't need to be baptized by any human being now because Jesus himself had baptized me. The next time the pastors offered to baptize me I shared my dream with them and said it wasn't necessary.

Some dreams that were a complete mystery at the time became clear later on. One of these was a dream that I was behind bars but did not know why. Then God spoke to me in the dream saying, "You will get arrested and go to prison in the near future. It is necessary for you to pass through this experience."

I woke with a start and was a little bit scared because I had talked to many women at the cosmetology school about Jesus. Had one of them reported me? Was I about to be arrested?

My only concern at the time was the possibility I might deny my faith in Jesus for fear of being imprisoned or tortured. After this dream, I prayed for the strength not to deny Christ if I was arrested. The apostle Peter denied Jesus as soon as he felt threatened, even though during the Last Supper he had promised he would never betray his Lord. Jesus predicted Peter's betrayal when he said that "before the rooster crows tonight, you will say three times that you do not know me" (see Matthew 26:31–39 and Luke 22:54–62).

I could not imagine denying Jesus no matter what the circumstances. I was in love with him from the beginning of my faith. I could never forgive myself if I failed to defend him. "If I ever get arrested," I prayed, "give me the strength and courage to pass that trial with victory. Please never allow me to be weak." I didn't ask God not to allow me to go to prison. If that were ever to happen, it would only be because God had a reason for it. Instead, I asked him only to give me courage to stand on my faith under any circumstances.

When I shared the dream with some friends, they thought I might have had it because I was afraid of going to prison. In fact, I had never considered the possibility of going to prison until after I had the dream. I told them I wasn't afraid.

"But they torture, rape, and kill prisoners there," my friends said.

"I know," I said. "I realize what horrible things could happen to me there. But I trust my heavenly Father to protect me no matter where I am. Even in prison, nobody can touch me unless he allows it. And if he allows horrible things to happen, I trust him still because I know he has a purpose behind it. Everything is under God's control. My only fear is denying my faith in a moment of pain and weakness."

God would one day show me the full meaning of this dream.

———— • ————

Mrs. Taheri and I continued our wonderful friendship as the two of us stayed busy with the cosmetology school. Her mother lived in the northern part of Iran and came to visit once. Mrs. Taheri's children called their grandmother Madar Joon. She was a kind and thoughtful woman who I liked right away. Soon we were friends and I was calling her Madar Joon too.

I was surprised and saddened when Madar Joon had a stroke. She was transferred to a hospital in Tehran so that Mrs. Taheri and her two sisters could be responsible for her care. One of the sisters lived in another city and wasn't able to help, while the other one lived in Tehran but had two small children. I offered to sit with Madar Joon at night so the two sisters taking turns at the hospital could spend evenings with their families. Every afternoon instead of going home, I went to see Madar Joon.

Madar Joon shared a hospital room with several other elderly ladies. Before long they assumed I was another one of her daughters because I was there so much. Due to the stroke, Madar Joon was completely paralyzed. She couldn't even talk.

One night Madar Joon seemed very restless and in pain. She looked at me with pleading eyes, trying to communicate what was the matter. Finally, I realized she was hurting because she could not empty her bowels. The muscles that normally served this purpose were paralyzed along with everything else, and she was unable to relieve herself. (Again I was reminded that we can lose anything or everything in this life in the blink of an eye.)

I know this embarrassed her, but she had to have some relief. When I told a nurse about the problem, she gave Madar Joon a stool softener. After a while it was clear the pills didn't help, so they decided to try suppositories. However, they didn't insert them but left that job to me. Still the problem remained. I got a pair of medical gloves from the nurse and manually massaged the waste out of Madar Joon's body with my own hands. The other patients in the room looked on in disgust. It was indeed a nasty job, but I couldn't have cared less about their opinion. If no one else was going to do what was required, I was. The nurse was nowhere to be seen.

Embarrassed as she was, Madar Joon was very grateful to be comfortable again and soon went to sleep. In the morning when Mrs. Taheri came to relieve me, everybody started talking at once, telling her what I had done.

"Your family should be proud to have such a humble and selfless sister," one of the other patients said. "Your mother is very fortunate to have a daughter who takes such devoted care of her."

"But she is not my sister," Mrs. Taheri said. "She is our friend."

The room was stunned. "That's unbelievable," one of the women said. "She takes better care of your mother than you or your sister. We never suspected for a second she was not her daughter."

After that, Mrs. Taheri and her sister learned to massage their mother's body the way I had. After Madar Joon went home, they got a physical therapist to help her with some exercises so she could relieve herself naturally once again. I continued visiting and caring for Madar

Joon at home. Though she never recovered her speech, she made it clear with her gestures that I was her daughter as well and that everyone should accept and respect me as such. What an honor!

When I came to visit I read the Bible to Madar Joon and talked to her about Jesus. Once when we were alone I prayed that she would give her heart to Christ. She agreed and accepted him with a gesture and a nod, acknowledging that she believed.

Caring for Madar Joon taught me lessons I never forgot. I learned especially about the power of love. It is the most powerful force we have, more powerful than money, influence, fame, or anything else. Most important of all, she taught me that you don't need words to tell someone you love them. Your actions, behavior, acceptance, smiles, and service to others speak louder than any words ever will.

CHAPTER 17

A New Chapter

It had been four years since Ali and I had gone our separate ways after our marriage. We never lived together as man and wife and hadn't even seen each other in all that time. I lived and worked in Tehran while he stayed with his parents in Rafsanjan. Though it was convenient having an ID card that showed me as his wife, I felt the time had come to move on. I decided to formally file for divorce.

I knew that for a woman in Iran to get a divorce without her husband's permission was almost impossible. I hadn't considered it before because I was busy with my work and had no interest in starting a new romantic relationship. It didn't seem worth the trouble. But after four years of matrimonial limbo, I needed to turn the page on a new chapter in my life.

I called Ali and told him what I wanted. He agreed immediately to help me. "It's the one thing I can do for you," he said. I could tell he was crying. "You have been the most amazing person in my life. No one knows how precious and worthy you are. You sacrificed everything to save me, and I repaid your kindness with failure. I was never able to make you happy. Now I have a chance to bring you happiness." Ali said he would come to Tehran and sign all the necessary papers.

Friends in Rafsanjan had warned me that Ali was in poor health. He still suffered from addiction and the effects of his torture. He had severe headaches and seizures from being beaten with fists and police batons and from having his head bashed against the wall. At times he fainted in the street. When I saw him I knew there was nothing more I could do to help him. He was crushed, devastated, and hopeless.

We visited a lawyer to move the process along more quickly. Ali signed all the necessary papers in the lawyer's office giving his permission for the divorce. He explained we had never lived together formally and asked to have his name removed from all my personal documents. When couples announce they never lived together, the court removes the husband's name from the wife's official identity as though they were never married. It is legally similar to an annulment in the United States. This way I would not be labeled as divorced, meaning a woman of questionable moral character. Divorced women in Iran face many kinds of discrimination. Ali's cooperation should have allowed me to finish the process without delay. Ali felt sick and returned to Rafsanjan as soon as the papers were signed.

A while later I returned to the lawyer's office to follow up on my case. The lawyer had done nothing since my visit there with Ali. That day we had paid him a substantial fee to help us. Now that I had returned alone, the lawyer said I would have to pay a lot more money for his services. He hadn't mentioned any further cost when Ali was with me. I told him I didn't have that much all at once but could pay him over time. He insisted I pay the full amount in advance before he started working.

If I couldn't pay up, he said, he would accept a temporary Islamic marriage instead. He knew I was single and working and had only a modest income. He had inflated his fee so he would have an excuse to demand sex from me. He was, of course, a very religious and faithful Muslim. He was also a lewd, opportunistic scumbag.

"You should have told my husband and me up front what you would charge," I said.

"I don't see the problem," he said, looking me over with a sleazy grin. "I've offered you an alternative to paying me with money."

I was furious. "I would rather not have a divorce than give in to your shameful demand," I said. "You care more about satisfying your disgusting lust than helping innocent people."

I stormed out of his office and never went back. I was afraid he would rape me. Because of his position, no court would ever charge him with a crime.

Now I was in a quandary. The scumbag lawyer had all the papers Ali signed, and I had no way to get them back. To move ahead with the divorce as planned, Ali would have to come back to Tehran and we would have to pay a new lawyer. Ali was too sick to travel again, and I didn't have money for another attorney. To do what I wanted to do, I would have to go directly to the court by myself. I had heard many stories of how corrupt the court system was in Iran, but I had no idea how vast and deep that corruption actually was. I was soon to find out.

I quickly learned that many of the religious mullahs who serve as judges in Iran know very little about law but a great deal about how to satisfy themselves at the expense of people who appear before them in court. They expect as a matter of course that men will give them money and women will give them sex to move their case along to a favorable conclusion. No money or sex means no action on your case.

Morality police at the entrance to the courtroom would not allow any woman inside unless she was completely covered, preferably with a chador, and wore no makeup. Even so, judges often lost no time telling women that if they expected a favorable ruling they would have to sleep with them. Sometimes the proposition was subtle, and sometimes it was shockingly direct. As a woman pleading her case alone, I was a prime target for these religious perverts. Time and again I refused their advances. They responded by putting up endless legal obstacles or by transferring my case to another court.

I came home from every court appearance angry, frustrated, and with a severe headache. To release the tension I would scream as loudly as I could into my pillow. After one particularly hard day I sat on my bed, heartbroken and desperately lonely, and I prayed to God, "Daddy, I don't want anything from you. All I need is for you to hug me like a father hugs his daughter." This was the deep desire of my heart at that moment, but I didn't expect God to literally hug me like my dear earthly father would if he were there.

I fell asleep and dreamed that someone lay down gently on my bed behind me, wrapped his arms around me, and hugged me tightly like a lover would. When I reached to touch these arms, I woke up. At first I thought someone had snuck into my apartment and climbed into bed with me. Then I felt the overwhelming presence of God all around. It was God who had hugged me. What I had prayed for he provided almost immediately.

I could not believe how faithfully God had answered my request. I started praising him for his love and kindness and didn't stop for hours. His tender love melted my heart.

———— • ————

Of all the times God had spoken to me in dreams, the next dream was the most life-changing of all. In this dream God told me to leave Iran and follow him to a new place. He also told me to keep this plan a secret until the time was right. I could not believe what I was hearing. Why would God choose me for such a big responsibility? The thought of leaving the country was unbelievable, impossible. But God had spoken to me through dreams many times before, and I had always trusted him. I knew I should trust him again.

With God all things are possible. I remembered that God promised to give Abraham a son even though his wife was ninety years old.

Abraham wrongly chose a human solution by marrying his concubine. Even so, God fulfilled his promise after Abraham's sin.

I confided in Pastor Onnik and told him about my dream and the plan God had for me to leave Iran. He was the first person I thought of who could help me. I trusted him more than any other Christian I knew, and he had known me long enough to understand my passion for following Jesus.

I learned that church leaders in the Assembly of God were working with a Christian ministry in Great Britain. The Iranian church would send twelve students to study theology with this organization in London. Pastor Onnik chose me as one of the twelve. It was the most incredible miracle I could imagine. The path God had set before me in my dream was opening up before my eyes. The twelve of us would attend a conference in Turkey sponsored by the British organization to meet with their pastors there. They would then assess our qualifications and approve us for study in London.

In March 2005 I left Iran for the first time in my life and traveled to Istanbul. I attended the conference, met with the Christians from London, and thought I was on my way to study theology in the West. Every student approved for the theology program would later receive a formal invitation to come to the university in London. We were then responsible for going to the British embassy in Iran to get our visas.

I did not want to leave my life in Tehran behind unless I was positive I was going to England to study. I talked at length with one of the pastors to make certain I would be able to get a visa. He assured me that their invitation alone was all I needed. He warned me that I should settle my affairs and get ready to move as soon as I returned to Iran because once my visa was approved I would only have a short time before moving to London.

My head was swimming. What would I tell Mrs. Taheri? She was planning to turn management of her whole operation over to me. She had even converted an office into a private salon where she would keep serving a few favorite clients and have me run the school by myself. I had worked hard to earn her trust, get my certifications as a trainer and as a manager, and learn the business from top to bottom. God was asking me to leave all that behind. And what about my divorce case? It had dragged on for two years with no end in sight. Since I wasn't going to sleep with a judge, the case might never be settled. And what about the lease on my apartment? How could I get out of that?

I dreaded telling Mrs. Taheri the news, but I had to get it over with. She was dumbstruck and disappointed that I would leave her. She had counted on me to run the school. "You're the only one I can trust to take over," she said. "If you leave, I'll have to close the school or rent it out because I'm not able to run such a big place anymore." I felt terrible for her, but God had called me and I knew I had to follow. When I explained to my landlord that I had a wonderful opportunity to study in London, he kindly canceled my lease. Once again God was at work clearing the path for me to follow him.

Within only a few weeks, my formal invitation arrived through the church to study theology in London. Breathless with excitement, I went with the eleven other students to the British embassy, where we filled out forms and had our interviews.

Days later we learned that all twelve visa applications were rejected.

Now what? I thought. The eleven other students still lived with their parents. They simply went home and went about their lives as before. I had quit my job, given up my apartment, sold my furniture, and left everything in order to follow God to a new life. Fortunately, my landlord hadn't found a new tenant yet and let me return for the time being. Mrs. Taheri had advertised the school for lease and was going ahead with her move to a smaller place for a few exclusive clients.

I was so confused. Maybe I was mistaken about God's message. I prayed to him asking, "Why did this happen? If you wanted me to leave my job and everything I knew and follow you, why have you closed the door?" As the days passed I got more frustrated at my situation, losing

166

hope and thinking I had ruined my future. I began to doubt God and his message to me.

Then I had another visit from the White Horse.

I dreamed I was hiding in the middle of a battlefield, surrounded by enemies. Suddenly, I saw the White Horse on the ground. I thought at first he was injured and called out to him. When he recognized my voice, he stood and ran to me. As I climbed onto his back a big, heavy sword appeared in my hands. With both hands I held the sword straight out in front of me as the horse started running and carried me straight through the enemies. They all fell ahead of me before I could actually touch them with the sword. The White Horse ran like the wind, carrying me through the enemies as they fell one by one. At the end of the battlefield, I looked back and saw the enemies were dead. I had defeated all of them.

Then the horse took me to a place like an embassy where someone handed me what looked like a passport. The people there only gave these passports to someone who was victorious on the battlefield. As the White Horse and I were passing across the border, I woke up. *Thank you, God, for reminding me you're always there. Always.*

A month went by. It seemed like the door to theology school in London was closed for good. Should I try to pick up the pieces here in Tehran? How long could I manage without any income? When would I have to leave my apartment for a new tenant? In the midst of all these questions, God spoke to me once again in a dream.

I dreamed I was in a church in a foreign country. I didn't know where I was, but I could see the faces of the worshipers very clearly. I would have been able to recognize any of them in the street. As I looked at the faces, God said, "This is the place I have chosen for you to start your first step." Although this was an exciting message, it was still a mystery to me. From the dream I could not understand what God's will for me was. I prayed that I would understand where I should start the journey God had in mind for me.

Sixty days I waited for an answer. I had to trust God and be patient. God was testing my faith and trust in him and teaching me always to be patient for his timing.

When the answer came, it was another miracle from God to help me walk the path he had chosen for me. The theological school in London had reconsidered their offer in light of my personal circumstances. They had learned I was living on my own and that denial of my visa application had turned my life upside down. They reached out with an alternative offer to work with some Iranian Christians they sponsored in Turkey. If I worked for them in Turkey, I obviously wouldn't need a British visa.

I was elated that God had opened a new and completely unexpected door. The only cloud in the picture was my divorce case. If I abandoned it now there was little chance I would ever see it through to the finish. Months earlier the case had been transferred yet again to yet another lecherous holy mullah who offered to expedite matters if I would sleep with him. The law was on my side. What I had to do somehow was bring the judge onto the side of the law. I prayed that God would give me the courage to face my judge and confront him boldly. It was the only chance I had left.

That same day, I made an appointment with the judge and met him in his private office. I knew he had the power to cause trouble and even ruin my case. But in that moment God made me fearless.

I cut to the chase. "You are the same age as my father," I said. "You should be ashamed of yourself for expecting sexual favors from me in exchange for following the law and granting my divorce. You may have daughters my age. What would you do if someone like you suggested such a thing to them? I would rather die than accept your vulgar, disgusting offer. My faith and trust are in a mighty God who can deliver me from your filthy hands.

"You can do the right thing and finish this case that has dragged on for years. Then I will pray that God forgive your sins and bless your life. If not, I will ask God to send his harshest punishment upon you. If you want to keep playing with my case, God will take his holy revenge on you. I pray your daughters never have to go through the insult and misery you have put on me."

I turned and left his office. He followed me out the door immediately, turned to his secretary, and said, "Resolve this woman's divorce case as soon as possible." Then to me he said, "I admire your courage and faith." He went back into his office, closed the door, and I never saw him again. He could just as easily have sent me to jail on the spot. Instead, he set me free with a few strokes of a pen.

Five days later, I stepped off an airplane in Istanbul, alone, nervous, apprehensive, and excited beyond words to see what miracle God had in store for me next.

———— • ————

One experience that shaped my life the most over the next few years would be not where I lived but rather what happened in my personal life. In the past, my disappointment in marriage convinced me I should not make a long-term romantic commitment with anyone. I had a love relationship with God that was very comforting and fulfilling. At the same time, I had the natural desire any young woman has for human love.

Even though Ali and I never lived together as man and wife, I did not date anyone during the whole time we were married. Friends kept asking, "Marzi, why don't you date? Why don't you have some fun? You have a husband in name only. You should get a boyfriend!" But I was determined to honor Ali and be faithful to our marriage as long as his name was on my ID as my husband.

After my divorce I dated a few men but never found true love. Looking back, I believe I intentionally dated people I would never marry in order not to be tempted to start a serious relationship. I knew they did not meet my standards, but I spent time with them anyway.

In those cases, they began to pressure me to be more serious and consider marriage, but I refused. I knew we were not a good match for the long term. When they started getting more controlling and insistent, I said goodbye.

Even so, one of those relationships was a long-term one. It was my first experience falling in love, and I was so happy! We were happy together for years before our romance started to unravel. One cause of the trouble was that although I loved this man and wanted to be with him, I had no interest in marriage. My sad life with Ali and the endless divorce proceedings made me unwilling to go through any of that again. I believed that love was enough to keep two committed people loyal to each other. We didn't need a legal document to hold us together.

My boyfriend disagreed. This eventually led to the pain, sorrow, and heartbreak of ending our relationship. As much as I loved him, I could not consent to marriage.

These relationships were wrong in God's eyes. Sometimes I still feel shame at the sins of my past and ask God why he allowed me to fail. But he never left me alone. Our heavenly Father is always patient, even when we choose the wrong path. As we understand the ugliness of our deeds, he is ready to forgive us and wash our sins away. I'm grateful that God allowed me to fall and, by falling, to learn what true love and commitment are.

Even in that sadness, God was teaching me. My romantic relationships helped me better understand God's love by comparing it with human love. God wanted me to experience compassion, affection, and emotional love in order to show me the difference between that and divine, true love. Human love is not durable but fragile. Human love is sweet but needs constant nurturing and attention to keep from turning sour. Love requires protection, sacrifice, and patience.

The Bible reminds us of this so beautifully in 1 Corinthians 13:4–7: "Love is patient, love is kind. It does not envy, it does not boast, it is not proud. It does not dishonor others, it is not self-seeking, it is not easily angered, it keeps no record of wrongs. Love does not delight in evil but rejoices with the truth. It always protects, always trusts, always hopes, always perseveres."

In a dream God told me that by experiencing a few flawed human relationships I would understand what true love is. I feel ashamed of those times in my life and wish I could take them back. Yet if I hadn't made those mistakes I would not fully understand God's love for me. God allows us to fall, choose wrong paths, make mistakes, and even commit sins in order to teach us his lessons. He waits patiently for us to repent and return to him.

God allowed me to fail, be broken, and experience a lot of emotional pain in order to teach me what true love means. He also taught me that mistakes and sin cause us to harm ourselves and then we have to face the consequences. It is always from our mistakes that we learn the best lessons.

CHAPTER 18

Ministry with Maryam

In Istanbul I lived in an apartment with two other Christian girls, one American and one Iranian. Since Iranians couldn't get visas to travel to London for training, those of us working together decided to bring the training to students in Turkey, where Iranians could travel without a visa. After four months and several meetings, our sponsors made plans to set up formal classes in Istanbul instead of continuing to try to get students into the UK. Rather than hosting us in England for four years of college, they would give us a few months of leadership training and Bible study and then send us into the mission field. Professors from London could rotate into Istanbul to teach the courses. The organization rented classrooms in the basement of a church. (Today, by God's grace, the ministry has its own purpose-built building there and is still going strong.) Meanwhile, the other Christian girls and I started looking for apartments in town that our sponsors could rent for the new students.

The first time I went to church during this trip to Istanbul, I was astonished at the faces in the congregation. These were the people I saw in my dream before I left Iran! I recognized every one of them. The sight made me so happy because now I was sure I was in the place the

Lord had chosen for me. God closed the door on my travel to England because he had something better in mind.

I had another dream a few weeks after arriving in Turkey. In the dream God showed me that Madar Joon had passed away. I immediately called Madame Taheri, who confirmed her mother had just died. I went to a quiet corner of a cemetery and cried for hours. Caring for Madar Joon had taught me unforgettable lessons about the power of love, a power greater than money or status or anything else. She taught me that love doesn't require words to express it. It can be conveyed by an act of kindness or something as simple as a smile. In his first letter to the Corinthians, the apostle Paul reminds us that love never fails. It is the great gift we share with one another.

As a handful of students started our theology and leadership courses together, new students began to arrive. I moved into an apartment with a newcomer from Iran named Maryam Rostampour. She and I had met on my first trip to Turkey and immediately formed a strong friendship. Maryam and I were both from nominal Muslim families that did not follow traditional religious practices. She discovered Jesus as a teenager and faithfully attended Bible studies at a home church in Tehran. At nineteen she was secretly baptized in a church basement. Like me, she had the gift of speaking in tongues.

Maryam and I lived together, studied together, and joined other students in serving the refugees in Istanbul. Meeting with these displaced people and families—mostly Iranians—and listening to their stories helped us better understand the condition of refugees in Turkey. We talked to them about Jesus, prayed for them, and tried to help them with their needs. Some of them were already Christians and members of the church.

On one hand, it was a joy to serve those people and spend time with them. On the other hand, it was heartbreaking to see their pain, poverty, and struggles. Some had been stranded in Turkey for ten years without official identity papers, and the United Nations would not resolve their cases. They could not even return to Iran because of their political status and lack of passports. Desperate to work, they took any jobs they could get. Turkish employers took terrible advantage of them, paying them far less than they would give a Turkish worker because they knew the refugees were powerless to complain. Some of them lived in a single stuffy room where it was dark, damp, and hard to get even a single breath of fresh air. Most of them felt hopeless, depressed, and frustrated with the UN. I had no idea refugees coming from other countries would face such hardship.

About this time I had a dream. I was flying through the sky on huge wings fifty yards long. My body felt very small between them by comparison. I flew effortlessly like an eagle. While I was flying, God opened my eyes to show me how the wings could move. Shining rays of light, coming from above like glistening ropes, held up every inch of the wing tops. These rays were the power of the Holy Spirit that moved the wings up and down.

God told me, "It is always I who move these wings for you to fly."

This was a message that God had given me freedom and an opportunity for serving him and his people in Turkey. He was the one who moved me forward with his mighty power. Without his power I was nothing: an ordinary person with all my flaws, sins, and weakness. Without God's protection and power I would fail. I thanked him for all the power he had given me, for his protection and blessing. I knew he had started my journey to fulfill his promise in the future.

Living, studying, and serving refugees in Turkey was the best time of my life. I enjoyed the beautiful country, the sea, and the freedom. I had been there seven months when my pastor asked me if I was ready to be baptized. He knew I was the only student who had not had this sacrament and suggested I do so along with two Christians who were coming to Turkey specifically for baptism. I had been a Christian for seven years, but since Jesus had baptized me in a dream I did not think I needed to go through the process again. Also I remembered how some people were baptized just so they could use their baptism certificate to help them leave Iran. I didn't want any part of that sham. Moreover, I never wanted to go through the ceremony in secret or even inside a building. I always wanted to be baptized in the sea. My pastor told me since there were only two Christians coming for this service, he would baptize them in the sea.

When my pastor first invited me to be baptized, I immediately said no, just as I had in the past. But later that day when I was reading my Bible, the Holy Spirit spoke to me through the verses and put it in my heart to be baptized in water. I didn't know why God wanted to do this again when I had already done it in my dream. Still, the Holy Spirit strongly pressed on me and changed my heart. I went to the church and told my pastor I would like to be baptized after all.

The next afternoon I went with the others to the shore of the Sea of Marmara in Istanbul. My turn came at just before 7:00 p.m. I stood in the water as the pastor started praying, and I acknowledged my faith in Jesus. Before he could finish his words and put my head under water, a big wave washed over our heads. We both laughed.

"I don't need to put you under the water," my pastor said, "because God has already baptized you and washed you from head to toe!"

I felt so happy that after my obedience to God he himself baptized me and not a human being. Afterward, my pastor and I were surprised as we counted the number of sevens in my baptism day. In the Bible this number represents spiritual and physical completeness and perfection. I was baptized at the age of twenty-seven, in the seventh month of the Persian calendar (Mehr), seven years after giving my heart to the Lord, seven months after arriving in Turkey, on Friday, the seventh day of the Persian calendar, at 7:00 p.m. when God himself washed me in the sea and baptized me. That made seven sevens all together. It was amazing to us how God had planned everything so perfectly. I have never forgotten the joy I felt that day. Also, I had followed through on my vow never to be baptized in Iran, and I never asked for or received any certificate of baptism.

After completing our courses in Turkey, Maryam and I returned to Iran to serve the Lord together and give the message of salvation to our people. At first we were unsure how best to proceed. There were many restrictions for Christians in Iran and many more restrictions for women. We knew that if we depended on our own power and wisdom we would fail. What was God's will for us? We needed God's wisdom. We needed his guidance, plan, and strategy. And so we prayed, asking God to guide us with the Holy Spirit and tell us how we should serve him and send his message to the people despite all the restrictions.

One day as I read the Bible the Holy Spirit told me that Maryam and I needed to evangelize Iranians by distributing Bibles throughout the country. He showed me that Iran was a big, dry land where not enough seeds had been scattered and sown, and that we should scatter as many seeds on this land as we could. He said that after we scattered the seeds, he would irrigate and grow them with the power of the Holy Spirit, bringing hundreds and thousands of fruits from each one of them.

The only version of the Bible generally available in Iran is a false and distorted Farsi translation called the Barnabas Bible. People don't have access to accurate Bibles in churches or bookstores. I realized that Maryam and I could sow seeds by distributing accurate Bibles in the Farsi (Persian) language. This is the original and historic language of the people of Iran, not the Arabic that many Muslims use. At the same time, Maryam had a dream that she and I were distributing Bibles in Tehran. After receiving these confirmations from God, we knew that our mission was to distribute Bibles all over the city and the country.

I called our pastor in London and asked him to smuggle thousands of Bibles to us. He was worried about our plan. "Are you serious?" he asked. "What you're talking about is very dangerous."

"Please trust us," I said, "because we're going to do exactly what God wants us to do."

That convinced him. It took a few months, but eventually we received Bibles by the thousands. We divided a map of Tehran into squares. Every night that we could, we visited a square with 140 Farsi New Testaments in our backpacks, putting them in mailboxes. We also left them in public restrooms and sometimes in coffee shops or other places. With God's power, miracles, and protection, the two of us distributed almost 20,000 New Testaments throughout Tehran and a few other cities in three years.

During those years we also evangelized people every day. Wherever we went—shopping, eating at a restaurant, or doing our errands—we spoke with people and offered them a Bible as a gift. God also gave us a vision to start a house church for youth and another for prostitutes. Before we started our church for prostitutes, we were invited to travel to India to share the gospel with prostitutes there. We learned that while the role of prostitution is the same everywhere, the attitude toward it in India was very different from the way it is viewed in Iran and other Muslim countries.

In Bombay (also known as Mumbai), we met Indian Christians whose mission was to save prostitutes and their children. With these missionaries we visited the red-light district in Mumbai. It was a dangerous street, and we had Indian bodyguards with us. Prostitutes lived in the most horrible, filthy homes under the worst conditions. Some had been sold to pimps and could not escape. They couldn't depend on the police to help them because police were in league with the pimps. Those poor women endured a living hell.

We sat with the women and listened to their heartbreaking stories. A number of them were there by force. Some were kidnapped, while others had been born there. Most of them had AIDS. Some of them begged us to save their children. Christians in India were trying to save those women and help them start a new life. In some cases they would buy the children of prostitutes in order to raise them in freedom.

Despite all the sadness of the red-light district, we tried to encourage the Indian Christians working there and help them in their ministry, speaking at churches in the area. The Christian community was very strict and followed rigid rules like a bunch of machines. We encouraged them to relax, enjoy God's wonderful world, and take a more personal, less legalistic approach. When I wanted to visit the jungle near the church compound, some of the boys there told me they weren't allowed in the jungle. "In Turkey they called me the Wild Horse because no one could tame me!" I said, half joking. I still wanted to go into the jungle, and so we went, including taking a dip in a pond where snakes were commonplace. The cook was angry at us when we returned late (and very dirty) for dinner, but that was the price of making the point that God isn't opposed to fun.

After fifteen days in India we returned to Iran, where the idea of prostitution was very different. Islamic mullahs teach that a temporary marriage, or *sigheh*, is legal and morally acceptable. Mohammad himself had four wives and many temporary marriages. He also married a nine-year-old girl named Aisha. Therefore Islam teaches that temporary marriage is acceptable under Islamic law and not a sin. Yet a "temporary marriage" may be for a couple of years, a couple of months, a couple of days, or even a couple of hours. To be granted a *sigheh*, a man and woman only have to sign a contract in front of a mullah and pay a fee.

Temporary marriage in Islam is nothing more or less than an act of prostitution, but mullahs try to manipulate and brainwash people by calling it a "marriage" because the fees line their pockets and it gives men a legal way to satisfy their physical desires. Therefore women, especially widows, could enter into temporary marriages without any problem in order to support themselves and their children. These women never consider this sexual relationship to be prostitution because what they do is completely legal and according to the command of their prophet Mohammad.

Working among these women was very difficult because we had to convince them that *sigheh* was in fact prostitution, not marriage. We started the house church for prostitutes with one person. Then God started blessing the church, and it grew every day. As our ministry expanded, the danger of consequences also grew, but I never had a moment's fear. God was always with me.

CHAPTER 19

Under Arrest

Whenever Maryam and I started a new mission, we could be sure Satan would attack us in different ways. It was a spiritual battle. We felt his anger, especially after we started our home church for prostitutes. The evil one was furious with us for evangelizing people and saving more lives for Jesus.

One afternoon when I was taking a nap, I envisioned that the door opened and standing there was an ugly demon. He said, "I have come to kill you today. This time I am not alone. I have brought hundreds with me to destroy you forever!"

I was paralyzed with fear. The demon lay down on the bed beside me, put his arms around me, and said, "Now I'm going to break your back." I felt sharp pain in my back, especially the spinal cord. I didn't know how to get rid of him. All I knew was how much Satan fears the name of Jesus. As he grabbed me to bend my back even farther, his hand was close to my mouth. I bit his finger as hard as I could and shouted, "In the name of Jesus, get out of here!"

As soon as I spoke, he loosened his grip and disappeared. I woke with a start and sat bolt upright on the bed. I had terrible pains in my back. I wanted to go to Maryam's room to tell her what happened and ask her to pray with me, but when I tried to get up, I couldn't stand straight because of the pressure on my back. At that moment Maryam opened my door. Seeing me bent over and obviously in distress, she asked what had happened. When I explained, she said that after leaving me, the demon had come to her room in another form and attacked her. Satan was trying to destroy us for carrying the gospel of Christ to the prostitutes of Tehran.

We prayed daily for protection from the enemy. Almost every day we saw how God's miraculous hand was with us everywhere we went. Later, when the authorities started closing in on us for distributing Bibles, they thought there must be some huge international organization behind the project. Our work was the subject of discussion in the Iranian parliament. They had no idea that all those Bibles were from two girls with backpacks who were under God's protection in countless ways.

During the three years of my Bible ministry with Maryam, God sent two dreams to remind me of his purpose for my life. In the first, my mother came to me and said she knew what God had promised me. "I know the secret that you have hidden for years," she said, and repeated the dream I had that I would leave Iran. In the second dream, I saw one of the Assembly of God pastors I had known for years. He said the same thing my mother had said and that he knew God had chosen me for a specific purpose. He also said he and some other pastors had prayed, and my name was selected from among many for the specific purpose of fulfilling God's promise to me.

Every couple of years or so, God repeated his promise that he had a specific purpose in mind for me. He kept reminding me so I would not lose faith in his promise and would always look to him, not to myself, for the strength to do whatever it was. While I was happy that God had chosen me and was passionate to do his will, I had no idea exactly what my purpose would be or when I would fulfill it.

Knowing God had a purpose for me made it easier to understand the hardships and difficulties. He wanted to train me, prepare me, and increase my faith. Whenever I focused on my weaknesses, sins, flaws, and mistakes, I concluded that my sense of purpose was only a dream. It couldn't be true.

It is hard to believe God's promises and trust him for impossible things. To do so requires patience and obedience. It also takes humility, sacrifice, and resistance to temptation. God taught me all those lessons by passing me through many hardships and allowing me to experience pain. Hebrews 11:1 tells us, "Now faith is confidence in what we hope for and assurance about what we do not see" (NIV). In this same letter, we are told that it was by faith that those chosen by God—Abel, Enoch, Noah, Abraham, Isaac, Joseph, and many others—could do seemingly impossible things and, through the power of God, transform the world around them.

———— • ————

Maryam and I moved into an apartment with a beautiful view of the mountains surrounding Tehran. We also had a view of the wall of the notorious Evin Prison, built by the shah of Iran in the 1970s to hold political prisoners. The apartment was our refuge, the place where we taught converted Christians in our home church.

One day when I was feeling sad and heartbroken, I decided to climb the mountains near our apartment. Since I was a child, mountain climbing had always given me a sense of peace. I enjoyed the quiet and solitude, where I could pray to God and talk to him about anything on my mind. This particular mountain was not a high one, but it was out of the way and no one else was in sight. I sat down to rest and talk to Daddy, my heavenly Father.

After a few minutes I saw a young woman climbing toward me. *Oh no*, I thought. *Please don't come this way. I just want to be alone with God.* But she was definitely headed toward me, and there was nothing I could do.

When she got close enough, the woman said, "Sorry to bother you. I just came to deliver a message." She pointed to a hut partway down the mountain. "The owner of this land lives there. My friends and I have come to visit him. He asked me to invite you to come by when you're ready to climb down."

I was embarrassed to be on someone's land without permission. "I didn't know this was private property," I said. "I'm sorry I came up without asking first."

"Don't worry," the woman said, smiling. "The owner is a kind old man who doesn't mind you being here. He just wants to meet you."

After spending time talking to God and praying, I felt like I should at least go apologize for trespassing unintentionally. An elderly man was sitting outside his hut. The man met me as I walked toward him, welcoming me with a smile.

"I'm sorry for being here without permission," I said. "I didn't know this was private land."

"That's no problem," the man said. "You are welcome here. I only wanted to meet the person who was scaling this mountain like an antelope. Watching you, I realized you weren't climbing just for recreation. There are plenty of mountains only a mile away that people climb all the time. It seemed you had a purpose in going up. In all the years I've lived here, you're the first person I've ever seen climbing."

"You're right," I admitted. "I didn't come for recreation. My apartment is very close to your property. I just wanted to climb a mountain to be alone and talk to God."

This made the man curious, and he invited me to sit down with him. After chatting a few minutes, I shared my faith with him. He was very curious and interested. I promised the next time I came, I would bring him a Bible.

"I'm glad God sent you here to give me this message," the man said. "Any time you want to be alone with God, please come climb my mountain."

Over time I learned the story of his life. In some ways it reminded me of my father's. He had been a wealthy man with lots of property and important government connections. Then his political opponents conspired to confiscate most of his property and even sent him to prison for a while. When he lost his wealth, his family abandoned him as well. The one property he had left was the mountain where he was living. His ownership documentation was so strong even his enemies hadn't been able to take it from him.

In order to keep the property, he had to live there. His big concern was that to stay, and especially to plant crops or develop the land in any way, he had to find a source of water. Otherwise he would eventually have to move, and when he did, he would forfeit his ownership. Though there was a lake nearby, the government blocked his effort to bring water from there. Two men were drilling a well inside the hut. Despite digging very deep, they had not reached water because of the huge rocks in the area.

I asked the man if I could go down into the well and pray for water. I remembered climbing into a well on a dare from my brother when I was a girl. I had no fear of going down. The two young workers were very surprised at my request. The man agreed to my plan and finally convinced the workers to help me. They showed me how to use their safety rope and gave me a miner's helmet with a light. Down in the well I prayed for water. When I came up, I told the men that if they had faith, they would find water soon.

"We admire your courage and faith," one of the young men said, "but we think it's almost impossible to find water here."

A few days later I went back to visit the hut. As soon as the man saw me he started calling my name and running toward me. "It's a miracle! It's a miracle!" he shouted.

"A few days after you prayed, the workers moved a huge stone at the bottom of the well and found water just below it. God answered your prayers! I am so happy that Jesus sent you here for me!" Seeing God's miracle in his life, the man gave his heart to Jesus.

"Now that I have water I will become rich again because the value of the land will increase greatly." He said he planned to build a recreation area for the public. "I'm also going to build a church on top of the mountain for you," he added, "so people can come there to worship God. I'm going to call it Church of Marziyeh!

"This property is yours," he continued. "You are welcome here any time."

I visited him regularly after that and also invited him to attend our home church.

———— • ————

For years now, God had been telling me he had special plans for me. He had also sent me dreams about being in prison. When God told me I would pass through a prison experience, I had no doubt it would happen. In March 2009, God finally put his plan into action.

For three years before that time Maryam and I distributed Bibles all over Tehran and elsewhere. We led two house churches in our apartment. We talked to everyone who would listen about our faith and the message of salvation in Christ. All these activities were illegal and dangerous in Iran because no one there is allowed to promote any religion except Islam. Yet God protected us, and as a result of our work, hundreds of people came to Christ. (Today Iran has one of the fastest-growing Christian populations in the world.) Through it all we continued our mission until finally someone reported us to the authorities.

It started with a call about my car documents. The caller, who was a stranger to me, asked me to come down to the police station to answer some questions about my auto registration. Suspicious of this request, I called a friend who was a lawyer. He assured me there was no problem and advised me to go to the station. When I arrived, police confiscated my documents, handcuffed me, and told me I was under arrest for being a Christian and evangelizing. Three guards escorted me back to our apartment where they ransacked every room—without a warrant of any kind—and took all our belongings along with our Christian books, CDs, and Bibles. Maryam was arrested too, and we were both hauled back to the police station.

The police interrogated us until midnight. Though they threatened to torture us, we survived that first day without physical harm. We were taken to a dark, filthy cell in the basement. As he locked us in our cell the jailer warned, "You'd better tell us everything about your friends, your network, and your activities as Christians. Otherwise we will beat you until you vomit blood."

I had heard stories of women being tortured, raped, and even killed in Iranian prisons. As terrified as I was, I knew in my heart that God was with Maryam and me every minute. We prayed for each other, asking the Holy Spirit to strengthen us. As the hours passed, we kept thinking any moment we would be taken out and tortured. Finally, after a long day behind bars, we were transferred to the Vozara Detention Center, a short-term jail for prisoners facing minor charges or awaiting trial.

Our new cell was also in a basement. Since we had no beds, we slept on the freezing, filthy, bare floor with only urine-soaked blankets for cover. Cells were locked from 8:00 p.m. until the next morning, so if a prisoner had to relieve herself the only choice was to go in the cell. The only drinking water came from horrible restrooms with backed-up toilets and toxic waste everywhere, including feces and used sanitary pads. Prisoners were fed like animals from a dirty pot on the floor without any utensils.

We refused to eat for fourteen days. For the first few days we prayed for our release. But then we realized God had put us there as a tool to bring his message to our fellow prisoners and even some guards. In those close quarters, we had more opportunities to share the gospel than we did on the street. Every day we were surrounded by prostitutes, drug addicts, and homeless women who desperately needed Jesus in their lives. We started having daily church services. Most of the other prisoners were very interested in hearing about God's forgiveness in Jesus.

Later we learned that some of the guards were curious to know more about Jesus because they could see how much the prisoners wanted to spend time with us. As we left the detention center after fourteen days, some guards came by, held our hands through the bars, and asked us to pray for them and forgive them. What a miracle!

CHAPTER 20

Obama's Betrayal

From Vozara, Maryam and I were transferred to Evin Prison, the most notorious prison in Iran, which we could see from our apartment window. As terrifying as it was, I knew we would survive somehow because God had told me I would go *through* a prison experience. He knew all along what was in store for us. At Evin we were charged with apostasy, blasphemy, promoting Christianity, and anti-government activity.

Maryam and I wrote a detailed account of our prison experience in the book *Captive in Iran* (Tyndale Momentum, 2013). While I won't repeat our whole story here, I will summarize some relevant points and events.

Evin Prison is the heart and brute manifestation of the power of the ayatollahs and a symbol of their dominance and strength over Iran. It is infamous for the torture, rape, and execution of many innocent people. Students, lawyers, journalists, doctors, intellectuals, and others are interrogated and tortured there for violating the government's harsh and restrictive rules.

The first few months Maryam and I spent in Evin the guards and interrogators treated us harshly. Other prisoners also criticized us because they believed anyone who converted from Islam to Christianity

189

or any other religion was dirty and an infidel. Rather than answering anger with anger, we tried to show them by our actions what the teachings of Jesus were. Instead of criticizing them, we loved them, respected them, and prayed for them. Jesus tells his followers to "love your enemies, bless those who curse you, pray for those who mistreat you." It was not always easy. I prayed for the power to love these people and also for their well-being. The Holy Spirit taught us to pray for them and even for the guards, and gave us the grace to reach out to them. Our behavior encouraged most of the prisoners to start respecting us and listening to what we had to say. We remembered the words of Jesus in Matthew 5:11–12: "Blessed are you when people insult you, persecute you and falsely say all kinds of evil against you because of me. Rejoice and be glad, because great is your reward in heaven" (NIV).

Although it was very difficult to rejoice in persecution, with the power of the Holy Spirit and the grace of God everything is possible. It should be an honor for every Christian to be persecuted for having faith in Christ. In Evin Prison we had many opportunities to share Jesus's message. In fact, this dark and brutal place became our church.

Most prisoners, including the two of us, suffered from the lack of medical care. There was only one small, dirty, understaffed, and undersupplied clinic for the whole prison. Doctors were radical Muslims whose first question was not "What is your problem?" but rather "What is the charge against you?" When they learned we were Christians they refused to treat us.

The food was awful. Besides being served in a pot on the floor without utensils, it was unhealthy and disgusting. One regular meal was a stew of water, fat, and a few unpeeled carrots and potatoes. The vegetables were unwashed so the water was full of dirt, more like eating mud than stew. Another meal was dried, tasteless rice without cooking oil or spices. Once a week we had horrible sausage that gave us all diarrhea. Prison authorities also added chemicals to the food, supposedly to suppress inmates' sex drive, which made the food smell and taste even worse and was dangerous for a woman's reproductive system. Six days a week, all that Maryam and I ate was the bread and cheese at breakfast. One day a week we had potatoes and boiled eggs, which was the only decent food we saw.

Because we were Christians, the prison administrators refused to allow us to go to the prison library or attend classes or any other activities. They separated Maryam and me and sent me to the ward where the murderers were housed. After I had been there a week, they executed one of my cellmates, thinking it would break me by showing the price of resistance. The unmistakable message was that if I continued to resist, I would be hanged just like she was. Later, shortly before our last court appearance, they executed our best and closest friend in Evin Prison, a beautiful young woman named Shirin Alam Hooli. She was hanged after being violently tortured for months. Her crime was that she was born a Kurd. She was charged with anti-government activities and accused of being a *moharebeh*, meaning an enemy of God, which carried a death sentence. During her two years in prison she was tortured repeatedly to force her to reveal the names of others like her. She was hung by her heels, whipped on the soles of her feet, kicked in the stomach until she vomited blood, and beaten unconscious for days. But she had the will of an ox and the heart of a lion. She never betrayed her friends. She was hanged before dawn with four other Kurdish prisoners. Their bodies were secretly buried in a single unmarked grave "to avoid a public protest or family reaction." Her family never received her body or even knew the location of her grave. Her execution left a wound in our hearts that will never allow us to forget the savage atrocity of her murder by the Islamic state.

In prison God continued communicating with me through dreams. I dreamed about when other prisoners would be released and what would happen to them. God foretold Shirin's execution in a dream. I knew months ahead of time that it would happen and suffered terribly with this secret knowledge. I was desperate to save the life of my best friend. Every time the guards took her away for another interrogation I expected something bad to happen. I prayed to God to spare her life and begged him to take my life instead of hers. Every day I saw her beautiful smile, yet my heart was full of pain.

During our months in prison, many prisoners became curious about our faith and gave their hearts to Jesus. How ironic it was that on the street they never had a chance to hear about Christianity, but now they could learn about it in prison! The filthy environment and bad food made me sick. But God spoke to me in a dream and said, "Do not be afraid, because I am always with you." Hearing that voice gave me strength and courage to go on. I knew that even in prison, everything about my life was under God's control.

With the Green Movement of 2009, the reelection of Iranian president Mahmoud Ahmadinezhad, and the brutal crackdown that followed, another dream of mine became clear as that bloody conflict spread through the streets of Tehran.

A year or so earlier I had a dream about Ahmadinezhad, a short, ugly little man. In my dream God showed me Ahmadinezhad's true image, which was a tall, huge, scary monster. In my dream he captured thousands of people in a dark, horrible place where everyone sat in long rows. As Ahmadinezhad gave the order, his henchmen took the people out one row at a time. As the rows close to me emptied, I could see the people were being taken outside and killed. I could hear their cries. Before it came time for my row to leave the door, I woke up.

That dream was a preview of the Green Movement crisis after the 2009 election. Protesters demanded that Ahmadinezhad resign because he had won reelection by cheating. Thousands of people assembled peacefully in the streets to show their objection to the fraud and cheating that kept an incompetent president in office. Government soldiers and thugs shot many people in the streets and tortured and killed hundreds more in prisons.

Evin Prison was suddenly filled to overflowing with people who had been arrested for protesting. When interrogators killed a prisoner, they dumped the body into an empty pool inside the prison until they could sneak out to bury it after dark. I talked with other prisoners who saw this pool full of dead students. Many of the people who were arrested during the Green Movement completely disappeared. Their families never heard from them again, and their bodies were never found. This was what happened to our dear friend Shirin. Her body was never returned to her family, and to this day they do not know where it is.

When the Iranian government started murdering innocent, peaceful protesters, the Iranian people asked the United States for help. Crowds chanted, "Obama, are you with us or with them?" This is a play on words in our language. "Obama" in Farsi means "He is with us": *O* (he), *ba* (with), *ma* (us).

Despite the people's hope and expectation, President Obama stood with the criminal regime in Iran. He not only failed to help the Iranian people who were fighting for their freedom, he also later made the worst deal in history with the Iran nuclear agreement known as the Joint Comprehensive Plan of Action, which allowed Iran to pursue its nuclear program while the United States and other countries lifted their trade and economic sanctions. Obama shook the bloody hands of mullahs and transferred billions of dollars into the pockets of murderers who used that money to expand terrorism in the Middle East.

The Iranian people will never forget Obama's betrayal. He is the most hated president among a majority of Iranians for his foreign policy toward Iran and his support of the criminal Islamic Republic. He evidently has no idea that his hands are soaked in the blood of innocent Iranian citizens, because he gave the regime more opportunity, time, and money to kill more innocent people instead of standing with the freedom fighters in Iran. History will remember this atrocity by the Islamic Republic and those who helped them cling to power.

I myself saw crowds of people arrested, imprisoned, and tortured for protesting election fraud. When I asked God why he didn't end this horrible situation, he answered me in a dream. He said, "I am giving these cruel people a chance to repent and come back to me. But if they don't, I will destroy them all." At first I couldn't understand how God could give such cruel, ruthless people a second chance. God's answer made me realize how much God loves his people, even the cruelest ones, and gives even the most savage of them an opportunity to repent. However, do not be misled. His patient kindness does not mean his justice won't come.

———— • ————

Besides the mental strain of imprisonment and expecting to be tortured or executed without warning, I was physically sick from the lack of fresh air, sanitary facilities, decent food, and a comfortable place to sleep. The last few months in prison I spent most of my time in bed, weak and aching. During this time I had a dream that I had a big hole in my right hand. Looking at the hole, I remembered Jesus's sufferings for the human race. The thought of his suffering made me cry. I heard God's voice saying, "I have allowed you to taste what it's like to suffer." When I woke up, my face was wet with tears and I kept on crying, praising God and thanking him for allowing me this small taste of what suffering truly means.

I thought to myself, *How could Jesus endure so much punishment?* He sacrificed himself on the cross for every one of us because of the power of unconditional love. My suffering helped me better understand the meaning of the cross. I only wished I could share my revelation about the love of God with everyone on earth. I wish I could help them understand how much God loves them. That amazing love has the power to push away all hate and darkness. Compared to what he endured on the cross, my suffering was nothing.

In another dream God told me, "It is only pain and suffering that can polish your soul and make you valuable and beautiful." Still another time he told me, "If you want to understand the truth, you should be brave enough to pass through and experience hardships. You should go toward them, not try to escape from them." From this dream I understood that there is a secret power in pain and suffering that makes the human soul beautiful and pure. Only they can open a channel to God that lets us get closer to him.

Most people want a secure and normal life. They don't want to take risks or give up their happiness. No one in this world prays for pain and suffering, but I learned the secret behind those conditions. People think pain is bitter and dark, but I learned that it can be very sweet— especially when it takes you closer to the source of love, which is God. I could now taste the sweetness of the pain.

Maryam and I spent part of our imprisonment in what were called 209 cells, solitary confinement cells in a separate building where our interrogations were the most intense. We were separated, though we figured out how to leave hidden messages for each other. One day a week I was bombarded with questions by two interrogators for hours at a time. The rest of the week, the only sound I heard was the screams of other prisoners being beaten. The cell was so small I could scarcely move. The light was kept on 24 hours a day, so I lost track of whether it was day or night.

Hour after hour, week after week, the interrogators relentlessly insisted I had to renounce my faith in Jesus. If I would give up my Christian beliefs, they would release me immediately. This continued later in the courts. All we had to do was write one sentence renouncing our faith, and we would be free. But we refused.

I hadn't just become a Christian; I was in love with Christ. No one had forced me into anything. No one had manipulated me. No one cast a spell on me when I received the flames of the Holy Spirit. My personal experience led me to give my heart to Jesus. I met him when I received the Holy Spirit. I touched his love in my dreams and in all my suffering and pain. I had seen miracles. It was an honor for me to suffer for my faith. In dreams God had shown me how much he suffered to give me a new life. Every human being has the right to choose a personal belief. The Iranian government was trying to take that right away. I would resist. I would stand up for my rights.

Our interrogations in the 209 cells continued. Maryam and I were questioned separately and were blindfolded so we could not see our interrogators. We had infuriated our judge, Judge Sobhani, because we refused to retract our statements of faith as Christians. Instead, we encouraged him to go ahead and execute us. Since our case was now attracting international attention, the court needed us to make some kind of confession or admission so they could drop the charges against us without losing face.

At my next interrogation, a university lecturer in Islamic theology came to "coach" me in how to express my religious belief in a way that would allow the court to resolve our case. He questioned my reasons for "abandoning" Islam, though I had never been a Muslim, and spoke for an hour about the brutal acts committed by Christians during the Crusades.

I admitted I couldn't match his knowledge of history. But I pointed out that Islamic police and courts were currently arresting, torturing, and killing people in the streets and that women in Evin Prison were routinely beaten, raped, and executed on religious grounds. "I saw these women every day," I said. "Some of them were my friends. Protesting students were murdered in cold blood or disappeared without a trace. I was arrested by Islamic authorities and sentenced to death. And Islam is the religion of peace?"

The university lecturer said he wanted to let us go and that by simply changing the language of our statements we could be free. The court wanted to release us but, he said, our "defiance" made it impossible.

My interrogators said repeatedly that they had never had a prisoner like me before. I trusted in God to protect me and to guide my thoughts and words as I was questioned. They were used to people cowering in fear and begging for their lives. I stood up to them, never aggressive but never yielding. It wasn't a matter of bravery or my own strength, but an invincible power that came from God alone.

One of the most painful injustices of our time behind bars was to see prisoners we lived with, women we came to know and care about, taken away and executed. Every time this happened it left a spirit of sorrow and death. Following an execution there was nothing but silence. We stared at each other and wanted to speak but were forced to remain quiet. Knowing someone you lived with was in another room being hanged is an indescribable feeling.

In spite of such tragedy, the great miracle of our story is that Maryam and I were able to bring light into that dark place with our faith. Our prayers and actions led many women to give their hearts to Jesus. We showed them who he is by loving them, praying for them, and respecting them no matter how they behaved toward us. We demonstrated to them God's miraculous power. Before we were released, even guards came to apologize for the way they had treated us. The government was only able to imprison our bodies in that dark place. They could not imprison our souls. Prisoners who started out insulting us became some of our best friends. We led a quiet revolution inside Evin Prison that made our interrogators furious and desperate. They couldn't break us, couldn't hold back the power of God's love. With God's help, we transformed the dark, miserable cells of Evin into our church. This is the best victory of all: changing the world around you with faith, love, and respect instead of disappointment, anger, and revenge.

I remember one particular conversation with an interrogator after the Green Movement protests about other prisoners who were interested in our Christian faith. He was furious, screaming, "You are brainwashing these young people with your fake religion!"

I stood my ground. "First of all," I said, "you're the one brainwashing students with your Islamic ideology, not us. If Islam is the truth, why are so many students here in prison instead of at the university?

"Second, it's your fault that I'm sharing my faith with these women. You and your cohorts are the ones who put me in here. Prisoners are always curious to know what others are charged with. When they ask me why I'm here, I tell them."

He was so angry and confused he couldn't speak. We were already in prison and being threatened with torture, so there was nothing else he could do. He was desperate but in a way completely helpless. I was freer to share my faith in prison than I had been on the outside. In Evin I could share the truth about Jesus without fear.

Maryam and I were sentenced to death by hanging. Yet, as we later learned, the Iranian government was under intense pressure to release us. We felt lonely and isolated behind bars and had no idea there was a worldwide effort to set us free. Christians around the world prayed for us and sent letters to the Iranian government. As the letters poured in, judges and even the guards began to change their behavior toward us.

The United Nations made an appeal for our release, as did Amnesty International. Even the pope sent a letter to the Iranian government requesting they set us free. Other people and organizations worked behind the scenes, seeking dialogue with Islamic leaders out of the public eye. In the end, the rulers of Iran had to release us to show the world there was freedom of religion in Iran. What irony! Once our case became widely known, keeping us in prison on charges of blasphemy and apostasy would only prove how rigid and ruthless their regime was. Though they broke their own laws to set us free, it was better for their public relations than keeping us in prison or hanging us according to the law they now claimed didn't exist.

Our last court hearing was on the seventh day of the month of Mehr 2009, the fourth anniversary of my baptism. That experience had meant the world to me as a Christian. The day I was baptized was one of the happiest days of my life. I could never have imagined that a few years later on that same date, I would be standing before a judge proclaiming that same faith even in the face of death. Though my faith had condemned me to die, I never wavered in proclaiming my love for Jesus.

Throughout our arrest and imprisonment, there had never been a written order for our execution. In high-profile cases, these charges were often limited to verbal rulings. That way the authorities had no accountability for their decisions and could always deny whatever they did.

At that hearing, after 259 days in prison, we were released.

Though we were out of Evin, we were still charged with apostasy and had to remain in Iran until the case was settled. Twenty days after our last court appearance our lawyer told us we were free and our files were closed. Just as there was no written record of our death sentences, we had no written confirmation that we were acquitted, only a verbal statement from the judge. Before our release, our interrogators and the judge were not happy that international pressure forced them to let us go. They said they would monitor us constantly. We were required to tell them where we lived and when we moved.

After our release we could see that people followed us everywhere we went. Though we were outside of prison, we had no freedom. Authorities threatened us, saying, "We cannot guarantee your safety because there are many prejudiced Muslims who are angry that you were released. You may die in an accident. Your house may catch on fire."

They also warned us we might meet the same tragic end as Haik Hovsepian and Mehdi Dibaj, two Christian pastors who were murdered by government agents. They wanted to make sure we knew that even though they had to release us, there were other ways they could easily kill us without attracting attention from Western governments or human rights organizations.

After thinking the matter through, Maryam and I felt that our mission in Iran was finished. There was no more for us to do there. It was time to leave the country.

CHAPTER 21

On to America

God had talked to me in dreams several times over the years, both before and after my imprisonment, about going to the United States. I never imagined he would open this door by leading me through the worst prison in Iran, and I still didn't know how it would happen. I only knew that my next step was emigrating to America.

My pastor in London did not want me to move to the United States. He said he and the other pastors had prayed for God's will about where Maryam and I should live to continue our ministry. He insisted we come to London; all the pastors agreed it was God's will I should move there. I told him about my dreams and how God told me I should move to the United States.

This pastor meant well, but he could not understand that all my life with Jesus, it has been Jesus alone who tells me what to do. I listen to Christ, not men. I prayed about what to say, then told the pastor, "You are my pastor, and I always respect you and your decisions. But I am a follower of Jesus, not human beings, and I listen to Jesus in my own way. Jesus himself has trained me, built my faith, and taught me how to communicate with him. I cannot allow people to make decisions for me or give me direction."

I knew my answer would hurt his feelings, but I had to do what I knew was right. Finally, the ministry agreed to let Maryam and me go to the United States. To do that as Iranian citizens, we had to move back to Turkey, register with the office of the United Nations High Commissioner for Refugees, and wait for our immigration applications to be processed.

Before we left Iran, Maryam and I both visited doctors to treat the problems nine months of imprisonment had caused, including dental problems, kidney problems, and sore throats. My back was worse and now hurt all the time. A friend of mine suggested a chiropractor who would make house calls. He was very expensive, but because I was in such pain I decided to try to negotiate a price. To my surprise, he agreed to treat me for only a little more than half his regular fee.

When he arrived for our first appointment I knew immediately something was wrong. As he stood in my doorway, I had an overpowering sense he was sent from Satan. He certainly didn't look the part. He was a short man in a crisp white suit who walked with a limp. I went to Maryam's room and told her I felt uneasy about this man though I didn't know why. I asked her to come out of her room and pray for me when the treatment started.

As the man prepared to treat me, I asked him why he agreed to reduce his fee.

"I knew you were going to call me," he said mysteriously, "and if I insisted on my usual fee, you wouldn't allow me to treat you."

"Why do you want to treat me?" I asked.

"I know who you are," he said. "I know many things about you."

This made me even more uneasy. "You've probably heard about Maryam and me on the news."

"I know you were on the news," he answered. "But I also know who you really are."

I felt this weird little man knew the secret of God's promises to me. I felt Satan had entered my home in the shape of this human being.

Maryam came into the room and sat down. The chiropractor didn't like her being there but didn't say anything about it. I asked him how he knew I was going to call.

"I was a witch in the past," he said. The man explained that when he was a child his parents dedicated him to two Islamic prophets, which gave him the ability to practice witchcraft. He added that he was a witch for powerful government leaders and that they made their decisions only after consulting with a witch and making a sacrifice to Satan—especially those who make national and foreign policies.

"I was once the private witch of President Ahmadinezhad," he added.

This was all astonishing and terrifying news to Maryam and me.

"There are hundreds of agents in the city," he went on, "working to control the country and the people. They meet in dark secret places underground. There are dozens of them who wear long black robes and stand in every square in the city. Only other witches can see them. To everyone else, they're invisible.

"Government officials and mullahs have to sacrifice the blood of others to Satan's agents for the success of their policies and plans. That is why once in a while they kill a large number of people: they dedicate the blood to Satan."

Maryam and I were speechless. Without hesitation or shame, this man was proud to claim he was a witch with supernatural power bestowed by Satan. As soon as he left, we prayed for me and for the protection of our home. I canceled all future appointments, and we never saw him again. I wondered later why, having the strong negative feelings I did, I even let him in. I realized it was because at that moment I was temporarily paralyzed until I gathered my own heavenly power in Christ.

———— • ————

After our court case file was closed we moved to Turkey and registered with the UN as refugees who wanted to go to the United States.

One of my last visits before leaving my native country was to the man who owned the mountain. Almost every day during the months Maryam and I were in prison, he stood on the spot where I had climbed, faced the prison in the distance, and prayed for my release. I went to see him, and we shared a tearful reunion and goodbye at the same time. I gave him money to buy some sheep and make improvements to his land. "One day I will return," I said. "And when I do, I'll come back and visit you. By then I'm sure you will transform this mountain according to your vision."

He repeated his promise to build a church for me there. "Go now," he advised, "and save yourself from the savage people who persecute you."

It took almost a year in Turkey to process our application. During that time we wrote the story of our Christian ministry and imprisonment in Iran. We had not been allowed to keep any sort of journal in prison, so we now wrote down everything we could remember in order to explain our ministry and honor the many, many people who were imprisoned or executed by the Islamic regime. We ended up with more than 1,500 handwritten pages in Farsi. This memoir became the basis for our book *Captive in Iran*, written in fulfillment of our promise to be a voice for our friends and others who had no voice. We were determined that their stories would be heard.

During our time in Turkey I also had two dreams in which God spoke to me about the future. In the first one, the wonderful White Horse reappeared, galloping out of the sea toward me. As he got closer I heard the voice of God ask me, "Do you promise to give my message to the whole world forever?"

"Yes!" I nodded my head.

"I am not satisfied with most churches and pastors."

Why would God tell me that? Especially when I was on my way to a Christian country where so many people were true believers? It was only later, after I moved to America and started speaking in churches there, that I realized what God was talking about and why he gave me that message.

In American churches, God opened my eyes to the difference between a relationship with him and merely following religious rules and laws. I saw that some churches are run as businesses, not as houses of worship. I saw that many Americans attended church not because they loved God, but because they were afraid of hell. Many Christians gave gifts to the church to receive rewards in this world such as tax deductions and an ego boost, not for the purpose of helping someone in the name of Jesus. I saw that in some American churches there is no place for the Holy Spirit.

God showed me how denominational squabbling was carried out selfishly and falsely in his name. God let me see and experience many things that broke my heart. Along with the disappointment, however, I had many good experiences in churches where the truth was proclaimed and the members sincerely and selflessly served God. I felt the presence of God in those places. I had the honor of meeting and becoming friends with many amazing Christians who were true believers. They remain a great blessing in my life today.

My second dream was only a few months before I moved to the United States. In that dream I was captured by a crowd of people. They took me to a cross to crucify me. As some tried to nail my hands and feet, others tried to tear my clothes. Though I fought with them, they got my clothes so that I was naked and embarrassed. As I tried to stop this mob, God reminded me of what happened to his son, Jesus. He showed me how Jewish religious leaders did the same thing to Jesus. He reminded me that Jesus never fought back but allowed them to do whatever they wished. After I remembered Jesus's suffering and crucifixion, I stopped fighting. Then I woke up.

Later in America my dream was partially interpreted. After we moved to the United States, some Iranian Christians tried to hurt us and damage our reputation. Because of some disagreements with people we had worked with in the past, we decided to be independent and not be associated with any ministries for a while. Our decision was not acceptable to these Christians because in their eyes we were two girls who needed to be managed and controlled.

I have found that life can be hard when you decide to follow God's will instead of people's will. Many people have mentors they go to for advice because they cannot find God's will for them. The book of Proverbs talks a lot about listening to the advice of our elders and our parents. We need the wise counsel of others to make good decisions. However, my true leader, mentor, boss, advisor, king, and commander is Jesus Christ alone. I listen for his directions for my next steps. When he tells me something directly, I obey even if the whole world stands against me.

Unfortunately, some people cannot understand this and are hurt by my decisions. But my ears hear only the voice of my love, Jesus Christ.

———— • ————

Maryam and I had to go for interviews with UN representatives to finish our applications for emigrating to America. They were more like prison interrogations than interviews. Afterward we came home with headaches that lasted for days. My last interview was very tough and very insulting.

Our lawyer had prepared all the documents we needed to explain our case, including news accounts of our imprisonment and copies of statements from organizations and important people like the pope who worked to free us. The file was 300 pages of proof that we were condemned and imprisoned because of our Christian faith. In my last interview, the UNHCR interviewer asked me if I was a Christian or not. His question was ridiculous and strange since I had been in prison for nine months and sentenced to death because I was a Christian.

"Yes," I said, "I am a Christian and was in prison and sentenced to hang for my faith. All these documents on your table are about my imprisonment on account of my faith in Jesus."

The interviewer stared at me with a blank look in his face. "If you're a Christian, where is your certificate of baptism?"

I was confused. "I believe you have it right there," I said, pointing to it in the stack. "It was issued by the ministry I was working with."

He held up the document. "This is doesn't prove you're a Christian and is not acceptable. A genuine certificate of baptism is issued by an official church, not a ministry. So I cannot consider you a Christian because you don't have a certificate of baptism from an official church."

For nine months I had fought for my faith as interrogators insulted me, threatened me, imprisoned me under miserable conditions, and pressured me relentlessly to renounce my faith in Jesus. Now in the free world some arrogant bureaucrat from the UN was insulting and mocking my faith and demanding "proof" that I was a Christian. It was likely that everyone in Iran knew by that time that I was a Christian, and now this man presumed to tell me I was not a Christian because I didn't have the paperwork he considered acceptable—the same certificate of baptism I had declined to get years earlier because to me it stood for a false faith that people claimed just as a means of escaping the country.

I tried to explain the situation to my interviewer. "I stayed in Evin Prison for months under a sentence of death because I refused to denounce my faith in Christ. Now you're telling me I'm not a Christian because I don't have a letter from a church that says so?

"Do you know what it's like living in a country with religious persecution?" I went on. "How do you expect me to show you a document from an official church in Iran? Most churches are closed by the government or monitored to pressure people not to attend." But my interrogator wasn't interested in explanations. He just kept repeating that he couldn't consider me a Christian because I didn't have proper documentation. The interview lasted almost an hour. This clueless and ignorant UN employee insulted my faith and broke my heart.

Later I got an explanation of sorts for this unexpected and disappointing experience. Most of the UN staff in Turkey were Muslims who resented Christians and had no interest in helping them. The United Nations is responsible for protecting human rights, not further violating the rights of people who have already been persecuted. I could not understand why they chose Muslims to do our interviews. But finally, our asylum was granted, and Maryam and I moved to the United States in 2011. Once again, God had opened a new door for me to walk through in faith.

CHAPTER 22

Jesus the Rock

Coming to the United States was like landing on another planet. Everything was different. The language and culture were unlike anything we had ever experienced. Though we had been to other foreign countries, none of them was anything like the United States. We came first to New York City, and then to Atlanta, where our sponsors were and where we expected to live.

We were grateful beyond words for the ministry that brought us to America, but it wasn't long before we realized our vision of life in our new home country was very different from theirs. I barely spoke English. We were dealing with culture shock. We had spent nearly a year as refugees in Turkey waiting to make the trip. We still dealt with the physical and psychological damage from our time as prisoners and convicted criminals in Iran. We needed time to settle in, rest, and get used to our new world. Yet the ministry wanted us to go on a speaking tour immediately. They had already booked us into forty churches to share our testimony. The reason, we found out eventually, was in part to encourage our listeners in their faith but also to raise money.

It was too much too soon. The thought of sharing personal details of my persecution in halting and inadequate English made me very uncomfortable. Speaking and conversing in English forced me to concentrate so hard that I developed severe headaches. Also, we needed time to reflect on what had happened to us, what it meant, and how to express it effectively. Emotionally, spiritually, and practically, we were just not ready to take our show on the road.

When I shared my concerns with the ministry, they assured me it wasn't necessary for me to speak in English. They could translate for me. God's work was too important to wait. I asked them why we had to be in such a hurry. "It's not good to postpone God's work," they said, "because God wants to use your story to save people."

"We don't save people," I told them. "Jesus is the savior, and a little delay won't harm God's purpose. I'm sure God has a great many servants and believers who can serve him and carry out his plans. God can save the world without us."

The ministry also insisted we allow them to take over the entire process of writing and publishing a book about our experience in Iran. They said, "The ministry will manage everything for you."

However, we didn't want the ministry to manage everything for us. We didn't want the ministry to control the process of publishing our book. For us it wasn't a story, it was our life. We wanted to be involved in every meeting and every decision. It would take time for us to be comfortable with a manuscript in English. We had to be sure it said what we wanted it to say. They also wanted to draw up the publishing contract in the name of the ministry, which was not acceptable to us.

It became clear to us that we would have to part company with the ministry that had helped us so much. I will always love and respect the pastors and others who made it possible for us to come to America and start a new life. I'm very grateful for their support in helping us serve the Lord in Iran and Turkey. They are amazing servants of God who serve thousands of people in Iran every day. Many people have come to Christ through their dedicated effort.

Our intention was never to be hurtful or ungrateful. However, my prayer is that they can also see their mistakes. I am absolutely sure it was God's will that we separate. It's unfortunate that separation often comes with disagreement and bitterness. I will always admire them and their passion to serve the Iranian people. My prayers are with them still.

Going our own way had immediate practical consequences. Suddenly, we had to find our own housing, a source of income, and make our way as best we could. My most frustrating problem was the language barrier. Not being able to communicate was like being paralyzed. I'm a very active and social person. Being suddenly dropped into an English-speaking world was a nightmare. Maryam's English was much better than mine, and I had to depend on her to translate conversations. This went against my independent nature and was extremely stressful.

Gradually, our situation improved. I registered in an English language school and studied hard. A refugee organization that was helping us with our living arrangements found us an inexpensive house to rent that belonged to a church in Atlanta. We also met some wonderful American Christians who soon became like family. They had worked with the same ministry we had and had separated from them because of some issues and disagreements. This family took us under their wing and helped us become independent. They even donated jewelry-making supplies to us so we could make bead bracelets to sell in churches and conferences where we spoke in order to earn some income. I passed the TOEFL (Test of English as a Foreign Language) exam and registered for college.

Finally, in 2013 Maryam and I published our book *Captive in Iran*. We also got involved in advocating for religious freedom and exposing the ongoing human rights violations in Iran. From that time until now, we have spoken at churches, conferences, universities, and government events across the United States and Europe. We were surprised that the American media did not do more to highlight the stories we shared. They were hesitant to criticize Islam despite overwhelming proof of that religion's brutal and inhumane policies. Fortunately, we met several policymakers in the United States and other countries to discuss the conditions of millions of Iranians, including religious minorities.

Moving to the United States was a dream of mine from childhood. When I was in school, the students were required to chant "Death to America!" every morning before class. The level of brainwashing in Iran would shock most Americans. But even as a girl I loved America and only pretended to join in the chants. Even then I wanted to be an American citizen. My brothers laughed at me at the time. They aren't laughing now! The day I became an American citizen was one of the greatest days of my life. I love this country, its people, and all that this great nation under God has done for me.

America is the most powerful, most free country in the history of the world. Even so, I faced many difficulties after I arrived here, including poverty, health problems, and culture shock. As a result of all the stress and trauma of imprisonment, being a refugee in Turkey, and building a new life in America, I got very sick. I suffered from horrible pain almost every day and had to take a lot of painkillers.

Attending college classes was hard because I couldn't focus. The pain distracted me and took away all my stamina. Throughout the years I was in college, Maryam stood beside me, explaining lessons and helping me get through the work. Some of my notebooks are stained with tears of pain that I shed while taking notes. Without Maryam's help and support, finishing my education would have been much harder and taken far longer. Yet Maryam and I both managed to complete our studies and earn masters degrees in international affairs from the Georgia Institute of Technology in Atlanta.

Most wonderful of all, my father was able to come to Atlanta for my graduation. I had not reunited with him for almost twenty years. I didn't see him at all for five years, and then only for a few short visits that were ruined by my brothers' interference and refusing to let us talk in private. But through yet another series of miracles, he arrived the day before my graduation and fulfilled his long-held dream of seeing me receive my diploma. Today it is my honor to have him living with me in America.

I am grateful every day for Maryam's friendship and companionship. We were like sisters, closer to each other than our own family members. Our relationship helped us survive the most difficult times of our lives. Though we were two different people with different personalities who had plenty of disagreements over the years, we grew together and learned from each other. There was power in our unity. Whenever we decided to do something in spite of all the obstacles and difficulties, we were victorious. Even in prison it was a special privilege that we were together. Through interrogations, sickness, and isolation because of our beliefs, we always supported and prayed for each other. If either of us had been alone in prison, it would have been much more difficult to endure.

I was sick for almost three years. Because my health insurance didn't cover visits to an experienced specialist, I had to deal with doctors who weren't as able to help me. Each one had a different diagnosis and recommended a different kind of surgery. Finally, one of them convinced me that she was "100 percent sure" about my problem and that her surgery would relieve the pain. But after surgery, she backtracked and said she had been wrong, her diagnosis was incorrect, and there was nothing more she could do. I was not willing to risk having other doctors make the wrong decision or keep doing surgeries in order to experiment and improve their medical knowledge.

During this time there were people who judged Maryam and me, thinking we had a comfortable life because of our speaking, writing, and receiving support from various churches. The reality was that I struggled with pain every day because I couldn't afford to see a competent specialist. A church that learned about my situation kindly offered to help me see a holistic doctor. Unfortunately, my problem was a lot bigger than what a holistic doctor could manage. The treatments made my pain more tolerable, but the underlying problem remained.

During these dark times I actually thought of suicide—anything to end the horrible pain. The only thing that helped me to endure was my faith in Jesus. I had experienced healing by Jesus in the past and couldn't understand why he did not heal me again this time. I prayed, questioned him, and complained. There was bitterness in me against God.

After months of suffering, I had a dream in which I fell to the ground, weak and helpless. Suddenly, I saw Jesus standing above my head, dressed in a white robe with his kind face shining. He stretched his hand toward me and lifted me up from the ground with the power of the Holy Spirit. After the dream my pain became more tolerable even though I was not completely healed. I still couldn't understand why he did not heal my body when he had the power to do so.

Finally, after three years, an Iranian Christian who knew about my health problems offered to pay for me to see a good specialist. After this doctor performed major surgery, my pain was completely gone. In the recovery room and still under anesthesia after my surgery, I dreamed that I kept calling the name of Jesus. There was a very deep and strong love of God in my heart and all over my bed. My heart was shaken by the love and presence of God around my bed, and I was crying because I longed for him so badly. Then I heard the voice of God calling, "Agape! Agape! Agape!" over and over again. I woke up with that word, *agape*, which is the Greek word in the Bible meaning "unconditional love." As I lay there, God had allowed me to taste his unconditional love. He showed the world his unconditional love by sacrificing himself on the cross for our sins.

I learned an important lesson during my years of illness. Many times I cursed the day I was born and questioned God for bringing me into this dark world. I lived in a true hell because there was nothing but pain, suffering, and pressure. I had been through many difficulties in the past: I lost my wealth, security, pride, and my loved ones. I was persecuted and imprisoned for my faith. I saw the terrible result of torture and suffering in the husband who loved me. I experienced loneliness and poverty. My best friend in prison was executed, and I saw many other injustices there. But none of those experiences had driven me to consider suicide. I could scarcely believe that I passed through all those previous fires with victory and my faith stronger than ever, but this latest test I almost failed.

Even though my heart had been full of bitterness, the love of God broke through and kept me hopeful and alive. I couldn't deny the love I felt deep in my heart. God's love was much stronger than my pain, suffering, and bitterness. Jesus himself built my faith during those difficult times and taught me every day how to walk with him, how to trust him, how to live with him, and how to hear his voice.

My faith was not built in a church by human beings or religious rules. My faith was built on the Rock of Jesus himself. As Matthew 7:24–27 reminds us, "Everyone then who hears these words of mine and does them will be like a wise man who built his house on a rock. And the rain fell, and the flood came, and the winds blew and beat on the house, but it did not fall, because it had been founded on the rock. And everyone who hears these words of mine and does not do them will be like a foolish man who built his house on the sand. And the rain fell, and the floods came, and the winds blew and beat against that house, and it fell, and great was the fall of it" (ESV).

I learned that when we only follow religious rules without a personal relationship with God, when we make people and religious laws our idols and follow them instead of Jesus, we will get tired and fail. I have learned that many people follow and obey God not out of love but out of fear. I have experienced the love of God many times, and I never want to lose that love. The love of God is not comparable with any love in this world. From the first day he allowed me to taste his love he made me frantic with love for him. I long for him desperately almost every day, long to meet him and hug him. I have such thirst and desire to be with him. I never cared about what hell looks like. Hell to me means the absence of God. Hell for me is when I lose the presence of God in my life, when I can no longer hear his beautiful voice or sense his tender touch. I have told God many times to take whatever he wants from me but never take away his presence and his love. Without him I feel empty and selfish.

During my years of suffering I had another dream about the White Horse. In my dream I saw that the horse was in a lot of pain and could not move. His swollen belly was covered with a cloth. God's voice told me, "Whenever he has so much pain, he hides it and does not allow others to see how much he suffers." After that dream I decided to hide my pain and suffering, not to share my struggle with anybody. I stayed home most of the time. Whenever I was out of the house or with my friends, I took a lot of painkillers in order to seem healthy and fine in front of others.

I didn't know exactly why God asked me to hide my sickness. Maybe he wanted to protect me from people's judgment and ignorance. I remembered the story of Job and how instead of helping or trying to understand him, his friends constantly judged him. Sometimes people's unkind words are more painful than the physical pain.

Difficulties and hardships aside, I was so blessed to live in the beautiful country of America. This great country was so good to me, adopting me, a refugee from a foreign nation. In Iran, the nation of my birth, the Islamic Republic tortured and killed some of my best friends. Their torture finally killed my husband, whose dream was to finish his education and make me happy. After his beatings he was never healthy or normal again. Addicted to opium and wracked by painful headaches, he died miserably at a young age. His sister was there at the end and said the last word he spoke was my name.

Maryam and I have been blessed beyond measure by meeting so many kind individual believers and many dedicated servants of God in America's churches. God performed many miracles and enriched our lives with true believers who were connected to us by the power of the Holy Spirit. God gave me a great Christian family here, and I'm grateful to God that I've gotten to know each one of them. I am so grateful to live in the greatest and freest nation in the world. I love America and the American people. America is now my home, and I feel responsible to serve the American people and protect this country from its enemies.

CHAPTER 23

God's Kingdom Come

After moving to America I had a series of other dreams, all of them messages and guidance from God. I dreamed that Satan was furious with me and was throwing knives at me in order to kill me. "I know who you are," he screamed, "and I am determined to destroy you!" None of the knives hit me or injured me, and I realized that none ever will. Satan has tried many times to hurt me, torture me, and ruin my faith in Jesus, but the Holy Spirit always helped me stay strong and stand on my faith even during the toughest times of my life.

Before I believed in Jesus, I never saw Jesus in my dreams. And it was only after I became a believer that I could feel Satan's presence, his madness, and his attempts to take away my faith and ruin my life. The fact that Jesus is the only truth in the world makes Satan boil with anger. When we tell others about Jesus, Satan does everything he can to hurt us and disappoint us with his lies. I thank God for all the suffering and difficulties in my life that made my faith stronger and brought me closer to him.

One day when I was particularly depressed because of my sickness, I felt that God had brought me to the United States after so many hardships, only to feed me empty lies and let me suffer with relentless pain. I cried to him and called him a liar. Later in a dream, I heard God's voice loud and clear. He repeated his promise to me again, saying, "I am the mighty God who makes everything possible. I decide who will rise and who will fall." He told me again why he chose me and repeated his promise to me.

I woke up crying, my heart filled with repentance for my doubts about his promise and his power. Since that day, I have never doubted God's promise to me. I do not know how or when he will fulfill his promise, but I have no doubt he will when the time is right. He has a purpose for choosing me and bringing me to the United States. He will fulfill that promise.

When God baptized me with the Holy Spirit, I received the gift of praying and singing in tongues, the gift of heavenly language. Almost every day I sing for God, and I can hear the beautiful songs I am able to sing for him in some other languages. I once dreamed that God showed me all those beautiful words were coming from the White Horse. God showed me the White Horse in the sky and how he prepares those words and songs for me and sends them from heaven to my soul on earth.

I was in the middle of another hardship when God sent the next White Horse dream. I was floating above the clouds and saw the White Horse in the distance. When I called to him, the White Horse could hardly hear my voice at first. Suddenly, he heard me and, not realizing I was in the sky too, ran like a hurricane to make a hole in the clouds and come to earth for me. God was explaining how much he cares about my cries and prayers. As soon as he hears me, he immediately sends help to save me. It was his reminder that I am never alone and that God always hears my voice when I call on him.

Then I heard a voice in my dream say, "God loves you so much that whenever you pray and ask him something, he will come and dwell in you." Having those dreams and hearing the voice of God was so encouraging, especially during my sickness. Even during those times when I fell into sin he never abandoned me. He never rejected or judged me. He taught me and forgave me.

Now I understand why David prayed the way he did in 2 Samuel 24:14: "David said to Gad, 'I am in deep distress. Let us fall into the hands of the LORD, for his mercy is great; but do not let me fall into human hands'" (NIV). I wish people could understand how much God loves them and cares about them. I wish people didn't look at themselves through the lens of other people's judgment. Instead of living under religious laws, I wish people would see and celebrate the living God.

In another dream, God showed me the heavenly Jerusalem. It was like a big triangle in the sky, so shiny and beautiful that I couldn't take my eyes from it. In my dream I wanted to go to that city as soon as possible. I don't have the words to describe the beauty I saw.

In still another dream, I saw Jesus in a desert walking toward me from very far away through soft sand. There was only one tree in the desert, and Jesus stayed behind it as he walked. I could scarcely see his face. As he approached, I saw a big light around him. I felt that his coming to the world was very near.

I had a dream that many Christians were being murdered by Muslims. The Muslims were catching the Christians, then violently stabbing them in their stomachs with big, heavy, sharp crosses. It was horrible and painful for the victims. Then God opened my eyes and showed me that all these crosses were in the stomach of Jesus Christ. God was showing me that those who persecute Christians are in fact persecuting Jesus himself. It was Jesus who was suffering, being insulted, taking all those wounds, and enduring the pain of everyone's persecution in our place. Whoever persecutes Christians is persecuting Jesus who died for us.

———— • ————

Since the Iranian revolution of 1979, elections in Iran are empty symbolism. They mean nothing. The people of Iran have no role in electing their government representatives. Whoever the criminal Ali Khamenei, the Supreme Leader, decides will be president will only be in power as his puppet. A long as Khamenei is in charge, the Iranian people will never have a fair election and their opinions and votes will be worthless. Most Iranian citizens do not approve of the Islamic Republic, but they have no power to change the system. They have no hope for the future of their country until the Islamic regime is out of power. The people of Iran long to be free and live in a democratic country.

When I came to the United States, I was very happy to live in the greatest country in the world. I thought, *Here I will have my freedom without being suppressed or discriminated against. For the first time in my life, I can vote without my vote being stolen.*

After becoming a US citizen in 2016, I was so excited to be voting in America for the first time. I could vote for the candidate I wanted, and there would be no cheating or fraud in the election. Because of the toxic and biased America media, I got confused and wasn't sure which presidential candidate I should vote for. I prayed and asked God how I should vote.

God showed me in a dream that Donald Trump was the chosen president of the United States. In my dream, Trump was looking at the United States from the top of a hill. The hill and everything around it was dry like a desert. Then suddenly everything became green and beautiful. God showed me that when Trump came to power everything would change and become great. However, since 2016 President Donald Trump has been attacked nonstop by Democrats and wrongly impeached twice. Despite all these malicious attacks, he stood firm and fought for America and the American people.

Before the 2020 election I was worried about the result of the election because of the mail-in ballot system. This system is ripe for abuse. In fact, the only reason to use it is to manipulate the outcome. In a dream, God showed me that Joe Biden would win the election by cheating and fraud, by stealing people's votes. I saw his supporters cheering for him in the street but was sad because I knew he won by cheating, not by the vote of the people. I knew the election would be decided by fraud. Election night the Holy Spirit woke me at 3:00 a.m. and put it in my heart to pray for the president.

Joe Biden lost the 2020 election, but with the help of the fake news and big tech was able to call himself the winner. In my eyes there is no difference between what he and his followers did in 2020 and what the Islamic Republic does in the elections in Iran. The fake news media and big tech also helped him cover up the fraud and kept telling the world that Biden was chosen as president by the will of the people. This is a shameful lie.

Since Biden has taken office, he has hired National Iranian American Council (NIAC) employees as lobbyists for the Iranian Islamic regime. Members of this regime, who still chant, "Death to America!," have sent their own children to the United States to enjoy a life of freedom and privilege while suppressing the Iranian people and depriving them of their rights. This regime has also trained Iranian mercenaries and spies and sent them to the United States, funding their sinister work with oil revenue stolen from the Iranian people.

These elite Iranian children study at the most famous and expensive universities in America and bring their toxic politics along with them. The Islamic Republic regime has trained thousands of people and created an army of educated, Westernized agents who are devoted to Ayatollah Khamenei in order to deceive, manipulate, and brainwash politicians in the United States and Europe. They influence and even assume key roles in government. It is so sad—and so dangerous—to see how American politicians listen to these Islamic agents instead of to ordinary people who have been persecuted and tortured by the criminal Islamic government in Iran.

When I was studying at the university, I noticed that some of the research materials approved by the professors for use in assignments about Iran were written by Iranians trained and supported by the regime to reverse the truth and mislead American students and academics. I also noticed these same people had (and have) key positions as advisors in the federal government. It is sad to see that people like myself, who since childhood experienced firsthand the cruelty of this criminal regime, are very seldom hired or consulted by political institutions and departments in America. Our voices are ignored or silenced. Instead, those whose goals are to defend and expand the revolutionary ideology of radical Islam and promote the true enemies of the United States and Israel can easily find jobs with the most influential and powerful political organizations in the country.

It is shocking to find out how corrupt the government of the United States is, especially Democrats. They only care about power and money, not America's safety and the future of younger generations.

After moving to the United States in 2011 and becoming a citizen in 2016, I diligently studied politics in order to use my knowledge and firsthand experience—of living in a country with persecution, human rights violations, and a lack of freedom; of the government's tricks for suppressing the people's voices; of fake promises, lies, fraudulent elections, censorship, and socialism; and of misogyny—to serve America and its people, protect the country against its enemies, and help all who fight for freedom and justice in Iran or anywhere else. I love America. This country and its people have given me so much, and I always hoped that I could do something in return. Sadly, I've discovered that politicians and government agencies don't want to work with an ordinary person who has lots of experience in understanding and recognizing enemies of this country from the Islamic regime. I am a passionate opponent of enemies of America, Israel, and the Iranian people. My great hope and prayer is that someday Iran will become a free country and an ally of both the United States and Israel.

The Iranian people will never forget the American presidents and other politicians who stood with the freedom fighters and supported them. And they will never forgive those who stood with the criminal mullahs and betrayed the cause of freedom. The Iranian people will never forget those who not only shook the bloody hands of mullahs but also gave them billions of dollars, and made a deal with them that supported their hold on power in Iran. One day the regime will fall. On that day democracy will return and Iran will become a staunch ally of the US and Israel. God's kingdom will come to my native land and the people there will worship the true God.

But until that day the people of Iran will continue their suffering. The Iranian regime killed my best friend—sweet, kind Shirin Alam Hooli—and also killed my husband. The regime took away my rights as a woman, humiliated me, and insulted me. Even my own family members turned against me and denied me my freedom. Only my dear father loved and supported and encouraged me.

By contrast, America gave me freedom, hope, and the ability to worship God openly with all my heart. It gave me the opportunity to finish my education. This was one of my dreams and the dream of many young people in Iran like Ali and Shirin. I accomplished this goal for them and for the untold thousands of other young people tortured and killed while their only dream was to finish their education and live in a free country. My brothers were relentlessly taught to believe Islamic theology that says women are inferior to men. In America, God has given me spiritual brothers and sisters who are true believers and have always stood by me and encouraged me in all my difficulties.

Looking back, it was the struggles that taught me how to live. I learned the most important lessons of my life from family members and others who worked against me. They were my best "professors," whose lessons I could never learn in any university. Remembering those harsh realities is hard, but I know God had a purpose in allowing me to pass through all those fiery flames.

Those adversaries helped me to become strong, courageous, and bold. They taught me to trust and depend on God alone. Because of them I became closer to God, my faith became stronger, and God transformed me into a beautiful vessel for his own purpose. Therefore I am thankful for my family members and enemies who hurt me. How can

I not forgive them? I'm not going to allow myself to be held captive in their prisons by keeping hate and bitterness against them and replaying the bad memories. I love them. There is no place for hate in my heart.

I may never see them again, but I will pray for each one of them to learn from their mistakes and change themselves.

———•———

In Iran it would be unthinkable for a Christian to be involved in politics. It would be even more unimaginable for a woman to step into the political arena. To me, the opportunity to participate in American politics is one of the greatest miracles of my life. When I became a US citizen, I swore an oath before God faithfully to support and defend America from enemies "foreign and domestic."

I take that oath seriously. And to me, America's domestic enemies are more of a threat now than at any other time in history. Everywhere in our culture, forces are at work trying to undermine the principles that made America possible. Schoolchildren are taught false, distorted, and misleading versions of American history that damage their ability to understand and appreciate America's successes. Political institutions are threatened by liberal politicians and groups who are interested only in power and control. These same forces use irrational and dangerous identity politics to divide the country into opposing camps and to justify unequal treatment under law based on class, race, and other differences.

Lately, the COVID-19 pandemic has provided cover for restricting our personal freedoms to a degree unimaginable to our forefathers and illegal under the Constitution. The Christian bedrock beliefs that America's founders depended on to shape and preserve their government, the Christian perspectives that they believed would always inform the interpretation and enforcement of the law, are threatened from every direction. No law can protect its people when it is enforced according to the sliding standards of moral relativism.

As America's second president, John Adams, wrote in a letter to the Massachusetts Militia, dated October 11, 1798, "Our Constitution was made only for a moral and religious people. It is wholly inadequate to the government of any other." He also wrote in his private diary on July 26, 1796, "The Christian religion is, above all religions that ever prevailed or existed in ancient or modern times, the religion of wisdom, virtue, equity, and humanity." A generation later his son and our sixth president, John Quincy Adams, observed in a speech in Newburyport, Massachusetts, on July 4, 1837, "The Declaration of Independence laid the cornerstone of human government upon the first precepts of Christianity." In a summary of that speech, John Wingate Thornton wrote, "The highest glory of the American Revolution was this: it connected, in one indissoluble bond, the principles of civil government with the principles of Christianity" (*The Pulpit of the American Revolution* [Boston: Gould and Lincoln, 1860], xxix).

America's founders expected the law to be interpreted not according to political whims or some ideological tug-of-war, but to unshakable Christian ideals. Our schools, our courts, and even our legislatures have made an unprecedented assault on the Christian faith. While all Americans are free to believe and practice whatever faith they want, no one should doubt that Christianity was at the core of America's founding and is at the core of its continued prosperity and freedom.

The best way I can fulfill my oath as an American citizen to protect this nation from its enemies is to defend it against today's relentless effort to force us to abandon our founding principles. One way to do this is to participate in the political process. I don't know how God will call me to serve him in the future, whether in the political arena or through some other means. What I do know is that what God ordains is always right and that I will always follow where he leads with confidence and hope.

The Symbolic Story of My Life

I

There is more than one way to tell a story. So far I have shared the story of my life as a memoir grounded in facts and dates and experiences. But those are only part of the picture. There's also the journey I have taken in my heart, mind, and spirit. While you cannot see or touch them, they are as real and as essential as the other parts. And they require a different kind of communication: words from deep inside where dreams, dialogues, imaginings, and poetry are born.

Like all the facets of my life story so far, this symbolic, emotional side is unfinished. It's the kind of story where you and I both have to guess the ending. Stories with endings are easy because you can skip to the end and see whether they are happy or sad. This story is unfinished. You can guess whether the ending is happy or sad. It may take a long time to learn whether your guess was right or wrong, whether your imagination and intuition led you to the truth. You should be patient, wait, and watch.

This story began when my eyes could see this world for the first time, beautiful and full of colors. There were many beauties and each one attracted me. I stole parts of this beautiful world and made them my own. *They are eternal, immortal, last forever.* But the world was

229

deceiving me. I was immersed in the world, intoxicated by its beauty. I was desperate to have that beauty. Every day I tried more and more to make it mine.

My heart became a cage. I wanted to put the world with all its greatness into the cage of my small heart. I wanted to go through the labyrinth of the world and make the world my own. But even as I passed through this maze I grew more and more tired of the effort. The more beauty I put in my cage, the more I lost myself.

One day my eyes fell on the sky. That day I lost my heart to its beauty and purity. I noticed that unlike the world, which has many colors and faces, the sky had only one color and is sincere. Unlike the world, which was full of darkness and hatred, the sky was full of purity. I found it a loyal friend who was with me in all my loneliness. It cried with my cries and laughed with my laughs. I fell in love with it.

I decided to leave the world. But I discovered that the world had tied me with many chains. There were chains all over me. I shouted to the sky, "Release my chains so I can fly."

The sky heard my voice. "There is a condition," the sky said. "It hurts. There is suffering. Can you endure it?"

I said, "Get me rid of these chains. I'm frantic to be free when I look at you, but I can't fly."

"I will call your heavenly Father," the sky said.

"Who is the Father?" I asked.

"Come and meet him," the sky answered.

"I cannot," I said, "because I am full of darkness, guilt, and sins."

"You do not know your Father yet," said the sky.

"What difference does it make?" I asked.

"Don't rush," said the sky.

"Whatever you say," I answered. "Just get me rid of these chains. I want to fly!"

Then I heard the voice of my heavenly Father, who said, "If you wish to get to know me, get to know my son first."

"Who is the son?" I asked.

"Someone who can help you to get to know me," he explained. "Believe me. Don't listen to the world, so that you can believe me."

Then I closed my eyes and ears to everything. When I stopped listening to the world I could hear the beautiful voice of God. I became restless. I became delirious with waiting. "I don't want the world anymore!" I said.

I saw God. I saw God on the cross. I saw God in Jesus. "When I looked at my heart, you were here," I said. "And to think I was searching for you all around the world!"

I entrusted myself to him. He took me until I was captured by his love. He taught me many things as we traveled together on this long journey. When I saw how much he suffered because of an insignificant one like me, when I saw how much he had paid as the cost of my freedom, when I saw how he had sacrificed himself for me and endured all that pain, when I touched his love, when he revealed his unconditional love for me on the cross, it drove me berserk. My little brain could not comprehend the infinity of his love.

"How is it possible?" I asked. "You loved me so much, and you were looking for me! It was so important to you that you searched and found me to give me your love!"

"I knew you from the beginning," God said. "I knew you before you were born. You were mine even then, but you were far from me. You were lost, and I was looking for you. I looked and waited until I found you."

I had just recognized my Father. I could not comprehend his love and sacrifice. He opened his arms and hugged me.

"Wait!" I said. "What do I do with all my sins? How can I touch you or even look at you?"

"My love is a gift to you," God gently explained. "I found you by sacrificing myself on the cross. My love is unconditional. I don't want anything from you except your precious little heart. Will you let me live in your heart?"

"My heart is full of darkness."

"It would turn light with my presence."

"Who am I to deserve it? I am nobody."

"I am everything."

"What do I do in return for all this love?"

"Just be yourself, and let me be me."

"Do you think I can do that?"

"*I* can do that."

"I am very weak."

"But I am very powerful."

"I am ashamed when I look at myself."

"Then always look at me and be proud."

"I want to follow you. Take me with you. The world is meaningless without you. I have so many chains! Free me!"

"Be patient and come with me."

"I want to be like you, to see like you, to talk like you, to love like you, to forgive like you, to be sacrificed like you, to perish like you, to fall in love like you."

"Be patient. How hasty you are!"

"I'm not in a hurry; I am restless. I am restless because of you. I am restless to reach you."

"There is a cost."

"I will pay the cost."

"It is a long journey."

"I will travel with you."

And so my journey began.

II

I asked God to release me from three chains that bound me to my earthly world.

1. The Chain of Material Comfort

   I said, "Untie this chain from me." But while God was breaking the chain of worldly treasures, I thought I would perish without it. The world means material things. With that chain I had made myself powerful and proud. *If that chain is broken, I have no more power, no more respect. I have no place in the world.* When that chain was separated from me with great pain, I became light. I felt comfortable. I had nothing to worry about because I had nothing to lose. When I experienced poverty with all its difficulties, I felt how sweet it was. When I experienced hunger with all my being, I felt pleasure. When I saw I no longer had money to rely on, my Father said, "I am the richest. Do you believe that I can make you rich? Not with the wealth of the world but a wealth greater than the wealth of the world." *I believed.*

2. The Chain of Loved Ones and Dependency

   Breaking the chain that bound me to others was even more painful. "Even my family and loved ones?" I asked. Some of them, like my earthly father, were my idols. *I will die without them.* "Please do not take them. I will be so lonely!" There was only silence. I cried and begged and cursed and said, "You are the cruelest!" Still there was silence. Breaking that chain was the most painful of all. I could feel the pain to my bone marrow. But still there was silence. After this chain was broken, I found myself in his arms. I cried. I hit him in the chest. He caressed me. "I understand you and your pain," he said. "I am in pain with you. You are not alone. We suffer together so you can be free." After my blows and childish screams, I fell asleep in his arms. When I awoke, all my wounds and pains were healed. He had put ointment on my wounds. Ointment of love. Then he said, "I am with you, and I am everything to you." *I believed.*

3. The Chain of Hate and Unforgiveness

    This chain was forged from hatred of the suffering that human beings had inflicted on me. I hated those closest to me who hurt me and caused me so much pain for all those years. I could not forgive them. I said I would never forgive. Resentment and hatred grew like a cancer until it had poisoned my whole body. I said, "It is not possible to get rid of this chain." My body was covered with wounds caused by human beings. I could smell the stench of them. He said, "Forgive them." I said, "I can't. Don't expect this from me because I can't do it." He said, "Then come and look with my eyes." He gave me his eyes for a moment. Then I saw that those I hated were the ones helping me. I saw that they taught me great lessons with their evil. Also I realized what a great pain it was when I was not forgiven by others for my own mistakes. When I saw that God had forgiven me despite all my mistakes and sins, I was able to forgive them. Little by little the scars were healing. After forgiving them, my wounds started healing. When I forgave, I was filled with love. (Colossians 3:13: "Forgive as the Lord forgave you.") *Forgiving is better than not forgiving. Giving is better than receiving.* God said, "I forgave all your sins." *I believed.*

III

After that journey God asked, "Can you trust me now?"

I answered immediately, "Yes, I will trust you will all my heart." I became proud. I thought it was all over. But I stumbled again. I would fall every time I took my eyes from him and looked away. As soon as I looked at him, I could stand once more. He taught me a lesson every time I fell. I had thought I was released. I thought I could fly without a chain. But I was oblivious to many inner chains. One day he opened my eyes, and I saw I was full of small chains.

"I thought I was released," I said.

"This is just the beginning of the story," he replied. "You should rid yourself of all that your soul and body demand, of your selfishness. You have to forget yourself."

"I do not understand," I said. "That's impossible."

"Start loving others," he said. "Don't think about anything when you show your love to others. Don't expect anything in return for your love. Your love should be unconditional. No matter what others say or do, you should be able to love and forgive them."

I will definitely fail this test.

I tried to love other people despite their wrong behavior. I tried to love others, but sometimes hatred welled up. I tried, but I made a lot of mistakes. "I cannot do this!" I cried. "This is not my responsibility. I cannot love people when I see their evil behavior."

God said, "Try to see your own flaws; then you won't be able to see their evil. Remember Matthew 7:3, 'Why do you look at the speck of sawdust in your brother's eye and pay no attention to the plank in your own eye?' Instead of looking at their sins, look at your own sins."

When I looked, I realized I was the proudest and the worst of all. I realized how hard it was to change. I said, "I want to change myself, but I can't. I want to be like you."

"Allow people to slap and spit on your face and then forgive them," God said. "Allow them to break your heart and then forgive them. You have to see through my eyes so that you do not see their deeds."

"So this journey continues," I noted, "and the way is so difficult."

"You have to go a hard way to reach the cross," God told me. "Take your cross, and follow me every day."

When I decided to learn to love others, the world, self-desire, and love got into a fight. The world interpreted my love, questioned it, and looked at it skeptically. The world said, "This love is not acceptable. Because it isn't in harmony with the love of the world, it cannot be real."

It was then that I realized why humans do not understand God's love. They cannot understand the unconditional love of God because everything in this world is conditional. That is why people search every day for something to fill this void empty of inner love. They can't believe how much God loves them without any expectation or intention. People are used to looking at everything with suspicion. That's why they look skeptically at God's love. They're afraid of approaching God. Afraid of throwing away worldly loves. Afraid of losing the idols of the world. They cannot get close to God because they do not believe in such love. They can't believe how much God loves them.

My mistake was that I did not want to hide my love. My intent was that I did not want to lie. My thought was that I believed in my own love and that the world would believe it too. I had not learned true love and how to love. I was condemned because of loving others. They said there is a limit to everything, even love. I was confused. I doubted myself. *Maybe others are right.* Every day I checked myself and my behavior. I measured everything. I tried to prove that my love was pure. I became tired. "Father," I said, "I got tired. I could not continue. I got tired of loving others and being condemned. I did not learn how to love. I tried to prove my love."

"You got tired too soon," God said. "Now you understand what it means to be convicted for loving. Now you understand what it means to be slapped and hurt because of love. Your love was not pure. It was mixed with your self-desire. My love for human beings was pure, but they did not believe me."

"How could you tolerate us?" I cried. "How can you endure all this suffering and fall in love with us again?"

"This is the secret you did not know," God explained. "This is the love that you do not have and have not yet found."

"But I tried to prove it," I said.

"True love does not need to be proven," he said. "Your job is just to love. Nothing more. Go on and do not be weary. The day will come when they believe you truly love them." It was there that I realized it was the beginning of the story. That was the first step. God continued, "Are you ready to be with me until the end? Are you ready to travel and be my companion? Do you promise to follow me every day?"

In fact, I was impatient. I never learned how to love others. I was prideful and considered myself the kindest of all. I viewed my small love as very big. I thought I was at the end of the journey while I was at the beginning. I was ignorant but considered myself wise.

I must go now to sacrifice myself in this love. I know I chose the hard way. I should pay a high price. Must be slapped. Must experience humiliation. Must be broken to be rebuilt. *When I can be silent in the face of all this and love without any expectations, then I will become a bit like you.* I know I have to go with him. There is no way to return from this love. I have no way back. I was captured by love that is impossible to leave until I perish in it.

This is an unfinished story. The difference between it and other stories is that I am not the reader, I am the character. Now guess the end of the story. Like all other stories, this one will end one day. I hope it will end with love.

Longings of My Heart to God

I

I love you so much, Jesus, because you loved me
    beyond my imagination.
Your love is so deep in my heart.
You showed me the true unconditional love
    of the cross.
Nothing and no one can separate your love from me
    because you are in me.
You are my every breath.
I feel you in the depths of my heart.
You are in every cell of my body,
    under my skin.
My soul longs to worship you every moment.
My thirst for your love will never be quenched.

II

When you touched me, when you loved me, when you healed my
    wounds,
When you embraced me, when I was rejected by everyone and you
    came to me,
When I was hungry and you fed me,
When I was weak and you gave me strength,
When I was alone and you filled my loneliness with your presence,
When I was at the depth of my weakness and you called me,
When you wanted my existence because of me,
When you loved me unconditionally,
When you filled the empty corners of my being,
When you chose me while my soul was in darkness,
When I realized that I was nothing more than a particle in front
    of you
    (or maybe not a particle and just nothing),
When I realized you are love and I fell in love with you,
When you became my only idol and I became your worshiper,
When you became the precious pearl and I became the harvester,
When you became everything to me in this world,
That was when I perceived love.

III

I wish you were with me everywhere.
I wish you were my love and I loved you.
I wish you were my idol and I was a worshiper.
I wish your gaze was never taken from me.
I wish your eyes were always on me.
I wish your hands were always with me.
I wish your unconditional love was always with me.

I wish you were my way.
I wish you were my friend.
I wish you were everything to me.
I wish you were my support and my rock.
I wish you would build me as you should build.
I wish you were my guide everywhere.
I wish you were always with me.
I wish

IV

How beautiful it is to be with you, Father.
How sweet it is to live with you.
When your kind look is upon me
    I am not afraid.
When I cross the valleys
    I know that your eyes are always on me.
I know you will not leave me even for a moment.
When I look at your power and greatness
    I walk boldly,
Like a child who stares at his father's kind eyes to walk
    and walks with his powerful gaze.
When you look at me with a fatherly look,
When you take my hands in your kind hands,
When you empower me,
    it is easy to cross the valleys.
But when I look at myself and my strength,
Then it is impossible for me to take a step.
When I reach the top of the peaks,
    you are my pride.
My pride is your power and greatness
Because you are my power and strength.

V

You are so full of love
    that I sing only for an empty heart.
You are such a manifestation of love
    that I die seeking it.
You are such a temple of love
    that I gather my poems in its worship.
You are such a sea of love
    that I hide the drops of my love in the bed of the waves.
You are such an altar of love
    that I make my little love beautiful in your shrine.
You are so pure
    that I wash my ugliness in the mirror of your love.
You are the life of my poems,
Tracing my words on the soulless paper of my thoughts.
I long for the stream of my feelings in the boiling spring of your love
To irrigate the desert of my heart.

VI

Father, when I was weak you strengthened me.
You picked me up when I fell.
You made me happy when I cried.
When I was disappointed you became my hope.
When I was wounded you healed my wounds.
When I cried in despair you opened your arms to me.
When my legs were helpless you carried me.
You were the only one with me.
You were with me to the depths of the valleys.
You were with me to the depth of my sorrows.
You were with me to the depth of my frustrations.

Father, how kindly you became a father for me.
Father, how compassionately you loved me.
How kindly you tasted the cup of loneliness with me.
Father, stay with me, always stay,
Because without you I am nothing.
When you loved me, I did not need the love of people.

VII

O all people, let us praise God.
O earth and sky, let us worship the greatness of his mercy.
Earth and sky, come to worship the God of greatness and mercy.
Let us straighten our crooked paths.
Let us turn our hearts to God
    and raise our hands to his mercy.
Let us turn the darkness of our hearts
    into the brightness and purity of the sky.
Let us make our hearts repent.
Let us leave our pain, weakness, and sin to God.
Let us give him our thoughts
    and ask for his thoughts.
Let us trust and rely on him
    and leave our ways to him.

VIII

What a love that burns my soul!
What a love that makes me fall in love every day!
What a love that makes me wild and wonder!
What a love that I count every moment until I join the lover!
What a love that the more I know you, the more I fall in love!
What a love that the more I think in the depths of you,

the more I ask for you and want you.

What did you do to me, my beloved?

How can I praise you

    when my tongue is not able to speak the depth of me?

How can I express my love with these limited words?

O my invisible lover!

My eyes do not see you, but I see you everywhere.

My ears do not hear your voice,

But your beautiful songs and the whispers of your love have made

    me spontaneous.

I hear your song everywhere.

I cannot touch you, but I feel your gentle touch on my skin.

My whole being feels you.

What a love this is!

O my love, tell me how to praise you.

Can any words describe you?

My words cannot praise you enough.

My being and my heart are calling you.

I wish you had taught me a language so that I could describe you

    and praise you.

With which eyes should I see you?

With which ears should I hear your voice?

With which words should I praise you enough?

O God, my love, how I miss you! Why did you limit my abilities

    to praise you?

IX

My love,

With you happy, without you sad.

With you full, without you empty.

With you friendly, without you unfriendly.
With you strong, without you weak.
With you pure, without you defiled.
With you positive, without you negative.
With you light, without you dark.
With you hopeful, without you hopeless.
With you rich, without you poor.
With you generous, without you greedy.
With you painless, without you painful.
With you courageous, without you cowardly.
With you seeing, without you blind.
With you loving, without you hating.
With you everything, without you nothing.

X

I found you in my silence.
I found you in my despair.
I found you in my failures.
I found you in my sorrows.
I found you in my pain.
I found you when I was far away from you.
I found you in my cries.
I found you in my emptiness.
I found you in my poverty.
I found you in the darkness of my heart.
I found you in my spontaneity.
I found you when there was no hope.

I found love in you.
I found kindness in you.
I found truth and justice in you.

I found life in you.
I found all beauty in you.
I found purity and holiness in you.
I found loyalty in you.
I found friendship in you.
I found wealth and power in you.
I found everything in you
And suddenly
I found you in me, O God.

XI

Where was I?
Where did I go? What did I do? What have I said?
Everywhere it was you—
Everywhere you went. Everything you did. Everything you said.
Don't show me to me
    because I am ashamed of myself.
I'm ashamed of my lack of faith,
My frustration, hate, pride, selfishness, and flaws.

Did you really choose me?
Do you really love me?
How? Who am I? Where is my faith?
From whence cometh my strength?
Woe to all this pain!
Woe to all my worthlessness!
I asked you to give me pain and sorrow.
I asked you to give me poverty.
I asked you to test me
    and pass me through valleys and fires.
Do you know what I saw after all?

O my love, keep me away from me!
I can't see in all this darkness.
How do you tolerate me? How can you love me?
How can you embrace me while I hate myself?

Was there no one worse on earth that you chose me?
Was there no one more unworthy on earth that you chose me?
Was there no one more prideful on earth that you chose me?

Your burning look burns me.
Your lovely look makes me ashamed.
Your love makes me incapable of doing whatever I want.
Your love makes me delirious.
Who are you, such a love as that?
Are you creator or creature? God or human? Existing or existence?
There is no one like you, will never be one like you.
You are Love, my beloved God.
You are a sweet pain that can never be assuaged.
I feel this sweet pain deep in my bones.
I can't run away from this pain:
You are a candle and I am a butterfly.

O God, O God, O my love,
I have no way back. I have no choice. I cannot.
I am your captive. There is no way out.
Do not leave me.
I am the bird of your heavenly cage.
I am vanquished by your love.
The heart must be trusted, must perish in this love.
I have to empty myself from self and be full of you.
Tell me how to get rid of self-love.
How should I empty myself from my self-desiring?
How should I die to myself, my love?

XII

Where are you, O pain?
You are in me even as I seek you.
Where are you, O love?
You are in me even as I look for you frantically.
Who knows how bad I am except you, O pain?
You touched me to the marrow.
You suffered to the depth of my pain and sorrow.
You became pain itself, my love.
Where are you, O pain?

There is no cure except the pain.
My pain treatment is pain. The cure is the pain.
Who knows the depth of my pain except you, O pain?
Who knows the intensity of my pain except you, O pain?
Who knows my feelings?
O my loneliness!
O my loneliness, loneliness!
O pain, only you came to the depths of my loneliness.
I am frantic, crazy from this pain. Crazy from this loneliness
Where the pain and I sleep in your arms, O love.

XIII

My chains are tied to me.
I look at the sky and long to fly,
      but my chains are tied to me.
I long to fly. The sky is clear, blue, blue.
I long to fly. The sky is calling.
O, my chains are tied to me.
Must be abandoned! Must be broken!
The sky is calling me.

The sky is waiting. The sky is watching.
The desire to fly has made me restless.
O, my chains are tied to me.
Where is the key? How to be released?
How to get rid of them? How to break the locks?
The sky is calling.
My chains are tied to me.

XIV

I have such a pain of love, do not ask.
I have such a pain of separation, do not ask.
I wander frantically because of this love.
In which book should I read about you?
In what words can I hear you?
In which look should I see you?
In which song should I sing you?
In which poem should I interpret you?
In which love should I fall in love with you?
I do not feel you except in my heart.
Nothing could introduce you to me.
No words could describe you to me.
Where should I look for you?
You are nowhere but in my heart.

XV

I do not seek out others.
I do not follow the ways of others.
In exploring them
    I seek only your description and fall more in love.
Were they really able to describe you? I cannot.

Words cannot describe you.
I feel you in my heart. I feel you in my most delicate senses.

XVI

Give me flying wings! Teach me to fly!
Teach me how to be released. Teach me how to break chains.
Teach me how to fly in the sky of your heart.
Teach me the passion of love.
Teach me how to perceive your love.
Open my eyes to see the blue of your sky.

I am captive, captive.
The bird of my soul is captive, captive.
My soul is captive in my body.
Break this cage, O love! Break these bars of the body!
The soul, trapped in the cage of the body, longs for liberation.
A desire to be free, to fly.
Give me flying wings, O love.
Do not take away my longing to fly.
O, my body,
My life is coming to an end because of you.
O love,
My soul longs, O love.
I am captive, captive. Captured by this divine love.

XVII

O love, what did they do to my heart?
O love, what did these inhuman people do to my heart?
They wounded and ripped my heart.
O love, what did they do to my heart?
O love, save me!

XVIII

O father, O of this loneliness,
O father, O of this lack of compassion,
O father, O of this lack of sympathy,
O father, O of this absolute silence alone,
O father, O of this incurable pain
There is no helper.
There is no one but my loneliness.

XIX

I came from a land whose rulers are not human, not animal,
    but are savage beasts and vampires.
I came from a land whose rulers eat oil and gold instead of food
    and drink blood instead of water.
I came from a land whose rulers consider themselves God
    and God's successors on earth
While they worship the devil.
I came from a land whose rulers wear long, black garments at night
    and scatter darkness and fear throughout the city.
I came from a land whose rulers cover their ugly and savage faces
    under masks of long, black beards.
I came from a land whose people dance barefoot in rivers of blood
    to forget their captivity, the murder of their loved ones,
    and their own existence.
I came from a land whose rulers burn the beauty of women with acid
    and cover them under the black veil of captivity.

I came from a land where beauty, love, and joy are crimes
    punishable by death.
I came from a land where blood drips from mothers' hearts
    to irrigate the tulips that blossom on the banks of bloody streams.

I came from a land where ignorant, savage men,
     religious men under the protection of sharia law
Slaughter their beautiful wives, sisters, and daughters
     with sickle and axe.
They murder for honor's sake. For the law. They hold their heads
     high.

I came from a land of frozen brains and hollow hearts.

I came from a land whose people mourn every year for the deaths
     of criminals
     over a thousand years of history,
Who burn sacrifices on the altar
     mingled with the streaming blood of innocent sheep.
I came from a land where the hearts of its innocent animals are
     full of acid
     and bullets of anti-impurity.

I came from a land whose beautiful green forests have turned to
     gray ashes.
I came from a land whose every high cliff holds the name of a hero
     carved in blood.
I came from a land whose children watch their heroes dance on
     gallows in the street.
I came from a land where freedom has been hanged and liberty
     buried alive.

My heart is full of fire
     and
          silent
               screams . . .

XX

When God is with you, you do not need a big army.
You can win the battle with only a small one.
When God is with you, you have an army of angels fighting for you.
When God is with you, you do not need the weapons of this world.
You do not need to calculate the risk.

XXI

Love helps you to see the world differently,
To see people differently,
To see life differently,
To see your friends and even your enemies differently.

Love helps you to act differently,
To talk differently,
To hear differently,
To understand and comprehend differently.

Love helps you to smile
Even when life is not what you want it to be.

XXII

Pain, you alone
Came with me to the depths of solitude.
Your sweet taste became immortal in me.
You became love in the depths of my being.
I cherish you every day.

A Letter to My Earthly Father

My sweet father, all my childhood took its meaning from you.
I will never forget your fatherly hands. They were the most
beautiful hands. In their deep calluses I could see God's love. You carried the wounds of any thorn for your children's comfort. My childish
hands were in your hands. You were the god of love to me. I thought
I could never walk without you. I kiss your kind hands that for many
years carried a father's pain in order to be a comfort to his children.

I look back at the nights I spent as a child with you, nights when
together we looked at the stars in the sky and talked about the secret of
God's love. Sometimes I miss those sweet days I had with you, sweet
days when we interpreted the love poems of poets.

Alas, I was with you for only a short time. I will never forget your
fatherly support. I will never forget your kind looks. I always felt inside
the great love you had for your daughter. I think of the precious days
when we ate and laughed together. Where did all those times go? Sometimes I think the world was jealous of our wonderful relationship.

After your illness, I complained to God many times. I was lost like
a child who no longer had a foothold. I shouted many times at the sky,
"Why did you take my father from me?" The answer was nothing but

silence. I tried to replace losing you with the fake loves of the world. I tried to find love like you in others. Alas, I did not.

You are a sweet memory for me. Your memory is always alive in me. Father, I will never forget your vigilance for the comfort of your children. I will never forget your restlessness for the comfort of your children. I will never forget the sweat on your forehead for the comfort of your children. I will not forget your struggles with the world, your sufferings, enduring the world's hardships so that your children could sleep comfortably. My father, I will never forget the great love you taught me and your kindness with your little daughter.

I wish I could understand your fatherly love. I wish I could understand a little of your heavy burden for your children. I wish I could be an ointment for your weariness. I wish I deserved to kiss your kind hands. Forgive me for not understanding you. My sweet father, my dear, there is nothing in me that deserves your dedication.

My father, your little girl is like a migratory bird and loves to fly, loves to reach the love of God. I love crossing borders, love to cross the boundaries of empty human relationship, love to reach the peak of liberation. Forgive me if I am not by your side. Forgive me if I did not deserve your parental kindness. Forgive me because your little bird has no place to sit, no nest to stay in. The desire to fly and be liberated in the love of God is an ointment for the restlessness of your little bird's heart. I am captivated by the love of God, which draws me wherever it goes. I have no desire but captivity in this love. I am captive of love that gave me a fatherly love like yours.

My kind father, I will always cherish the memory of my childhood. The image of your kindness is inscribed on the heart of your little bird, who carries it in its heart wherever it flies. I miss you and your warm fatherly caresses. Alas, this also has become only a memory. Now your little bird is in the fatherly arms of the heavenly Father who will never leave her.

Reflections Upon God to God

Written as a Refugee in Turkey

I

I am beside the sea, the sea beside me.
We are both alone, full of words for each other.

II

It's been a while that my pen cannot write.
It's been a while that my heart does not beat.
It's been a while that I cannot hear
    the voice of my heart and its whispers.
Where are you, my love? Where are you?
My heart is depressed without you.
Where are you? My soul is death without you.
Where is the light of my darkness?
Where are you so that your light can open my eyes?
Bring me back to me.
O, for a while everything is quiet and cold for me without you.
I have been away from you for some time.

I have not touched you in a while.
I don't feel you. I don't see you.
Where are you, my love?
I seek you in the seas and look for you in the sun.
Why are you running away?
Why do you hide yourself from me?
Why do you walk away when I want to get close to you?
Can you not hear the moans of my heart?
Can you not hear the desperate voice of my heart?
Can you not hear the silent screams inside me?
You were not so cruel. You were not so unfaithful.
Don't leave me alone! I'll die without you!

Sometimes I think of myself and my loneliness in this strange land.
I am displaced in search of your love.
I am like a ship with no sail, seeking you everywhere.
I cross the seas like a bird in love, dreaming of being with you.
I migrate like a bird to the world of homelessness.

I walk in the valleys of your love.
I pour my tiredness into the calm bed of your seas.
I travel the land of love to find my beloved,
To forget my tiredness and grief
      in being away from the beloved
While I'm sleeping in your arms.
Will I rest in your arms one day?
Will I ever forget my difficult journey in your arms?
Will reaching you end my loneliness one day?
Will reaching you one day relieve the grief of being away from you?
Will the day I reach you quench my thirst?
Will this journey even end?
Where are you, my beloved,
      that my life is ending without you?

Where are you?
The flames inside me are not extinguished except by your love.
I burn with your love.
Find me!

III

O Father, what should I do?
I want to be free.
I want to be separated from this land, this earth,
To be released from this earth to the top of the sky.
I want to fly, to come to your heart, O God.
I want to say I love you.
I want to shout I love you, God.
How do I shout? How do I call you?
Come into my heart, God.
Come take me with you
To the top of the sky.
I want to say I love you.
Let me go. Separate me from this earth.
Come take me. I will die without you.
Come listen to my heart.
Come stay in my heart.

IV

My beloved, how should I express my feelings to you?
I am unable.
How can I say with my cries that I love you?
The whispers of my heart are silent inside me.
How can I tell you the cries of my heart?
My voice is muted within me.

My screams remain inside without reaching you.
Where are you? I will die without you.
Come teach me to fly!

Come, teach me how to let go,
    to be left in your arms.
Come separate me from me
    so that I can have meaning in you.

V

Daddy, for a long time I have been confused. It's been a while since we used to see each other, used to be together all the time. I was used to our habit. Whether or not we talked verbally every day, I got used to being together and feeling the assurance of your presence. I got used to talking to you for a few moments every day about everyday issues.

Love has been forgotten for a while. For some time now, love has lost its meaning, lost its color. The freezing of love has turned me into a numb human being who doesn't feel any pain. I did not even notice the distance between us. I didn't see that the distance was getting greater every day. Without realizing it, the distance made my heart more distant from you.

I used to practice the empty rules and laws with no love. I was so far away from you that I suddenly felt your absence. Suddenly, indifference reminded me of the difference. I was at the point of falling when I saw the distance. I had approached the cold precipice of love. My feet fell on the slippery slope of indifference and coldness. Suddenly, I noticed the danger. The love within me had become a stagnant force that had no movement.

We have not activated our love. When I got away from you, I turned the power of love into a stagnant force of confidence. I did not notice that my heart was dying in its coldness. I did not notice the contagion of freezing love in my heart into the veins of indifference. I was at the peak of my downfall. I had accepted my death amid the cold storms of love. Suddenly, I found you in the cold storms of love.

I had become so preoccupied with the things around me that I forgot the warmth of your love. Forgive me for forgetting our love! Forgive me for ignoring your precious love with worthless pursuits. Forgive me for forgetting the sweet moments of intimacy and being with you. It was at the moment of my fall, in the death of my love, that your love brought me back. Forgive me if I did not protect our love. Forgive me for replacing love with stupidity. In the end, your love prevented me from falling. Where I fell on the edge of the abyss, your love prevented me from slipping.

Now I want you again. The moment I put my head on your kind shoulders, the moment I have my head on your chest, I hear the sound of love beating in my chest. Now I demand your presence again. Now I am counting the moments for the moment of connecting love. Once again, I find security in the warm embrace of your love.

Give me a new love. Give me a new birth in love. Let me be born again in your love. Let your love alone be the cause of an eruption of love and my emotional outburst. Let us feel each other's breath again. Let us feel our hearts beating again. Let me fall in love again. Let me learn loyalty in love. Let me learn to stay in love. Let me learn to love and truly fall in your love. In the end, let my death be in your love.

VI

Daddy, the pen in my hand, without thinking about what is flowing from it, only rubs itself on the white of the paper to reveal a little of its inner secret to you. What the ink of the pen is trying to reveal is the strange force that has wrapped us from birth. A strange word that made us wander through it to seek it and, in the longing of approaching it, to take a long journey through the desert of our lives to find it and get to know it. A familiar yet strange word in which every creature was born. A meaningful word that humans interpreted during his lifetime and walked many paths to try to recognize. Humans tried to capture it in the cage of their ego. Humans, according to their egos, thought that this beautiful gem could be owned like everything else. What many paths humans have taken and what many sufferings man has suffered in search of this word! How many beautiful words, meanings, and interpretations were made for this word! What poems were written for this word! And how beautifully you interpreted this word on the cross. You are the word itself: You are Love.

VII

I do not know what I am looking for.
I am looking for something outside
    that I do not find except in myself.

VIII

How can I tell you how I feel?
How to assess the deep value of my feelings
    in the worthlessness of the world?
How to express my feelings in small words and their limitations?
In which poem should I include the deep whispers of my feelings?
On which sonnet should I sing my love to you?
In which gift should I give you my deepest feelings?
Can love be included in the words?
Can love be expressed in words?
Can love be given as a gift?

Forgive me for not finding a gift
    so that I can express my feelings to you with a gift.

Forgive me for not finding a word
    so that I can express the amount of my love to you with a word.
Forgive me for not finding a poem
    so that I can sing my love song to you with a poem.
Forgive me for not being able to give you the deep sea of love
    in the small drops of my tears.
I did not find love in the outside world.
I only found love inside me and in my little heart.
That is the source of your love and your presence.

IX

The blossoms of feeling
Blossomed in the empty space
Of the desert of my heart.
My soul is thirsty
And the springs of my dry and loveless feelings
Nurture the dream of the sea
In the desire to be refreshed from the remaining drops.
Where is the sea
Where I hide the drop of my love
In its infinite vastness?
Where is the veil
In which I hide the shame
From the smallness of my love?
I burn with the lack of love.

X

You are my beloved, my dream,
My beloved, my life.
You are my God.

You are the light of my eyes and my tangible feelings.
Without you I am empty, nothing, invisible.
You are my everything, my being and existence.
You are my reason to live.
My beloved, come with me. Stay in me.
O, my heart longs for you!
Take my hands. I cling to your lap.
I will reach my hands to your throne.
I set my eyes on your eyes.
I set my ears to the words of your mouth.
I set my lips to your lips, my beloved.
Take me to the infinite border.
Take me with you to lose consciousness.
Take me to separate from me to become you.
Take me to the end of surrounding and submission to you.
Take me to complete devotion in you.

XI

The dove of my soul is flying, aimless,
To the end of freedom, separation, and absence.
Tell me where my true home is.
Where is my safe nest, except in death?
Who am I? What am I
Except a silent sound in the heart of the wind,
A howling wind in the heart of the soul
That laments its emptiness in its nothingness?
I fill my nothingness with tears.
Maybe my death is the beginning of a sea.
I wash my nothingness on the canvas of life with my tears.
May it be a drawing of my being on the body of life.

XII

The heroes died,
The right seekers were killed,
Innocents were hanged,
The child inside us was looted.
Who am I? Is this you or me?
My heart cries for lack of love.
My heart mourns in its loneliness.

XIII

Eye saw and did not see what it should have seen.
Ear heard and did not hear what it was supposed to hear.
Open the eyes of the heart to see with the eyes of the mind.
Open the ears of the soul to hear with the ears of the body.
If you want to find your way, do not follow the path of your flesh
astray.

My lostness is my soul in the forest of my flesh.
My way is through my heart beneath the secret of my body and soul.
The fountain of my love crosses the silent border of your love.
My true road is through my heart behind my flesh.

XIV

It is a rainy night. I hear the heavy raindrops falling desperately on loveless souls in the cage of false belongings. The sprinkle of raindrops wakes
me, refreshing the dry ground of my thoughts to release the springs of
my feelings. In this deep silence of the night, while only the sound of
raindrops resonates with the silence of my heart, I write to you, dearer
than my life. I write for you, who inspire me to express my feelings.

I want to tell you alone about the rotten complaints in my heart, about a strange world where I was born a stranger, about the moment I was born of the lust of frozen bodies of love: the bodies that chose to join with no heat of love to make me a stranger to the world. I was born into a loveless generation spawned from the hot lust of dead bodies. Mine is a strange generation: the generation without love that seeks love.

The roots of my generation were grown in the cold lust of souls. Where are my true roots? Where are the true roots of my generation? I am a stranger looking for roots I have never had. I am a tired bird flying in search of a nest I have never known. Where is my nest? Where is the earth of my roots?

Why am I a stranger among those who call me one of them? Why am I a stranger in the nest they say is your birthplace? I am like a strange bird flying in search of my nest. In search of my roots. I travel land and sea looking for a clue. I scour the earth in vain. Could the mirage become reality? Is it possible to find the warmth of love in frozen hearts? To find roots anchored deep in the barren earth?

Once again I console myself to believe in things I never had, in reaching the heat of the sun and embracing the warmth of love. It is only God's love that gives me the power to fly, the power to search among the disbelief of my strange generation. I fly with faith because I believe in the dream of eternal love. I believe in God to nourish my dry roots with the warmth of love. I transcend the boundaries of false love that human beings believe in their frozen hearts. I go beyond their false principles and frameworks. I go beyond loving and believing in the cages of empty belongings.

There is no nest for me. I will not attach myself to such false nests. I seek my nest and my roots in the warm nest of God's love. May my roots be eternal. May my nest always be warm with the eternal love of God. What a love, that the more it takes root in me the more it quenches my physical desires. What a strange force, that it makes me a stranger even to myself.

XV

Hello, Daddy. I don't know how to start. I don't know if you still remember me or not. This is me, your daughter. The same daughter who could not live a moment without you. My heart is broken because I broke your heart. I know you may be mad at me. I know I broke your heart. I know I had forgotten you for a while.

Daddy, please forgive me. Please forgive your daughter. I did not notice how far I had gotten from you. I went so far that I was miles away from you. Suddenly, I noticed I was alone in the middle of a desert. What happened, Daddy? I did not understand how I got here. I forgot your caress, your lullaby. I forgot you wait for me every day to chat with me, to laugh together, and to cry in your arms.

O, what did I do to you? O, how could I forget you? I accidentally forgot about you. I forgot you love me, you are waiting for me, you look at me. I forgot that you are waiting to hear from me every day. I do not know where I went. I do not know when I went. Where did I get lost? I just know I went too far.

Once I came to myself I saw that I was alone. I missed you, Daddy. I missed your lovely and tender words, your lovely voice, your lovely caress, your lovely whispers, your lovely cuddle. I missed your strong shoulders that have always been my refuge.

What did I do to you? How long have you been waiting for me to come back? How many messages did you send to me? I got engaged in the nonsense work and glamour of the world. I was confused. I got so far from you and suddenly noticed I was lost.

Oh, how I miss you! I am in love with you. Please don't leave me. I will die without you. Daddy, I need you. I need your love. I will die without your love. I'm nothing without you. Please don't leave me alone. I am poor, very poor, without you.

It's been a while since I have sung for you. It's been a while since we've danced together. It's been a while since I've written any poems for you. Give me back to me. Do not take yourself from me. Forgive your daughter, Daddy.

XVI

Take away whatever you need to take away from me.
Take my pride, my selfishness,
But do not take your presence from me.
Do not take our lovely moments together from me.
Do not take yourself from me.
Do not take the depth of my feelings about you.
Do not take your warm fatherly embrace from me.
Take from me that which drove miles between you and me.
Take from me what is empty, vain, and deceitful.
Do not take from me the look of your kind love.
Do not take from me your fatherly loving kisses.
Do not take the deep feeling of being in love from me.

O how much I missed you!
How much I am sad. How much I am tearful and distressed.
Embrace me!
Embrace me because I am nothing without you.
How I miss your embrace!
How I miss your caressing hands!
Where are you?
Where are you to look at my torn heart?
Where are you so that my empty heart
    is immersed in the waves of your love?
I want to be a child in your arms.

Where are you to melt my frozen heart?
Where are you? I'm dying without you!
I will die of lovelessness.
I will die of lovelessness.
I will die of lovelessness.

Take me away!
Take me away from myself.
Save me from futility.
Give me another wing to fly to the horizon to reach you.
Do not say that it is too late;
    the soul is trapped in the body.
Do not say there are no flying wings;
    it is not impossible to fly without wings.
Do not say it is sunset.

It is dark.
Your light illuminates this narrow path.

XVII

Where are you?
Where are you in this dark, insecure path?
I am in the middle of the valley,
In the middle of a dark valley,
In the midst of the silence of terror of the valley,
In the midst of loneliness of the valley.
My scream is the reflection of the peaks
    that bring it back to my ears with a deeper sound.
Except for my ears there are no ears to hear my screams
    because I am surrounded by a fence of peaks.
I shout and I hear my screams.
Among the syllables of the cry within me

I was captured and imprisoned.
I am trapped in the midst of my unanswered questions.
Maybe a dove at the top of the peaks
Will send a particle of the reflection of my voice
    to the blue sky of my God.
Maybe . . .

XVIII

I am surrounded by the spirit of love.
It is not me but the songs of love
    that cry from the depths of the valleys of my being.
I am free in love.
I found freedom in breaking human laws.
I am the one who crosses the borders
    in search of the spirit of love and freedom.
I am the love of freedom.
I am a tireless fighter
    who crossed the border of my homeland to the land of freedom
By tearing the bonds of slavery and captivity.
I will never die.
I walk toward eternity because the blood of love boils in my veins.
I am the fiery arrow in the heart of oppression and evil
    that immortalizes victory with the fire of love.
I am the same woman
    who flips through the pages of history with the soul of her love
To give it a mythical spirit by showing her love.
I fight.
I fight in breaking inner ties
    to learn to fly in freedom by freeing love from bondage.
I give birth to love
    by breaking the bonds of my inner attachments.

I see the birth of love
    in the pain of tearing cuts and separation.
A deep pain burns all over my being
    to give birth to love in me.
And what a sweet pain when love is born!
Love is born of pain.

XIX

Flow in me.
Flow in me and my feelings.
Flow in my heart, my thoughts.
Be my life and my hope.
Be my path and my guide.
Flow in my mind and my soul.
Flow in my heart and my dreams.
Flow in my feelings, deep into my empty heart.
Flow in the house of my thought.
I will cross the dark valley with you.
I will pass with you from the fear and terror of darkness.
I will go through the darkness with you.
With you I am at my peak. Without you I am silent and cold.
Flow in me, Holy Spirit.
Flow in me, Holy God.
Flow in my words, my tongue, my feelings.
In you I found you. I found you in me.
I passed through the darkest valley
Until I reached you in light and brightness.
Shine in me the light of hope, love, and freedom.
Give me divine light.
Pour in me the pure heart of God.
The pure spring of love has flowed in me.

XX

I think of you.
You are far from me
   but you are always by my side and in my heart.
I think of you behind bars,
Behind these high walls and barbed wire.
Behind the bars that have taken only my body away from you,
From behind the sharp thorns pointed only at my body,
From behind the bars that only separated my body from you.
Walls that can never enclose love.
Which bars are able to maintain love?
My body is weakened, but my body is full of love.
How foolish are the people who tried to enslave love!
How foolish are those who want to tie chains to the hands and feet
   of love!
How glorious love laughs at them!

Thoughts and Wonders

I

Crazy people are their real selves, and we are the crazy people who try to look wise.

II

Love is not learnable. The ways of expressing love must be learned, not love itself, because we were created with love.

III

Christ taught us how to love.

IV

The fruit of love is love.

V

Power is gained in complete powerlessness before God.

VI

How ignorant are the people who want to see God with the eyes of the head, not the eyes of the heart.

VII

Love of God is a disease that has no cure. It is a deadly pain that kills the desires of the flesh bit by bit and revives the soul.

VIII

Love is not separate from pain.

IX

Humans are accustomed to accepting lies easily but to doubt the truth.

X

It is difficult to be yourself because people do not accept your true self and you are always trying to be someone else in order to be accepted. As a result, you will lose your true self, and then you will have to look for your identity.

XI

The world is full of different words or terms, and human beings seek to know them and interpret them. Every word has special meaning for every human being. And the only word or term that human beings cannot interpret is "love." It was only interpreted properly by God on the cross.

XII

Don't love something that stops you from moving. Be in love with love that gives you love and moves you forward.

XIII

My whole being dreamed of having your love.

XIV

The world is big in the eyes of small people and small in the eyes of big people.

XV

Never seek to prove your goodness and intention because over time the truth naturally nurtures itself.

XVI

The only thing that remains is the memory of love.

XVII

Humans are deceived by worldly love while they look at real love with skepticism and seek its interpretation and meaning.

XVIII

Lies are the roles we play for each other. Humans believe in your role but question your truth.

XIX

Love means sacrifice, forgiving, separation, pain, nonexistence while you are existing. It means absolute silence full of words.

XX

There are a few who believe in their dreams and follow them. There are many who fear their dreams and run from them.

XXI

You alone create the moments. Try to make them real and true moments, not false and fake moments.

XXII

The world is full of lies and false things. The realities in the world are the theatrical form of the false things we show, and these are the realities of the world with which human beings live. They make them the principles and framework of their lives and build their lives based on them.

XXIII

Who knows the truth and reality correctly? Where is the truth? The truth is what you and I suppress, and we prevent it from being disclosed because it is not compatible with the reality of the world, and no one believes it, and they laugh at you.

XXIV

The truth is inside you, the inside that you cover so that you are not embarrassed. Fear of revealing the truth, fear of seeing the truth, fear of confronting the truth—these are the things that make the truth silent inside you and you never hear its screams.

XXV

The principles and frameworks that human beings create for their world are false and meaningless principles and frameworks.

XXVI

My brain is so full of confusion that only my heart can feel it.

XXVII

Where are you, the truth seekers? You sacrificed your inner truth and ultimately knew nothing.

XXVIII

Life is like a dream, and for some it may be a nightmare that we all wake up from one day.

XXIX

The pen writes. And while I do not know what is in its essence and blood, what flows is the blood of my pen. Blood that sacrifices itself in order to reveal the truth. While its blood is running low and ending every moment, it tries to reveal the truth inside itself. And this is how we should flow.

XXX

In the human eye, the vulture is an ugly animal. In the eyes of God, a vulture is a beautiful creature. In the human eye, the vulture is a dirty animal because it eats from the impurities of the earth. In the eyes of God, the vulture is a good animal because it cleanses the earth of impurities. Humans do not like vultures and do not keep them in cages. But God loves the vulture and gives him his beautiful sky to fly in. Does the vulture understand this? Does the vulture know this? The world has imprisoned man, who is the most beautiful creature of God, in the cage of his belongings. Does man understand and know this?

XXXI

Believe in yourself so that others will believe in you. If you do not believe in yourself, the world will not believe in you.

XXXII

The sun of God's love shines on everyone equally, while you deprive yourself of this sun with colorful, worldly umbrellas.

XXXIII

Most people help the poor from a need to satisfy themselves, not to please God.

XXXIV

God sees the hidden truth within us, not what we pretend.

XXXV

I wish the time of our reunion would run like the calm waves of the sea.

XXXVI

The road of life is the road we build and travel on. Sometimes it is a road of sadness, sometimes the road of happiness. You just have to pass without stopping on it until you reach the destination of true love.

XXXVII

Miracles mean the power of love, and the power of love causes miracles. Christ performed miracles with the power of love.

XXXVIII

The strongest force that overcomes the force of death is the force and power of love.

XXXIX

Human dreams are countless and innumerable. People have many dreams in their thoughts without having faith in the manifestation of their dreams. It is only the force of faith that manifests our dreams. What makes our dreams come true is the power of faith. I wish we could believe our beliefs. Believing our dreams empowers others to believe. Believing our dreams is only the beginning of the manifestation of dreams. Having faith in the manifestation of dreams gives them symbolic form and makes them tangible. Our art is not in making dreams, because if that were the case, everyone would be an artist.

An artist is someone who depicts and creates dreams on the canvas of life. The spirit of faith brings their dreams to life, makes them a tangible reality, and gives others in turn the power to believe in their own dreams. True artists are those who draw their dreams on the canvas of life and make them a tangible reality. Such a faith brings us to know the great power of God's love and his wondrous work.

XL

The greatest miracle of love is release from the captivity of death and the acceptance of change.

XLI

Many who shout their slogans the loudest cower in the most secret hiding places on the battlefield.

XLII

There is no fear except the fear of God. All other fears are nothing but cowardice.

XLIII

The turbulent waves of my thoughts, the waves of my mind, sleep only in the bed of your love.

XLIV

I wish my heart was a bed for your weariness, my feet outran my many sorrows, and my eyes laughed at the flood of my tears.

XLV

The wave of love passes through the tumult of the world to take refuge in the security of your heart.

XLVI

The presence of your love is the security of my heart in the restlessness of my emotions.

XLVII

The dawn of your love shines on the sunset of my sorrows.

XLVIII

To be with you, to be by your side, to be without you, I am in your imagination.

XLIX

The cries of my feelings in my quest for you harmonize with the silent melody of my words.

L

I give the roots of my feelings in the land of my heart to the fountain of your love to sprout again in the freshness of the new year.

LI

The peak moment of my flight is the peak moment of my feelings.

LII

Poets wrote of love. Mystics praised love. Lovers walked the path of love. If you want to love yourself, you should not want yourself. It is easy to see love. To live in love is death. Living in love means love. Death in love is the peak of love.

LIII

Which tree should I water with my tears so that its blossoms can tell me of the beginning of my spring?

LIV

Which spring is the true spring? My heart is still restless.

LV

I want to grow all the flowers of spring in the warmth of your heart.

LVI

Shine like the sun. Maybe the flowers will make us happy and green.

LVII

I am doomed to madness because my crime is love.

LVIII

The heart is agitated and the soul is restless if you do not set fire to love in yourself.

LIX

The one who ignited love within was inflamed. The one who danced with the flame of love became ashes.

LX

Get intoxicated with the warmth of love. Be destroyed by the fire of love.

LXI

Our restlessness is not from fire. The fire of love dances restlessly for us.

LXII

I wish the feet of love would run to the bed of your heart until death. I wish the heart of dying love would beat again on the entrance of the altar of your love.

LXIII

Fear and quitting are the destiny of an unbelieving person.

LXIV

The world will pull you to what it wants if you don't stand against it. This is called destiny. If you stand up to destiny and do not give up, you will move the world in the direction you want. Few people believe this. Only they will live the life they choose and not what the world chooses for them.

LXV

Taking the first step is always difficult and scary. Cowards don't dare to take it because they have a fear of falling. Only brave people take it because they want to learn to run after falling. Always the first step is full of fear. Small people do not dare to take that step because of the fear of falling. But big people take that step because they don't have a fear of falling. They want to learn to run. Now that you have taken the first step, do not be afraid of falling because you will soon learn to walk and run.

LXVI

I need you only. My eternal life is in you alone. With you, I don't need the whole world. Without you, I am a beggar and a disgrace to the whole world. If you are with me, what do I need from the world? If you sit with me, why do I need to sit with others?

LXVII

Come to me to see my fever in the thirst for love. Come to me to see me burn in the fire of love. I burned like a butterfly in your love. I became fire and ignited in your glow.

LXVIII

If the butterfly sees such flames, it will envy the flames of love that kindled me. It will forget to be a butterfly if it sees me burning from your love.

LXIX

What is flame except for the fire of love that kindled the soul?
What is life except for the flame that ignited only from love?

LXX

My mind tells me only one thing: that only with my heart and feelings can I conquer the world, not by my mind.

LXXI

The secret of life is to move against the thoughts and directions of human beings. This is hard. You will be considered crazy and be rejected by the world because you have broken its rules.

LXXII

I do not get tired. I fight and continue until the last day I am alive. I do not want to live like others. I struggle because I do not live for life but to learn and break free of fear because it comes only from the mind and not from the heart. It is only the mind that keeps us from taking risks, flying, jumping, celebrating the joy of madness.

LXXIII

How beautiful and sweet is the pain that gives birth to love.

LXXIV

I dance to the beat of raindrops. I dance to love songs. I dance to the melody of love. I warm myself in the sunshine of love. Love is here. Love is you. Love is born. Love is born every day. Love never dies.

LXXV

Raindrops are dancing. Raindrops are dancing at the birth of love. There is a celebration in heaven, love's birthday party. How crazy it is that I sob at your birth. I wounded you like crazy. How madly I shouted at your birth! I searched for the light madly in the dark. You were here. You were waiting for my birthday, O love.

LXXVI

What a sweet pain I have. What a sweet pain, the pain of love. Don't take this pain from me until the moment this body dies. My death in love is my rebirth. What a sweet pain is birth pain. What a sweet pain to enter the realm of the soul. Love, how beautiful you are! My ears hear fresh melodies. My hands touch you, love. You gave me flying wings, wings to fly again. How glorious you are, love!

LXXVII

Your flames, O love, polished me. The flames of the fire of love polish me. The flame of your love burns my impurities. Burn as much as you can! The fire of love is the beginning of me. Burn what you have to burn. Only you, O love, can make me.

LXXVIII

I am the arrow that rips the heart of the enemy. I am the fighter that never gets tired. I am a soul that burns and its flames burn. I am not straw to bend. I am a trunk, rooted in love. My roots never dry out.

LXXIX

The true meaning of love is in pain. So if you see someone in pain, know that this is the love that is being born in them.

LXXX

Love can be felt. Love cannot be hidden.

LXXXI

Love is born of pain, so touch it to the marrow and touch the pain with all your being. This is the birthday of love.

LXXXII

My heart is a shed whose walls are covered with memories that I enjoy.

LXXXIII

My heart is like a shed where many people came. They warmed themselves and left, never thinking that they would leave their footprints forever. Now I am left only with those footprints.

LXXXIV

I wash my wounds with tears and bandage them with my loneliness.

LXXXV

If you fight and paddle in the storms of life you will drown sooner. You have to trust the storms and surrender to them to reach the real destination. So don't be afraid of the storms. Trust them. God is in your boat, so do not be afraid. Trust God in storms. They take you to the destination of maturity.

LXXXVI

My heart is like a roaring sea that can destroy everything when it opens its mouth.

LXXXVII

My pain is not from being far from you, it is from love that has forgotten how to love.

LXXXVIII

I witness the pain. I witness the rebellion. I witness the wound. I witness death. I witness suffering. I witness sorrow.

LXXXIX

Daring to tell the truth is harder than knowing the truth.

XC

Prison is a place for two groups of people: criminals and heroes.

XCI

You have to touch and taste the pain—you have to experience the pain—to understand the true meaning of suffering.

XCII

My heart is sad, and hatred weighs on my chest—a hatred that is followed by another hatred every time, which makes my heart heavier.

XCIII

A lover who is in love follows a lover, but a religious person follows people.

XCIV

I wish we understood the meaning of some words before making them meaningless by endless repetition.

XCV

Some priests preach love well, while in practice they are strangers to the word.

XCVI

Some priests have special skills in showing people their guilt, unaware that they themselves live sinfully, cleverly every day.

XCVII

How hard and painful it is to watch cruelty and violence against your fellow human beings and be helpless to do anything about it.

XCVIII

It is very difficult to live in this world pretending not to see the facts.

XCIX

You are closer to me than me. I breathe you, my beloved.

Epilogue: Closing Prayer

My love, you are the most beautiful song of my life. You are the most beautiful song in my heart. You are my beloved. You are the most beautiful love, my love, my darling, always by my side. Be the most beautiful whisper of my heart. Be like a crystal spring in my veins. You are my every breath. You are everything to my insignificance. My beloved, come to my garden, darling.

Thank you, my love, for seeing me. Thank you for being by my side in the darkest valleys of life. Thank you for rescuing me from the darkness. You lifted me up. Thank you for paying the price of my sins with your unconditional love. You suffered instead of me. Beloved, how can I thank you enough with my words? You stood beside me in the darkest valleys of life. You heard my cries. You never left me. You healed my wounds with love and washed them with the water of life.

You taught me a lesson every time I fell. You covered and forgave my ugly sins with your purity. You did not let my enemies laugh and celebrate. You as a kind husband comfort me in the warm embrace of love and affection. You provided for me when I was hungry and gave me water when I was thirsty. You watered the dry desert of my heart.

My dear, my beloved, my love, my breath, my soul, Christ, I love you so much although I do not consider myself worthy of your love. My dear, you suffered until I was released. You hurt and broke on the cross so I could fly. My dear heart, my beloved, you healed my most painful wounds with your love. You suffered with me to give birth to love in me.

How small I am without you. How ugly I am without you. How helpless I am without you. How restless I am without you. You are the blood in my veins. You are my breath of life. You are my honor and pride. You are a precious crown on my head. You are the only one who can tame me. You are the only love that captivates me.

Do not release me from this bondage. Resurrect me from me with your resurrection. Give me a new life, a new mind, a new body, a mind and heart free from wounds and pain. With your resurrection, release me from the wounds of the past, from insecurity, darkness, and sorrow, and give me a new life. My dear, you took my ugliness to the bottom of the grave with you. You separated me from me and then buried me in the darkness of the grave. Let your light rise! Let your love boil in my veins. Let the bitterness of the past and the poison of my pain leave me and sweeten my pain.

My beloved God, greatness is in you, power is in you, beauty is in you, peace is in you, happiness is in you, wealth is in you, wisdom is in you, light is in you, joy is in you, goodness is in you. True love is in you, and I found you in me. Why does man seek all these things in the outside world and trample humanity to get it? You graciously, gently, lovingly bestow them on all who ask.

Made in the USA
Middletown, DE
30 August 2024